↑ ALLIED ☼ MOUNDS ↓

Touching the Earth, Modeling the World, Reaching the Sky

Jay Miller

~ Vital Communion with Volatile Cosmos ~

© 2019

Acknowledgements

All too often documents, historical and otherwise, end up halved from their original. The book before you briefly suffered that fate when Ancestral Mounds was published with only the Southeastern material. Allied Mounds is the comparative (and more fun) half, constantly corrected and improved. From an Oklahoma backdrop, my study soon cascaded across the continent and through the world as study of the array of ways to honor earth consumed my lifetime of Americanist research. Thanks, gratitude, respect, and appreciation ranges equally far and wide, starting with fellow backbenchers: Blue Clark, Ray Fogelson, Bob McKinley, and Ted Isham for sustaining aid and concern. Blue deserves special thanks, as always, as a constant source of documents, encouragement, and meals. Thanks too to Sherry Sullivan, Sanger Clark; John, Luceen, Peggy, and Stella Sara Dunn; Jason Jackson, and, most gratefully, Felix and Minnie Gouge family. Through them, especially Felix's "Why would that be?", I realized the continuing importance of localized song and dance for amassing power ~ energy (*puwah*) while revitalizing mounds.

Before he undertook a heroic review of the entire full manuscript, Robert Hall used his Christmas digital camera for interior views of the wonderful Pawnee Big Doctoring diorama that showed more details than texts could. In its wisdom the Field Museum soon took it off display, proving once again that it is best to plan for uncertainty.

For technical, factual, and emotional support I am grateful to John Swanton, Erna Gunther, Viola Garfield, Clara Sue Kidwell, Pat Galloway, Jon Gibson, Barbara Duncan, Joe Saunders, Sunny Meriwether, Jim Brown, Janet Pollak, Harvey Markowitz, Ray DeMallie, Doug Parks, Marilyn Richen, Vi Hilbert, Bob Walls, Laura Dassow Walls, Ann Richel Schuh, Kurt Reidinger, Rich O'Connell, Mary Laya, John Adams, Julian Baumel, Donna Ellefson, Ken Tollefson, Monday Nite, and Ashland Annuals.

At Ole Miss, the Sociology and Anthropology Department provided support and context, especially Jay Johnson, Janet Ford, Ed Sisson, Robbie Ethridge, Ned Jenkins, and Gabe Wrobel. Robbie became miner's canary ~ guinea pig for testing the climate of the academic South. Maureen Meyers kindly loaned Lamar site materials. At Ohio State grudging support came from Jackie Royster, Linda Schoen, Richard Shiels, Rob Cook, Mike Sherfy, Tina Bergsten, Brian Joseph, Natalie Yellowhammer Warling, Newark Earthworks Center, and American Indien Studies (Indies, not India), as well as helpful Brad Lepper, Jeff Gill, and others struggling with Ohio's awful time warp. The near final draft basked in a Fogelson Georgia Beneficence within the *puwah* of Nikwasi, North Carolina, and Southeast penumbra.

Meticulous editing and proofreading of the final version became a new skill for Amelia Susman Schultz, the last PhD student of Franz Boas, an ageless friend, and a dynamo who marked a century of fulfilling life in 2015.

Mounds, as *safe* banked havens in a precarious universe, have an amazing continuity over millennia, testifying to the saving grace of soil and stone as pledges of security and immortality in bulge, bulk, body, and ballast.

To those of the past, who still teach us, *mvdo vcululke*. To all, *Mvdo, Yakoki*.

Foreword

We Creeks are proud of our tradition of mound building. In our homeland (today's Alabama and Georgia), each ancestral town (*etvlwv*) had its own mounds, large and small. Every year, at the Buskita Green Corn, some were renewed along with the earth. Soils and mementos of these mounds were carried west to Oklahoma when we were forced to move away. From these heirlooms, new smaller mounds were started in our new towns. These mounds of today contrast in size to the huge ones of our past. Their size called for special techniques and abilities which faded. In the hope that all Creeks will soon come together to build a modern great mound, our basketmakers relearned the art of weight-bearing baskets with strong rims. Expressing shared effort, community wellness, and beloved heritages, this project moves forward.

Today, about a dozen towns maintain ceremonial grounds and mounds, while other *etvlwv* have converted into Methodist or Baptist church keeping the same name. Both communities have camps and arbors focused on the East, with the church in the central place of the fire. Hymns in our language hold us together, along with fellowship and communion.

Our towns and churches honor fours, such as the directions and seasons. At ceremonial grounds, the foursome of soil, song, stomp, and spirit are especially vital. Ancestral Mounds helps to explain why this is so, and why they will continue until the end of time.

Mvto,
Honorable Alfred Berryhill[†]
Past Second Chief (vpoktv, "Twin") of the Creek Nation
Cultural Preservation Office, Muscogee (Creek) Nation
Okmulgee, Oklahoma

[†] Rev. Berryhill crossed over 31 August 2013

i

Allied Mounds
Touching the Earth, Modeling the World, and Reaching the Sky

Contents

Conventions

Over the years, the frustrations of trying to discuss Native America using standard English have led me to publish certain usages based in native understandings. Within the global context, I use the European (French, Italian, Danish, etc.) convention of spelling **_Indien_** with an E, for the Indies, instead of A for India. Two vital concepts are expressed in translation by the words **_puwah_** (= for the all-pervading cosmic vital energy, cosmic mind) and **_tysic_** (= for time + space + center (with vowels pointing down and up) that is its multidirectional intersection, as well as source and summary nexus, within a circuitry that is very like a global spider web 🕸 with rings and rays 🕸). Both terms derive from crucial concepts embedded in native languages. Cosmic energy is termed _paw-_ in Eastern Algonquian and _puha_ in American Numic languages, hence _puwah_ serves as a better conjoined variant of words for "power". What linguists call deictics, from Greek, refer equally to time and space, as tysic does in graphic fashion.

Dates will usually be presented as BP (= before the present), though some will appear as AD/BC or as CE/BCE (= before current era). At the moment, this chronology seems to be involved in a reanalysis that has doubled the earliest dates of some mound features, yet continues to provide a general sequence of events.

<< Archaeological Time Frame >>

PALEO INDIENS ?15000 – 9000 years ago, BP = before the present
    Pioneers: Clovis, Folsom, Plano

ARCHAIC Settlers, Tenders 9000 BP, BCE = before Current Era
  Early 9-7000
     Windover, Dalton ~ pecans
  Middle 7-5000
     Watson Brake ~ mounds
  Late 5000-3500
     Poverty Point

WOODLAND Founders, Intensive Tillers, Pottery 3500 BP = 5500 BC, BCE
  Early 3500-2000
     Adena - Cresap 3685-2020 BP
  Middle 2500-1500 = BC 500 - AD 500
     Hopewell - Kolomoki (BP 1650 - 1250 = AD 350-750)
  Late 1500-300
     Fort Ancient, Oneota

MISSISSIPPIAN 1200-270 maize farmers, > 800 AD, CE = current era
    Cahokia > Natchez (shattered 1731 AD)

PROTOHISTORIC 500-300 disease, epidemics, slaving
HISTORIC 400 >

To deal with kinship more precisely, lone capital letters will be used for primary kin, emphasizing a proper matri-focus for the Southeast (SE).

<< Kinship Codes >>

C = child(ren)
Cz = cousin
ego = central point of reference
e = elder / y = younger
et = eldest / yt = youngest
+/- generations, up/down from ego
G = grand, great

GM = grandmother	+2	GF = grandfather	
M = mother	+1	F = father	
A = aunt	+1	U = uncle	
Z = sister	0=ego	B = brother	
D = daughter	-1	S = son	
W = wife		H = husband	
Nc = niece	-1	Np = nephew	
GD = granddaughter	-2	GS = grandson	

Cf. eZetD = elder sister's eldest daughter

<< Graphic Codes >>

= equal, equivalent to, same as, translation
~ similar, related, comparable, variant, overlapping, parallel, linked, also known as
' foot, feet
" inch, inches
+ plus, add, conjoined
> transposed, changed to, becomes

p.c. = personal communication

Please correct & report all Typo-Gnomes!

WHY MOUNDS ?

Centuries of Euro-American scholarship have been devoted to basic questions of mound research, especially Who, What, Where, When, and How, but as yet there has been no serious investigation as to Why?[1] A major reason is that the sources for that answer, without written documents, have to be today's native moundbuilders, particularly natives affiliated with Southeastern towns driven to Oklahoma in the early 1800s, in combination with reliable ethnographic and archaeological reports, as well as all-important linguistic insights.[2] Like all human traditions, natives say they do what their ancestors have always done, with some accommodations to modernity, but specific verbal explanations are not readily forthcoming. Instead, my research has involved active participation in Summer moundbuilding activities in expectation that "actions will speak louder than words" to reveal cultural understandings. Indeed, after almost 30 years, I have learned the meaning of safe, secure protection that has long been provided to members by Creek ceremonial town squares and their annual mound building. Accumulated understanding appears in my prior book, Ancestral Mounds, while this present work is concerned with comparisons across the Americas, as well as glimpses of "best cases" drawn throughout the mound building globe.

We begin by reviewing the basic questions just mentioned. The Who[?] was solved by recognizing native tribal ancestors as the builders, not the politically expedient notion of a separate race of Moundbuilders.[3] As to What[?], every mound, by common understanding, is a microcosm of the ethos of its culture community. Where[?] produced distributional studies, with excavators working in the South during winter and the Midwest during summer to stay on task. When[?] was long problematic, partially solved by ceramic sequencing, tree rings, and superimpositions until absolute dating techniques

---

[1] Watchwords for my analysis are serious, scholarly, and culturally informed, in stark contrast to "new age" ~ "metaphysics" of muddled reviewers.

[2] Building on my "Instilling the Earth: Explaining Mounds," Commentary, American Indian Culture and Research Journal 25 (3): 161-177 2001; this second work abstracts the main argument from Ancestral Mounds, and owes much to continued welcome among Oklahoma Creek *talwa* and their scholars, both degreed and traditionally trained, as well as repeated personal visits to mounds in the Midwest, South, Northwest, and places in between. From these experiences, I learned that mounds are never inert, instead they apply rhythmic pressure, provide buoyancy, and assure safe proximity within an uncertain world. For their aids of all manner, from insight and advice to critique and proofing, I thank Drs. Amelia Susman Schultz, Blue Clark, Raymond Fogelson, Jason Jackson, and Mikkos and *heles haya* ~ *hilis haaya* of several living grounds, both Seminole and Creek: *mvdo.*

[3] Robert Silverberg, The Mound Builders 1986 [1970]. In England, the "national disgrace" of abysmal losses from poor excavation records by arrogant archaeologists has been rectified by Wessex Archaeology's summary of Stonehenge (Clael and others 1995).

gave reliable chronologies.[4] How[?] continues to investigate basket loading, soil sourcing and types, and various architectural reinforcements.[5]

And Why[?] involves native cosmologies and human desires for safety and renewal. Though long regarded by scholars and others as a distinctive feature of the Native South, human-made mounds occur across the Americas, North and South, where the macrocosm is a dynamic world comprised of a sky dome above and sea bowl below, with the living earth between these as a floating island usually created from bottom muck retrieved by an Earth Diver. A central tree (pole, pillar, tube, or similar *axis mundi*) interlinks these three domains, along with other mediators such as fires, springs, and caves to allow passage between the layers.

Throughout the Americas, natives know their universe to be alive, full of life force which is volatile, precarious, and moving (as it really is), rather than based on a reassuring but false premise that the world is constant, reliable, permanent, and static. To gain some assurance, mounds were ~ are carefully and prayerfully constructed under human control, with many of them resurfaced periodically to add heightened levels as an obvious expression of this belief in a multi-layered cosmos.[6] Engineered under special conditions and observances, mound constructions were very human expressions, based in the hands-on manipulation of thought, word, and deed. Above all, cross-culturally, mounds remain primarily "anchor weights" providing necessary places of security in an uncertain cosmos.

---

[4] Several natives with academic degrees, some allowing their efforts to appear in my acknowledgements, others preferring not, have willingly read versions of this draft, with approval, unlike most archaeologists who have pretty blindly asserted a monopoly. This continuing distress assures that the study of Mounds properly belongs to interdisciplinary Native Studies. Mounds were not built for reasons of Eurobiased greedy consumerism, grasping individualism, materialist grant writing, or pretentious one-ups-manship.

[5] Mound engineering involved more than mere soils – since color, origin, and texture are important considerations; as were wooden planks, crisscrossed reed reinforcements, and other internal architectural braces, well seen in the lowest remaining level of the great mound at Troyville (now Jonesville), see Winslow Walker, The Troyville Mounds, Catahoula Parish, LA 1936; as well as Sarah Sherwood and Tristram Kidder, The DaVincis of dirt: Geoarchaeological perspectives on Native American mound building in the Mississippi River Basin [sic], <u>Journal of Anthropological Archaeology</u> 30: 69-87 2011.

[6] In a sense such remantling also helps the mound to "breath" over a year as the new surface expands what a year of exposure has contracted, ever so slowly, like the surface of a torso or chest. Indeed, today's mounds are said to safeguard or "watch the grounds" when no campers are there. Further, this imagines that the ancient huge mounds stand sentinel to their towns like upright torsos with houses ~ temples set atop like heads.

Both the earth and "her" localized expression in mounds are alive, with defining characteristics of mind and motion, especially a pulse ~ throb ~ beat, attuned to the flow of cosmic life force ~ *puwah*.[7] Animating all, *puwah* pulsates along a web of rings and rays beginning and ending in a focused center (✴ 🕸), often a godhead, demiurge, deity, or creator. Circulating along the earth's taut skin, *puwah* flows in water as its curved and in light (rays) as its straight channels, both serving as tubes to concentrate vitality, as in spinal column, heart, and other organs. Each location tapped into a concentrated flow of cosmic *puwah*, which funneled from the sun in the sky into the sacred fire of the town, home fire, and heart in a body. It has particularly close associations with song and with snakes, as discussed below, as well as heart beat and dance rhythms. Moundbuilding is thus an affirmation of life and a recreation of awakening consciousness when deity provided a center for the living world.

According to their earliest missionary, Alfred Wright, the Choctaw earth, before any other beings were made, was a "quagmire" with the [quivering] consistency of clotted blood or jelly.[8] The creator made a banked, blessed, ballasting, and bulging mound at the very center, which became their anchoring "mother mound" *Nanih Waiya*, in what is now the state of Mississippi. Then he summoned humans to come out from its interior. When there were enough, "he stamped on the ground with his foot" and all those not fully formed perished. He promised immortality to these emergent humans, but they did not understand him. When they asked him to explain, he decreed, in frustration, that instead they would now die because of their ingratitude (and dull wits). This death, however, was only transitional between existences, an uncovering, "as the snake sheds his skin." In this way Choctaws received vitality instead of immortality.

Mind – variously expressed as thought, will, and memory – is passed on by a Creator as a vitalized gift to sentient ~ intelligent creations, generally at the moment when birth served to establish outside contact with the living earth. As distilled from his extensive fieldwork, John Swanton reported, "For Creeks, the earth is mindful, vital, and thereby powerful … Matter was not something which had given birth to mind, but

---

[7] My own coinage, combining two widespread native terms for cosmic power from eastern and western language stocks, respectively Algic (*powwow*) and Numic (*puha*), *puwah* is all-pervading cosmic energy ~ vitality ~ charge ~ force ~ power at the heart of Native American cosmologies. As noted in the text, Creeks know it as *Ibofvnga*, though some personify it as energy ~ spirit ~ soul ~ ghost ~ *poyafikca*. By using a term similar ~ familiar to English power, the vast array of native terms for this essential life-force can be accommodated, while also respecting occasional taboos against naming this energy in public. My data rich argument appears in Jay Miller, High-Minded High Gods in North America, Anthropos 75: 916-919 1980; The Matter Of The (Thoughtful) Heart: Centrality, Focality, or Overlap, Journal of Anthropological Research 36 (3): 338-342 1980.

[8] John Swanton, Source Material for the Social and Ceremonial Life of the Choctaw Indians, Bureau of American Ethnology, Bulletin 103 1931: 216; Marcia Haag and Henry Willis, Choctaw Language & Culture ~ Chahta Anumpa 2001: 346.

something which had formerly been mind [whose] highest form [is] human mind [expressed in speech] … 'By a word' wonderful things could be accomplished".[9]

Most of all, in Creek belief, *Ibofvnga*, their deified mental energy ~ cosmic Mind, willed the conjoining of four elements at creation. Two were male (fire, wind) and two were female (earth, water). Within each pair, one is definite and specific (fire, earth) while the other is indefinite and diffuse (wind, water). As breath, wind animates all life. Winds individuate by direction, indicated by the crossed logs (+) at the sacred fire at the focusing center of a town square. From the sky, Grandfather Sun and Grandmother Moon provide moderating heat and light, and communicate with the earth through the fire. Today, Creeks know the Christian God as Breath Holder (*Hesagedamese*), prayed and hymned to at local churches in Mvskoki and English.[10]

Native cultures of the US Southeast emphasize three zones of their world – a lower, middle, and upper layer.[11] Something like a thin membrane (such as a drum head, surface skin, sheer curtain) stretches between each of them, with catastrophe and confusion resulting from any breaching of it. In stories, men turned into "tie-snakes" after wrongly eating fish swimming in tree stumps, where they never belong. Today, most Creeks, both Christian and traditional, carefully avoid the "new ground" (*ekvna mocvse* ~ *i:kana močasi:*) turned up for a fresh grave, and special purification is required

---

[9] John Swanton, Tokuli of Tulsa, <u>American Indian Life</u> 1922: 142-3.

[10] Jean Hill Chaudhuri, <u>A Sacred Path</u> ~ <u>The Way of the Muscogee Creeks</u>, Joyotpaul Chaudhuri, ed. 2001; Jack Schultz, <u>The Seminole Baptist Churches of Oklahoma. Maintaining a Traditional Community</u> 1999: 61. Moreover, patience and persistence eventually pays off. For some time it seemed Creek Christians, especially Southern Baptists, were utterly opposed to mound-building as well as "doings" at the ceremonial grounds. Mounds seemed to be banished from their practices, but that is an error. While there are indeed no multiple mounds, there is an all-important one: Calvary. The hymn called in English "" Christ Crucified" (Luke 23: 33, 44-48) is titled in Creek "*rvne kalfvle hocefken*", which means "the mound named Calvary [*kalfvle*]" (See Fred Long and George Scott, <u>Nakcokv Esyvhiketv</u> ~ <u>Muskogee Hymns</u>; General Commission on Religion and Race, the United Methodist Church 1998: 11 [1936 by Presbyterians]). For early Christians, Calvary was the pivot of the world, where the skull of Adam long lay buried so it could be washed by the blood of the crucified Christ to renew the world and end any further blood sacrifice. Thus, one mound remains central to many modern Creeks who are members of churches. Further, by missionary script convention, the letter /v/ is used for a short vowel /ə/ like English sof<u>a</u>, b<u>u</u>t.

[11] George Lankford, ed., <u>Native American Legends</u>. Southeastern Legends: Tales from the Natchez, Caddo, Biloxi, Chickasaw, and Other Nations 1987; George Lankford, Some Cosmological Motifs in the Southeastern Ceremonial Complex, <u>Ancient Objects and Sacred Realms:</u> Interpretations of Mississippian Iconography, Kent Reilly and James Garber, eds. 2007: Chapter 2: 8-38.

of those who do go to the graveside and carry off such soil on their shoe soles. Each open grave breached the surface tension of the earth's skin and grief added uncertainty, calling for these ritual precautions.[12]

Before the invention of ever-more-probing scientific technologies opened the way to viewing molecular structures and subatomic particles, humans relied on what they saw and knew to work (most of the time) – the body, the day, the seasons, the waters, and the skies. Obviously, food nourished a body to grow and age. In mid-life, men and women begat children, who renewed these (re)cyclings. Genders and procreation, therefore, figure prominently in rituals as a way to assume (and assure) vital bulging continuity. The seasons moved through regular yearly and longer cycles, mirrored in the appearance and behavior of plants and animals. Spring sprouted seeds and welcomed other newborns. Honoring these species renewals assumed continuities.

Waterways, both rivers and oceans, varied in their flows by seasons and by geographic climates. Long residence in an area taught people about ten, twenty, fifty, and hundred-year floods, and leaders kept careful count between these periods to provide warnings, as Hernando de Soto *entrada* survivors learned. Those living in tidal areas were aware of simultaneous pulls in moon and menstrual cycles, including women's physiological changes, within their ritual patterns, often set apart by distinct taboos. The proven power of women's blood, believed to be the kernel of a fetus, made it dangerous to the flowing of other energies, especially those of men and immortals.

Fixed observatories, such as stump seats or rock piles on elevations, allowed specialists to make sustained records by watching along skylines for the orderly movements of the heavens and to show predictabilities in the orbits and transects of stars and other sky phenomena. The rising and setting of the sun marked off each day, as its movements toward the north and south tagged the solstices (farthest standstill) and equinoxes (midpoint) of a year. The moon's phases traced each month, while its risings and settings around the skyline fulfilled an 18.6 year cycle. Meteors, eclipses, and other calamities shook public confidence in these regular observations, although some routine irregularities may have been anticipated by well-versed observers.

For rituals to partake of full communion with the cosmos, some part-for-whole (metonym) equivalences were invoked to reduce these enormities to human scale. Hair, blood, and bone stood for the body and genders, while seashells or water-filled pots reflected the aquatic world. The sky itself was mirrored in the shiny surfaces of mica,

---

12   This is current Creek funeral protocol, where each person in attendance, except close kin, decides how close he or she will come to the grave, depending on what other obligations they have in their lives. Walking on new ground means time devoted to purification, which is not always possible when there are busy schedules and many obligations. A distinctive feature of Creek churchyard cemeteries, small rectangular slat houses, the dimensions of the grave, emphasize that the body is not entirely below ground, in congruence with this belief. These grave houses, preferably on the west side of today's Creek churchyards, also continue the ancient tradition of burying a loved one under a section of the bench platform, along the inside walls of the home, that served as his or her bed during life.

copper, and rendered oil. Threading these together were pivotal links among the heart, the hearth, the tribal holy fire, and the sun, pulsing with song.

For the Native South and elsewhere, Earth is precarious: a vengeful living being, with thin skin and hollow heart, floating on a vast sea. Periodically, it is imbalanced by human faults and in need of rebalancing. Its denizens, especially their spirit leader "bosses," are shape-shifting, active, and judgmental. Decent people have the moral responsibility to make conscious choices that provide security for all beings by performing rituals of propitiation and acts of protection to assure the beneficial flow of vital energy. Mound building and resurfacing are highly responsible acts.[13]

Bulging in substance and weight, mounds are beacons: monuments of all-embracing vitality, which is enhanced via tribal rituals, added soils, songs, and dances that are specific to each builder community and locale.[14] They both anchor their environs in a world made unsteady by human faults, and provide a banked reserve (charged deposit) to dispense vitalizing power (*puwah*) flowing through tubes, webs, and networks (Creek: *toyá* "web ~ net"). Vitality itself is global, dynamic, impersonal, and immortal, with a range that includes general health, success, attraction, goodwill, and fertility (though often limited to the mortal and sexual).

In Jon Gibson's[15] wrap-up of his archaeological career, especially life-long research at ancient Poverty Point, he concluded it was arrayed within a security shield of raised earthen rings because "mounds are magic." Maintained by (his newly-named) Tamaroha ("Mound Cave") people, he wisely highlighted their abilities to perpetuate such vitality: "Mounds were permanent fixtures on the land, conspicuous vessels of lived history and attachment to place [as] Navels of the Earth [with] an enduring traditional, if not direct ancestral, connection between [ancient] and later groups … Even after falling into disuse, mounds continued to evoke emotion, history, and identity (as material

---

[13] Jean Hill Chandhuri, <u>A Sacred Path</u> – <u>The Way of the Muscogee Creeks</u> 2001.

[14] In her learning-Creek lessons, Linda Alexander tells the story of a smashed turtle who is given a song which he sings four times to heal himself. The song is specific to him, and its effectiveness depends on repeating it four times. Such is the vitalizing power of song. See Pamela Innes, Linda Alexander, and Bertha Tilkens, <u>Beginning Creek</u> ~ *Mvskoke Emponvkv* 2004: audio CD, #32, 33. Earnest Gouge provided bilingual texts that specify the lewdness that got turtle mashed, *Totkv Mocvse* ~ <u>New Fire</u>, <u>Creek Folktales</u>, Jack Martin, Margaret McKane Mauldin, Juanita McGirt, eds 2004: 33, 113.

[15] Jon Gibson, Navels of the earth: sedentism in early mound-building cultures in the Lower Mississippi Valley [sic], <u>World Archaeology</u> 2006 38 (2): 311, 315, 320; Seeking a more respectful term, the builders of this site have now been called Tamaroha, from Tunican words for 'mound' (*tama*) and 'cave' (*roha*) by analogy with the phrase "water mountain" that in MesoAmerica means a "city". The intent is to be "more appealing to tourists and more uplifting of the state's image". See J. Clark, Jon Gibson, and J. Zeider, First Towns in the Americas: Searching For Agriculture, Population Growth, and Other Enabling Conditions, <u>Becoming Villagers</u>: <u>Comparing Early Village Societies</u> 2010: 244.

memory)." Mounds are embodiment of throbbing vitality, rising up and pressing down, simultaneously leavening and leveling, as "the seen of and for an unseen source".[16]

All surfaces (skins) associated with mounds receive careful attention. A passageway under a mound is opened by removing top soil to allow, like opening a valve, for its inflation, giving its substance added weight, and then, while in use, its banked vital bulk is periodically expanded and again resealed. "Blocks of sod were also stacked up, generally with the grassy side facing downward ... [rock piles] stone platforms or simple structures made of stacked rocks were built, often covered by earth ... carefully prepared surfaces ... were periodically renewed by the addition of more soil ... of different colors [with] ceremonies held on these surfaces [for] lighting fires and erecting posts".[17]

Mounds are of the earth, and, as such, commonly associated with snakes and, by extension, other reptiles and amphibians with burrows. As noted, earth is fragile, and, therefore, precarious – aptly derived from a Latin word meaning "pray" – because it depends on the capricious will of others. Comfort and succor are provided by the ordered rhythms of the sky, both stars and planets, helping to schedule rituals and events. Comets, asteroids, eclipses, and lighting bolts, however, provide reminders of sudden change that can strike from out of the sky, imagined as dragons, snakes, and others emerging from the under-earth abyss. For Creeks, "The slitherings of debris from [off] the top of the giant earth turtle in the creation legend is the source of all evil and pollution [and] can take the form of a great horned snake".[18]

Native languages make more intimate connections of mounds to earth's breasts and pubic bulge, as well as heart, navel, and womb. The feminine associations of earth and mounds are particularly obvious in Tunica, an ancient Southeastern language of Louisiana with male (m) and female (f) genders.[19]

> *hali* f[emale] ground, land, "earth"
> *halitimura* f[emale] levee; mount; "earth hill."

The circuitry of this webbing includes channels that are tube-like. To add interest and protective force, the most common embodiment of this shape is that of a serpent, variously coiled, undulating, or turning upon itself.[20] Symbolically within the greater graphic universe, male snakes are usually portrayed as angular and females as sinuous, regardless of their own biological indicators.

---

[16] David Lewis and Ann Jordan, Creek Indian Medicine Ways 2002: 118.

[17] George Milner, The Moundbuilders 2004: 67, 73, 110.

[18] Jean Hill Chaudhuri, A Sacred Path ~ The Way of the Muscogee Creeks 2001: 130.

[19] Mary Haas, Tunica, Handbook of North American Indian Languages 4: 1-143; Tunica Dictionary, University of California Publications in Linguistics 1953: 6 (2): 211.

[20] Ephraim Squier, The Serpent Symbol and the Worship of Reciprocal Principles of Nature in America, 1851; after he broke with Edwin Davis during the 1848 publication of their monumental study of Mississippi Valley mounds, using observations that were cut from their final draft by the Smithsonian editor.

Earth, moreover, can combine the forms of both woman and snake, represented separately or fused together as a female serpent. Also associated, therefore, are leathery eggs and the Moon, both from its shape and its influence on menstrual cycles. While these relationships abound in mythology, they are best seen among ancestral Siouans.

Along the upper Mississippi River, comparable traditions of the Siouan Hochungara or Ho-chunk (called Winnebago by Algonkians) of Wisconsin illuminate mysteries of snakes, turmoil, earth, and the world.[21] According to their creation epic, after _Ma'una_ (Earthmaker) placed the land, it was never still.[22] Its constant spinning kept things from rooting and growing so it remained entirely bare. Anything that tried to settle down slid off into space. Only barely-anchored spider webs floated above its surface. Eventually, after his grass to grew, Earthmaker placed trees, but everything still spun.[23]

At last he had four Island Earth Weights, brother water serpents, pin themselves tail first at the corners of the four directions, all facing east and the sun, to stretch, steady, and hold the earth. But the earth still trembled, so he scattered rocks (regarded as females) and these finally made it quiet by their weight. The name used for these snake stabilizers in ordinary usage derives from _sewe_ "to be quiet, to reduce to silence, to press, to press down".[24] In depiction of the Mississippian cosmos, these four serpents feature prominently at the four directions, supporting this direct analogy to HoChunk beliefs.[25]

---

[21] They are particularly well known, thanks to 1908-1913 research, followed by lifelong publications, of Paul Radin (1883-1959), though his major monograph (1923) was never fully finished.

[22] Paul Radin, The Winnebago Tribe [1923] 1990: 302; David Lee Smith, Folklore of the Winnebago Tribe 1997: 19.

[23] Dr. Henry Roe Cloud ~ Wa-na-xi-lay Hunkah, a HoChunk with degrees in divinity (ordained Presbyterian minister) and anthropology (Yale MA) lectured on 4 May 1929 (The Ohio Archaeological and Historical Society Publications 18: 564) concerning the "majesty, sweep and greatness" of his tribe's epic of the efforts of the creator, "But the [new] earth shook and fell apart. To make it cohere he set into it trees, and, not succeeding, he set into it grasses and roots of every sort. Then he weighed it down with innumerable rocks and stones until rest and equilibrium were attained" [emphasis added]. The Chiwere branch of Siouan, which includes Hochunk ~ Winnebago, are the likely builders of Wisconsin's famous effigy mounds in the driftless regions.

[24] These snake stabilizers are named _widjirasewe_ = island-weights; _widjirawasewe_ = weights, island-weights (in ritual); cf. _cewe_, _xewe_; _witc_ island in Paul Radin, Winnebago Culture As Described by Themselves, The Origin Myth of the Medicine Rite, Indiana University Publications in Anthropology and Linguistics, Memoir 3 1950: 1, 9, line 23, 19, line 37, 63, 64 line 16; Mary Carolyn Marino, A Dictionary of Winnebago: An Analysis and Reference Grammar of the Radin Lexical File 1968: 388, 422.

[25] Richard Townsend, Hero, Hawk, and Open Hand ~ American Indian Art of the Ancient Midwest and South 2004: 127.

Among Mississippian descendants,[26] "Linguistic and traditional material from Mvskoke, Yuchi, Chickasaw, Choctaw, and Cherokee" sources yields a reasonably coherent picture that "Mounds possess symbolic associations with autochthony, the underworld, birth, fertility, death, burial, the placation of spirits, emergence, purification, and supernatural protection. They are metaphorical mountains, anthills, navels, or womblike 'earth mother' representations".[27] In mythology, hollow mounds serve as nests and dens, as well as passages from the underworld.

Underlying many other purposes and uses, mounds are foremost and primarily pulsing anchor weights: obvious, vital, bulging bulk (ballooning bubble, according to their Cherokee name)[28] poised for both rising up and weighing down a place in the volatile world. Each one provides a rhythmic surface tension of security, sanctuary, "honored earth", and "blessed ballast".[29] Their size, shape, fill, mass, density, and distributions reflect local conditions, but the basic intent is the same: common security drawn from community *puwah* vitality that has been concentrated, attuned, and consecrated as a monument maintained by human efforts, often to atone for admitted human faults. The soil inside mounds is special, composed of specific colors taken from certain places and directions in particular ways by designated people. Some inclusions, including burials, help to feed its vitality. Height, weight, size, and mass add to their bulging effectiveness along with prayers and rites of song and dance which are specifically localized to be attuned to focusing vitality, fostered by song and dance.

Twenty years ago, Robert Hall[30] noted that mound rituals, using colored marsh muds in Wisconsin and hides staked over Illinois Hopewell graves, probably recreated aspects of the Earth Diver epic in which the first land was formed from a speck brought up from the bottom of the primordial sea by an aquatic hero. A mound, therefore, was a frozen monument of ~ to dynamic creation. Once this earth grew outward and stabilized,

---

[26] Chickasaw *chikbichi* "make a mound" (Humes 1973: 127) is not in Munro and Willmond 1994: 187) where ittihalbish = navel, mound (Miller 2015: 137 #4).

[27] Knight, Symbolism of Mississippian Mounds 1989: 283.

[28] The Cherokee word for mound is *ugwelvtvi* "it's bubbling up"; thanks to Barbara Duncan of the Museum of the Cherokee for conferring with Wiggins Black Fox of Qualla, Roger Smoker of Snowbird, and others to provide this usage in a text message of Friday 4 April 2008 at 1:48pm.

[29] "Ballast" comes from the Danish meaning "bare load" as a noun, including the underbed of a road, track, or moral character; but it is herein used in its verbal sense of conferring weight, balance, security, and stability in an uncertain world. As mounds and other terra ~geo~forms, it is made blessed by the care, prayer, and rites associated with its transport from a certain direction or place, such as a barrow pit, as well as by the ongoing communal prayerful activities for the mound's upkeep to provide security and sanctuary. In the process, these soils move horizontally to the mound, then vertically within it, falling and rising over a long time.

[30] Robert Hall, In Search of the Ideology of the Adena-Hopewell Climax, Hopewell Archaeology: The Chillecothe Conference 1979: 260.

it supported a varied population of living, thinking denizens, who well knew its origins, took none of its features for granted, and reassured concern for its constant flux. In confirmation of such insecurity, the most solid of shapes was believed to be hollow – tubes ~ ducts inside bodies, caverns inside mountains, chambers inside mounds, and a chasm inside the earth. Periodic human effort, especially prayer, speech, dance and song, they correct for their own faults and, for a time, hold steady a thin skin suspended in time and anchored in place by an engineered effort.

While hills were occasionally reshaped into mounds, unmodified hills ill-served this purpose.[31] Only engineered mounds of faithful human construction provide this anchor weight because their pulsating contents and contexts were well-known in the community, usually for centuries, until Afro-European epidemics took their toll on populations and accumulated wisdom.[32]

Finally, as I have worked throughout Native America, including two decades among Southeastern peoples who were forced to Oklahoma almost 200 years ago, I became increasingly fascinated by indigenous analogies that crisscross the Americas. In particular, as part of a larger agenda to bring the North Pacific Coast[33] back into pan-American scholarship, I want to draw attention to ways in which the Northwest can help with understanding the Southeast.[34] Both contained ranked chiefdoms relying heavily on

---

[31] While Caddo ancestors built impressive mounds, their Pawnee linguistic kin revere a constellation of earth-lodge-like hills on the central plains, Douglas Parks and Waldo Wedel, Pawnee Geography, Historical and Sacred, Great Plains Quarterly Summer 1985 5: 143-76. Pawnee did build small mounds during certain ceremonies, and Wichita ancestors, also Caddoan speakers, dug out a snake effigy.

[32] At Cresap Mound in West Virginia, for over 1600 years, people reused the same place for a set of slowly conjoining mounds, each positioned in reference to the central fireplace kindled at the very beginning. Such continuous orientation, consistent ritualizing, and serial devotion to raising up that spot highlights the sense of place by long-resident Americans; see Don Dragoo, Mounds for the Dead: An Analysis of Adena Culture 1963.

[33] Late in this process, I realized that both mounds and totem poles are monuments of and to vitality, installed and maintained by song and dance. The totem pole, decorated with matriclan and family crests, represents the spinal column of the ranking hereditary name channeling revitalizing *puwah* energy into the hereditary lands, as the spinal vertebrae of the named house head does for its members. See Jay Miller, Tsimshian Culture ~ A Light Through the Ages 1997: 52. Tubes featured throughout this mound study also channel energy into persons, events, places, and, especially, mounds.

[34] Before his suicide, Wilson Duff made much of the Haida proverb about their own sense of precariousness as island people who truly lived on the edge on all fronts, Cf. Donald Abbott, The World Is As Sharp As A Knife, An Anthology in Honour of Wilson Duff 1981. John Swanton switched his early career from

the careful tending of natural resources (fishing for both, farming for SE), were devoted to elaborate rituals, and traced kin through strong matrilineality.

There are also striking differences.[35] Major ceremonies are held in the rainy winter in the Northwest, but the blistering summer in the Southeast. Most communities in the Northwest, especially in Alaska, remain in their diminished homelands, dynamically involved in their own place-based traditions. The Southeast peoples, by contrast, were mostly relocated, but sustained themselves as farmers relying on the later trinity of corn + beans + squash, which had embellished the early Eastern domesticates such as sunflowers, sunroots, sumpweed, and amaranth.

Focusing on mound vitalities and their cultural ramifications, this book marks my coming to terms with the last of the four quarters ⊕ of Native North America (SW, NE, NW, SE), as understood through place-based rituals with cosmic meanings. In hindsight, my work has been in terms of diagonals, starting in the Southwest with Keresan Pueblos and then adding the Northeast with the Delawares (Lenape). While several articles have made it into print, the book-length treatments of Keres and Lenape suffered "peer" review.[36] In sharp contrast, my research in the Northwest, where I am more deeply involved among Salishans and Tsimshians, has seen friendly support and ready publication. Now, with the Southeast materials presented here, that other diagonal is broached. Though an avid interest of most people, fieldwork in the Plains has never attracted me. Instead, reading its ample publications has served to provide necessary comparative data already rich in detail. Moreover, both Delaware and Creeks living in Oklahoma (on the southern plains) visit many neighboring Plains tribes so I have not escaped some involvement as a guest at Powwows, bundle openings, Sun Dances, and other bison-fed rites.[37]

This book, hence, is concerned with the dynamism of mounds, their core meaning and obvious physicality, across the Americas and the World, informed especially by their present-day use and significance among tribes from the US Southeast now living in Oklahoma, and already in print.

My comparative coverage includes North America, as well as examples to the South. Alternating chapters include comparisons from other culture areas, following a Z-shaped route that will begin in the Northwest, move across to the Northeast, then angle

---

Lakota to Haida and Tlingit, before turning exclusively to the Southeast, without a look back. I hope to rectify this oversight.

[35] Key differences are long-range influences, with much of North America impacted from the Valley of Mexico, while those to the Northwest came from China. Southeast contacts with the Caribbean did not include adopting Taino mound fields (*conuco* = each mound three feet high and nine feet across) for growing and storing root crops, See Irving Rouse, The Tainos 1992: 12.

[36] The Keres study is now posted on line at the Ohio State Library, Knowledge Bank, American Indien Studies. Peter Nabokov (2015) makes good use of it.

[37] Because today's Woodland rites coincide with those of Plains tribes during summer in Oklahoma, one is unlikely to attend both a Green Corn and a Sun Dance without advance planning and dispensation from either of these separately interlocked ritual communities.

through the Plains to the Southwest. The Pawnee appear in each contextual chapter, and provide the midpoint of the Z. This placement is more than academic convenience since the Pawnee (as well as other Caddoans) seem to have been at the vortex of many religious traditions, and they built mounded graves and ritual spaces into historic times.[38] Westernmost, Native California comes into its own during the discussion of cremation and its ramifications (Chapter 6), which include "cremains" inside mounds.

The actual backbone for any such broad comparisons is ideally the trunk of the Mississippi River, and its main branches: the Ohio from the east and Missouri from the west. This interflowing crux was the cradle for the Siouan language stock, which can be expanded into Macro-Siouan to include Iroquoian of the Northeast piedmont. The Ohio network saw the early blossoming of domed mounds, avenues, embankments, and earth constructions in the archaeological complexes known as Adena and Hopewell. The namesake Mississippians, living along this main trunk and building blocky temple mounds, belonged to several language stocks and traditions, which are still echoed today in living rituals and tribal beliefs.

Along other waterways, other regional traditions emerged, flowering under the broad rubric of the Mississippian, but my interest focuses on the overall pattern. Impressive research has helped to clarify the development of these local complexes, and it should be consulted by interested readers (see Bibliography). Most interpretations, though, are based in European notions of individualism, self-interest, and false permanence instead of a native one of sharing something obvious to stave off precarious uncertainty, and of moral obligations to the larger whole of all living and thinking forms. Where academics see the tools of political competition and control playing out on solid ground, natives teach a stockpiled means to survive in a very unsteady world by means of concerted communal action done in a prayerful manner to provide elevation, blessed ballast, and assured banked vitality.[39]

Beneath it all, mounds weigh and rest on the earth. From this basic and very obvious fact follow more complex associations, derivations, uses, and functions that have long challenged scholarly research. This touch-point truism is enacted every summer as soil is piled up at native harvest ceremonies, but this weighty activity has been overlooked by those who view the earth as inert and unaware. A mound, instead, is a steadying microcosm in the dynamic and dangerous world.[40]

---

[38] David Bushnell, Burials of the Algonquian, Siouan, and Caddoan Tribes West of the Mississippi 1927: Plates 36, 37.

[39] Jon Gibson, The Power of Beneficent Obligation in First Mound-Building Societies, Signs of Power 2004: 254-269, much to his credit, has tried to turn the academic discussion toward "beneficent obligation" (debt of gratitude) as a way of providing a better understanding of native motivation, as indeed it does, based in present tribal activities and beliefs.

[40] An idea to be pursued is inverting of sod pieces, placing roots up and plants down, which has the effect of closing an energy circuit into an endless loop of plant tops to plants tops. An analogy can be found in the use by canoers of swirling side eddies, turning back on themselves, along river shores to be pulled more easily upstream against the mainstream current in the middle.

2 EMBROILED SOIL

Mounds are obviously of and from the earth, partaking of its creation, continuity, and vitality. Built up of various extraordinary fills, "mounds are not simply earthen monuments constructed on the basis of least-effort principles".[41] Because of human effort via orderly ritual, moreover, the component soil is special because it has been blessed and consecrated by hallowed communal efforts. Thus, mounds are alive, and thereby share features with other beings, particularly those closest to the skin of the earth. Foremost among these are **snakes**, "who" live under, in, and on the land. Closely related are other reptilians. Trembling and turmoil are characteristically always lurking nearby because the cosmos is precarious, aggravated by humans, who are often at fault for worsening conditions.

For northern California, a prime example of earthquake-prone turbulence (Chapter 7), the Yurok struggle "to keep the earth [island] balanced upon the waters, in accord with the law [of the universe] and despite human breaches of it". To accomplish this feat, their immortals [called _wo-gey_] "instructed certain people in what to do to put the world back in balance when the weight of human violations grew too great for it". Rhythmically repeated like the tides and seasons, paired between major male and female towns, these leaders held world renewals, with matched pairs of dancers standing across from each other, to "fix" up the earth.[42]

Mounds embody vital substance, the seen of and for the unseen. They are obvious, tangible, manifested beliefs. They are dirt made special, but derive their material from past precedents. In the larger context, throughout the Americas, mounds follow from the creations, and therefore the origins, of the earth. Yet asking who, where, what, and how were involved in this American Genesis leads to many valid responses.

MultiGenesis

For Native America, there is no single answer to creation or recreation, unlike the Big Bang of science or the Eden of the Bible. Instead, Origin epics for the Americas include seven major versions, discussed more fully below.[43]

1) Earth Diver, who brought up a speck of dirt from the sea bottom to enable the world to be formed and spread out
2) Father Sky + Mother Earth who begat creation
3) Emergence up from an underworld

---

[41] Julieann Van Nest, Rediscovering This Earth: Some Ethnogeological Aspects of the Illinois Valley Hopewell Mounds, <u>Recreating Hopewell</u>, Douglas Charles and Jane Buikstra, eds. 2006: 417.

[42] Thomas Buckley, <u>Standing Ground</u>, Yurok Indian Spirituality, 1850-1990 2002: 214.

[43] Anna Birgetta Rooth, Creation Myths of North American Indians 1957; Jay Miller, <u>Earthmaker</u> 1992b.

4) Spider weaving together the world
5) Tricksters democratizing ("liberating" for the commons) private resources for future group benefit
6) Twins vying to create, producing either useful or harmful results
7) Dismemberment of a giant (like the Aztec Cipatli, Norse Ymir) whose parts become features of the world – skull into sky dome, bones into stones, hair into grass, blood into water, and organs into species

Of note, none of these epics is entirely unique to the Americas. Earth Diver is circumpolar and Sky + Earth occurs through Pacific islands and ancient Japan. Parallels might be reversed, as Ymir inverts the story of Adam (taking apart the human form that Genesis assembles). Though these types are presented for the moment as Origin epics, often beginning from nothing at all (*de novo*), many regions emphasize instead what are modifications or reshaping epics in which a Changer goes through the world making things as they are now or preparing the way for future needs.

It is especially relevant to know that the world is precarious, rather than a fixed or stable place, often suffering through a series of creations, catastrophes, destructions, and recreations over eons (floods, fires, earthquakes, etc.), like the Four Underworlds of the Pueblos. Though aspects and vestiges of these prior worlds continue, conditions on the whole improve. People in this volatile, unsteady world benefited from the vital stability provided by mounds, whose banked charge, ballast weight, and counter-tension (quivering, pulsing, trembling) made them protective havens.

Earthings

In greater detail, each of these epics provides a distinctive outlook on the world and universe. Each will be considered in turn, coded by number in the list above.

(1) <u>Diver</u>   The most widespread account, circumpolar across the Baltic, Siberia, and North America, portrays the motif called "earth diver", who brought up a speck of dirt from beneath the all-pervasive sea. This version could also explain a re-creation of the world after a flood. Beginning with a world of only water, birds or aquatic animals "come to" (gain self-consciousness) and decide, often at the mental instigation (sent thought, telepathy) of a deity, that one of them should dive to the sea bottom and bring up some mud (dirt) so that a firm earth island could be made. Generally, the last animal (the fourth and least likely) to try is the successful one, and this allows the earth to be created by mystically expanding outward from that muddy speck.

> "The Cherokee Earth Diver was a water beetle, a muskrat for the Ojibwas, Ottawas, Foxes, and Onondagas; a crawfish for the Shawnees and Osages; a duck for the Arikaras; a mudhen for the Cheyennes; and a red-headed duck and a turtle together for the Arapahoes."[44]

---

[44]   Robert Hall, <u>An Archaeology of the Soul</u>, North American Indian Belief and Ritual 1997: 19. Newman Littlebear, former official speaker at the Yuchi mother town, noted that crayfish uses its tail to fan stream-bottom dirt into a

(2) <u>Sky/Earth</u> In native southern California, the world was created by the union of Sky Father and Earth Mother, a belief also found across the Pacific. These met, bonded, and remembered each other before the wife gave birth to inhabitants and artifacts important for this region.

The sky was often the source for many features that came to earth. In the Plains and southern Northwest, accurate star lore is projected onto the landscape to describe the creation of leading families at specific locales where Stars came to earth. For example, Pawnee trace their chiefs, together with interlinked sacred bundles and town sites, to specific Star beings who landed in Nebraska. Pueblo theocracies of the Southwest are chartered and empowered by beings from the sky, duplicating on earth their celestial strengths. Among Salish, the Starchild founded chiefly families around Seattle's Puget Sound before he and his brother went back into the sky to become the Moon and Sun.

(3) <u>Upward</u> In Southwest and some Plains tribes, people lived in an Underworld oblivious to their surroundings. Eventually, they moved or were lured to the earth's surface passing through four separately colored layers of underworlds. Monsters and hardships are left behind in each tier. After temporary stays in the lower three, they begin life in the fourth world during known time and space. Twin sons of the Sun established current leaders and guided their careers. They also passed on remembered knowledge in order to vitalize the rituals which serve to record and sanctify these uses of a homeland. Such a stalk-like (tubular) upward growth is particularly appropriate for natives who relied on intensive farming, especially of corn (maize). Locust, sharing song with humans, plastered the sides of the tunnel or tube leading upward.

(4) <u>Spider</u> Sporadically through western North America, particularly in the Great Basin, where insects were vital foods, there are accounts of creation by Spider,[45] who wove the world's foundation as a weblike tracery. Though Numics (Shoshoni) provide the most explicit regional statement of this belief, spider and web provide the template for *puwah* flowing via rings and rays which are implicit in beliefs across the continent.

While most creators were in some sense male, in the southern Great Basin, Ocean Old Woman made the world, aided by Wolf, Coyote, and Cougar. She sprinkled particles of her skin over the primal ocean to create a speck of earth, then, through prayerful thought, she expanded it into a huge flat disk. The center from which she worked survives as Charleston Peak in the Spring Mountains just west of Las Vegas, Nevada.

---

mound, Cf. Jason Jackson, <u>Yuchi Ceremonial Life</u> 2003: 240. (Of note, Mr. Littlebear's father was Shawnee.)

[45] For Mississippians, this was not the "water" spider as many have long assumed, but rather an "orb weaver", as nicely shown by Duane Esarey, Mississippian Spider Redux 2004.

Even now, she lies on a side promontory called Mummy Peak, her own physical work done.[46]

Others finished her labors. Humans were created by the union of Coyote as father and Louse as mother, placed in a basket, and intended for careful array over the landscape. Coyote assumed the form of a water spider to transport the basket to be opened at the center of the world (a *tysic*, see below), the logical starting point for such an even apportioning. As he journeyed, curiosity got the better of him, however, and he prematurely opened the lid. Humans jumped out and ran all over the earth like lice, remaining imperfect forever (like Coyote).

(5) Transformers   Among tribes of the Northwest, along with the Ainu native to Japan, the world was finished by a Changer~Transformer, called Raven, who wandered over the mainland, tricking sole proprietors out of various resources and necessary elements -- such as salmon, sun, moon, tides, and fire -- to make these available to humans. In keeping with the communal life of the past, these Changers worked in teams, often brothers or siblings, but have become more solitary or individuated in recent centuries to accord with expected American ideals of loners.

(6) Twins   In the Northeast, among Iroquoians, the earth was created on the back of a Turtle to provide a haven for a pregnant woman who fell (or was pushed) out of the sky. She died giving birth to twins, Sapling and Flint, who finished the world as they vied to will into being either beneficial or harmful creations, such as butterflies or mosquitoes, squash or poison ivy, gardens or brambles. These alternating creations by the twins provided checks and balances that helped define the ways of the world. Thus, death highlighted life, while the benefits of squash vines set off the dangers of poison ivy or thorns.

(7) Scatter   Sagas having more limited distribution trace world creation from the dismembered body of an immortal. In such epics, the dome of the sky above is the inside of the giant's skull, directly linking the upward curve of molded earth with shaped cranium. This analogy of body with beginnings seems, moreover, to have extended to newborns, living out the process.[47]

In all, thought, knowledge, and wisdom are often central in these accounts, but not always a tribal divinity; or so it seems in the record. Usually, however, this is because a native is reluctant to mention cherished beliefs to doubting, hostile, or critical outsiders. This deity is assumed by all members of the community and (in that sense) taken for granted. While some scholars have charged that such a high god was an import from Christianity, as these sagas make clear, however, it is not the idea or portrayal of a

---

[46] Jay Miller, Numic Religion: An Overview of Power in the Great Basin of Native North America 1983a; Basin Religion and Theology: A Comparative Study of Power (*Puha*) 1983b.

[47] An intriguing corollary is the report that Adena, the Ohio natives first to build complex burial mounds, also reshaped (molded) the heads of babies by pressuring them against hard cradleboards.

godhead which is important, but rather His or Her or Its (epicene his~her) position as a deified Mind at the heart of the cosmos, [48] aligned with other aspects like hearth, temple fire, sun ~ moon, and north star.[49]

Such a centering is herein called a <u>tysic</u> from the first letters of <u>t</u>ime + <u>s</u>pace + <u>c</u>enter with vowel letters pointing up (i) and down (y) to fill out this cosmogram. This tysic is made clearest by looking at translations of native language terms for such a divinity. The Delaware refer to "The One Who Created Us By Thought", the Keres Pueblos to Consciousness Deity (literally "Thought Woman"), and the Basin Numic to "Ocean Old Woman". As variously expressed; thought, will, and memory are passed on as their vital gift to their intelligent creations, generally at the moment of birth establishing outside contact with the living earth.

While these varieties of epics describe how the world was made or modified into the way it is today, not surprisingly, neighboring tribes will often have very different (or deliberately opposing) accounts of creation, as if to confirm their own separate and distinct identities. Similarly, incidental stories within a body of regional literature might be singled out to become a tribal epic of origins. In this way, an account of how a grieving husband carved the wooden likeness of his dead wife became the epic explaining the revival of a lost or deceased family through divine intervention. Habitat also played a major role. Cultures along the Atlantic and Pacific coasts attributed the creation of some people, especially "white" Europeans, to the sea foam made by wave action against beaches. By implication, of course, such origins are a subtle snub of their substance and worth.

Balled Up Layerings

Regardless of the type of epic, all regions share a basic model of the world as a floating flat disk, highlighted by mountains and rivers, with at least one level above it as the sky upper world and another below it as the under world. In overall profile, the cosmos is a ball, with the flat earth disk across the middle, an air-filled sky dome above, and a water-filled bowl below. A central tree (pole, pillar, tube, or similar <u>axis mundi</u>) interlinks these three domains, along with other mediators such as fires, springs, and caves to allow passage between the layers. Animating all is *puwah* pulsating along a web of rings and rays beginning and ending in a tysic (⊛), often a godhead, demiurge, deity, or creator. Circulating along the earth's skin, *puwah* appears as water in its curved and

---

[48]   Jay Miller, High-Minded High Gods in North America, 1980a; The Matter Of The (Thoughtful) Heart: Centrality, Focality, Or Overlap 1980b; <u>Earthmaker</u> 1992b.

[49]   Native languages usually use the same word for sun and moon, translated as 'orb' modified to be specific as 'day orb' for sun and 'night orb' for moon. In mythology, however, they are often distinctly engendered with the Sun male and the Moon female, linked with tidal and menstrual cycles. Cherokee, Yuchi, and others of the Southeast, though, revere Sun as female. As noted, North Star represents the fixed stability appropriate to community leaders.

light in its straight channels, both serving as **tubes** to concentrate vitality in the spinal column, heart, and other organs.

Certain beings, such as birds and snakes, had the inherent ability to travel across these divisions. Better yet were beings like the Feathered Serpent with combined attributes of the avian, reptilian, and amphibian. As Peter Roe, a South American archaeologist, has shown, the cosmic model for lowland Amazonia and much of the Americas is like a layer cake inside a ball that is pierced by the world tree in the center. Indeed, the very title of his book The Cosmic Zygote (fertilized egg fusing female and male) underscores the crucial importance of gender for all of the Americas.[50] The earth is thin and danger lurks below, so mounding earth adds vital layers of protection and weighted security.

The US Southeast emphasized three zones of their world -- a lower, middle, and upper layer. Something like a thin membrane (such as a drum head, surface skim, sheer curtain) stretched between each of them, with catastrophe and confusion resulting from any breaching of it. In stories, men turned into "tie-snakes" after wrongly eating fish swimming in tree stumps, where they never belong. Today, most Creeks, both Christian and traditional, carefully avoid the "new ground" (*ekvna mocvse* ~ *i:kana močasi:*) turned up for a fresh grave, and special purification is required of those who do go to the graveside and carry off such soil on their shoe soles. Each grave breached the surface tension of the earth's skin and grief added uncertainty, calling for these ritual precautions.[51]

For the whole of North America, interlinked by intermarried regional high families, the universal metaphor of the cross inside a circle ⊕ was given actual geographical form by the confluences of the Ohio and Missouri Rivers entering the Mississippi above modern St. Louis. As confirmation of this belief, the huge Mississippian ceremonial center, now called Cahokia, thrived there, focused around Monk's Mound, the largest human-made earth platform in these drainages (and north of Mexico).[52] Surrounding it were sacred spaces and scattered settlements presided over by high chiefs and priests thoroughly involved in a vast complex of trade and ritual relations.

---

[50] Peter Roe, The Cosmic Zygote ~ smology in the Amazon Basin 1982.

[51] A distinctive feature of Creek churchyard cemeteries, congruent with this belief, are small rectangular houses, the outline shape of the grave, emphasizing that the body is not entirely below ground.

[52] Melvin Fowler, The Cahokia Atlas, A Historical Atlas of Cahokia Archaeology 1989; Sally Kitt Chappell, Cahokia – Mirror of the Cosmos 2002; Roger Kennedy, Hidden Cities, The Discovery and Loss of Ancient North American Civilization 1994; David Brose, James Brown, and David Penney, Ancient Art of the American Woodland Indians 1985; George Milner, The Cahokia Chiefdom, The Archaeology of a Mississippi Society 1998; Patricia O'Brien, Cahokia: The Political Capitol of the "Ramey" State 1989.

Of course, each of the Mississippian centers – such as the "big three" of Moundville, Etowah, and Spiro – was itself a world pivot for a native nation.[53]

Given the link between size and spiritual potency, Cahokia, as the largest in overall area and complexity, could and did make claims to paramountcy. Its location near the junctures of the Mississippi, Missouri, and Ohio Rivers also marks it as the "heart" (tysic) of the entire continent. Though some have argued that it was merely a larger version of its neighbors,[54] the enormous bulk of its main mound among all those surrounding chiefdoms bespeaks its assertions of primacy (hegemony?).

In addition to such hand-built sacred centers, all of the Americas were marked by numerous, widely scattered holy sites enhanced by rock art or portable bundles. On a cliff face near the mouth of the Missouri (near Alton, Illinois) was painted a huge Piasa, an underwater panther with antlers and long tail, "who" served as both marker (route, road sign) and warning for turbulent river conditions ahead. The image is appropriate because many Plains tribes regarded the Missouri as the embodiment of a huge snake that had once been human.[55]

Birger and Beyond

Mounds are of the nurturing earth, usually "conceived" as a mother (and grandmother). Stones are her bones, soil her flesh, and grass her hair. Native languages also make more intimate connections between mounds and her breasts and pubic bulge, as well as to heart, navel, and womb. The feminine associations of mounds, as noted above, are particularly clear in Tunica, an engendered language of Louisiana, where *hali* ~ earth and *halitimura* ~ earth mound are female.[56]

Earth, moreover, combines the forms of both woman and snake, represented separately or fused together as a female serpent. Also associated, therefore, are leathery eggs and the Moon, both from its shape and its influence on menstrual cycles. While these relationships abound in mythology, they are best seen physically in three dimensions. In Ohio about CE/AD 1066, as noted, the looping body of the female Serpent Mound was built of earth to have alignments with the Moon and Sun. Within its open jaws is an egg-like mound. Of especial note, the surrounding terrain is massively fractured, with meteor impact or gaseous explosion suggested as explanations for this "unique crypto-explosion geology".[57]

---

[53] Vernon James Knight and Vincas Steponaitis, <u>Archaeology of the Moundville Chiefdom</u> 1998. Moundville has 20 mounds, Etowah has 6, and Spiro has 12, though many are small presumably to raise up a house.

[54] George Milner, <u>The Cahokia Chiefdom</u> 1998.

[55] Alfred Bowers, <u>Hidatsa Social and Ceremonial Organization</u> 1965: 65, 165. Pottery making itself was a gift to an old Hidatsa couple from snakes, evoking their eternal battle with Thunderbirds, whose lightning bolts can crack drying vessels before or as they are fired.

[56] Mary Haas, <u>Tunica</u> 1941; <u>Tunica Dictionary</u> 1953: 211.

[57] Ohio Historical Society flyer for Serpent Mounds, 7/04, backside.

From a priestly suburb (BBB Motor site, in CE/AD 1050-1150 = Cahokia's Stirling Phase), where the honored Mississippian dead were processed, came the sculpted Birger Figurine.[58] It is the only motion-depicting effigy among Illinois stone images. Carved of red stone, a woman kneels down so that her hoe and hand directly engage the body of an enormous snake, whose forked tail turns into vines with gourds growing up her body.[59] Fangs and catlike eyes also indicate that it is no ordinary serpent.

Snakes, moreover, represent the much larger class of amphibians, such as turtles, lizards, alligators, and crocodiles. Many have strong associations with creation and cosmology. For Delaware and Iroquois, the world rests on the back of a Turtle, floating in a vast sea, whose domed shell parallels the sky and copies the mound form. The Maya creator is a complex crocodilian (reptilian) being called *Itzamna*.

The Birger woman's bland face, slack jaw, and exposed teeth suggest death to some, though her upright posture and hand-held hoe show that she was active (and perhaps in trance). Affirming life are her bare breasts and something carried on her back, in the same manner as a cradleboard. Such life and death juxtapositions associate her with the renewing abilities of both Moon and snakes. Waning and waxing, the Moon perpetually changes both within a month and by 18.6 year orbit. Among Hochungara (Winnebagos), snakes represent immortality, through the ability to shed skin (Chapter 8); Ohio Valley Siouan equates snakes with deity (Introduction).

In parallel fashion, much larger than life, the largest figure in the Pawnee earth lodge prepared for a Big (Medicine) Doctoring was the snake, set in an arc sixty feet long. It had a forked tail, and a large man could fit inside its sharp-fanged mouth. Resting her back along the side was a woman effigy identified as the Moon (Chapter 8).

Ramifications of such Woman ~ Moon ~ Snake ~ Egg imagery extend into seeds, and therefore plants. In particular, the spiraling radiation outward of vines is likened to spider webs, whose rings and rays covering the earth provide a ready arterial means for the flow of vital *puwah* throughout the universe. Equally powerful are the ebb and neap tides influenced by the Moon. The use of gourds as rattles to keep the pace of songs, which also pulsate with *puwah*, brings these associations, literally "in hand", back to

---

[58] Guy Prentice, An Analysis of the Symbolism Expressed by the Birger Figurine 1986. Though Prentice traced the complex symbolism of the Birger as Earth Mother in the ethnographic and mythologic literature, he would have done better to look also at ritual, where the Pawnee effigies provide a startling parallel that is also in three dimensions. He suggests that the figurine, if not made and smashed at the BBB site (as seems most likely), may have been manufactured in either the Missouri Fire Clay or Spiro Caddoan districts, and traded into Cahokia. The Pawnee are Caddoan speakers. Cf. Thomas Emerson, Mississippian Stone Images in Illinois 1982.

[59] According to Gayle Fritz, Levels of Biodiversity in Eastern North America 2000: 235, these vines "are depicted in such clear botanical detail that they can be attributed to the taxon *Cucurbita argyrosperma ssp. argyrosperma*, familiar to many eastern North Americans as the green striped cushaw".

humans. Women raise the gourds in their gardens, and men shape them for musical accompaniment in the town square.[60]

Snakings

Based on the Birger and other figurines featuring snakes, Jim Brown[61] identifies serpent images with the Mississippian fertility cult.[62] The use of their undulating form in mounds is much earlier. Ohio's Serpent Mound dates to CE 1066, as noted, while Serpent Mound (194 feet) in Ontario, near the famous Peterborough petroglyphs, yielded dates ranging over 174 years from CE 128 ± 200 years to 302 ± 150 years. It included burials that had been cremated in place, as well as full body inhumations. Burials 1 and 2 were a tightly flexed male and female sharing their grave with rolled foil beads of silver (1) and copper (4 of these), bird and mammal bones, and a timber wolf snout.[63]

As legless, cold-blooded, underground dwellers, snakes are closely identified (embellied) with the earth itself.[64] In general, they embody fertility because they are regarded as androgynous, making them both anomalous and mediating. Throughout South America, snakes have both male (tails) and female (mouths) aspects.[65] Except while egg-laying and nesting, females seem virtually identical to males. Of note, this same observation, with global comparisons, was reported by none other than Ephraim Squire (after he broke with Edwin Davis during the 1848 publication of their monumental study of Mississippi Valley mounds), using observations that were cut from their final draft by the Smithsonian editor.[66]

---

[60] In Timucua, a lapsed language of north Florida, <u>chucu</u> means dark earth as well as gourd, pumpkin, squash, See Julian Granberry, <u>A Grammar and Dictionary of the Timucua Language</u> 1993: 125.

[61] James Brown, The Mississippian Period, <u>Ancient Art of the American Woodland Indians</u> 1985: 123-140.

[62] George Lankford's "The Great Serpent in Eastern North America" reviews Mississippian images and motifs, including a link to the constellation Scorpio and star Antares on the edge of the southern horizon, an obvious panoramic departure from its habitual underworld constraints. See Kent Reilly and James Garber, <u>Ancient Objects and Sacred Realms</u>: Interpretations of Mississippian Iconography 2007: 107-135.

[63] W. A. Kenyon, <u>Mounds of Sacred Earth</u>, Burial Mounds of Ontario 1986: 10-12, 22-24.

[64] Dave Aftandilian, Frogs, Snakes, and Agricultural Fertility: Interpreting Illinois Mississippian Representations. <u>What Are the Animals to Us?</u> <u>Approaches from Science, Religion, Folklore, Literature, and Art</u> 2007b, Chapter 4: 53-86.

[65] Peter Roe, <u>The Cosmic Zygote</u> 1982: 196.

[66] Ephraim Squier, <u>The Serpent Symbol</u> and the Worship of Reciprocal Principles of Nature in America 1851.

In Origin Sagas (including the Bible), snakes feature prominently. Among the Cubeo of Venezuela, an ancestral Anaconda's body served as the canoe that delivered ancestral couples to their homelands along the various bends of their river. Similarly, as long and thin, snakes share attributes of the world tree that upholds the universe.[67] Often hollow, and sometimes water-filled, this tree, which grows from the earth island, was the abode of either the primordial woman or snake. For Mayans, its patron is Itzamna, with many reptilian features. Today, one living species replicates the world in microcosm when "crocodilians pile up earth amid water to make mounds where they lay their eggs. Trees take root in these mounds, forming miniature models of the earth".[68]

Snakes, because of their undulating locomotion, are closely linked with rivers and other waterways. Hidatsa believed that any lake and river was "inhabited by a snake that maintained their water level".[69] The snake in the Missouri blessed hunting, warfare, and gardens when given prayerful offerings. Mounds had been built during rituals associated with his ordeals when he was a human (Chapter 5).

Karl Luckert proposed, based on the mound and buried mosaics at La Venta,[70] that the Olmec world recognized its origin from the Earth Serpent, whose coiled body became a volcano whose lava streams, issuing from its open mouth, were regarded as snake children emerging from the earth.[71] At other times and places, this snake appeared in the sky in rainbow form, as among the Panare of Venezuela. Diverse Mayan groups regard the Milky Way as a snake. For Yucatec, it is the very deadly fer-de-lance.[72] In imagery during Classic Mayan times, snakes indicated transitions, appearing as "vision serpents".[73] Generally, they show passages, with their own bodies sometimes providing the means (**tubes**) of transport and of congress.

---

[67] Trees, sticks, and snakes are closely associated. Among the meager stories told by Catawba, successors of a thriving Eastern Siouan chiefdom visited by Soto, is "63. Sticks Turn into Snakes to Guard a Melon Patch. An old man stuck sharp sticks in the ground in his melon patch. The land was good. Some person stole some melons. Many snakes [ya] came from the sticks. The person ran away." Clearly, the sticks had been treated with dicta to animate them into snakes to protect the crop. Frank Speck, Catawba Texts 1934: 41.

[68] Susan Milbrath, Star Gods of the Maya 1999: 76.

[69] Douglas Parks and Waldo Wedel, Pawnee Geography, Historical and Sacred 1985: 168.

[70] Ignacio Bernal, The Olmec World 1969; Philip Drucker, Robert Heizer, and Robert Squier, Excavations at La Venta Tabasco 1959.

[71] Peter Roe, The Cosmic Zygote 1982: 285.

[72] Susan Milbrath, Star Gods of the Maya 1999, 40: 282.

[73] Linda Schele and Peter Mathews, The Code of Kings 1998: 47.

Slitherings

In a tour de force analysis, Trudy Sable[74] focuses on the Snake Dance of the Mi'kmaw (Mikmaq) of Maine.[75] Today, this dance is done by children at powwows, but this belies more ancient origins. While the Mi'kmaw word for snake is *mteskm*, this dance is named *jujijua'jik*, meaning 'emulating crawling'. It derives from *jujij*, referring to the distinctive movement ('slithering', 'crawlying')[76] used by snakes, lizards, turtles, spiders, toads, and others who move close to the ground (including "dragons", see below).[77] Slugs, snails, caterpillars, beetles, and inchworms also share this attribute, but are less compelling examples, unless they are explained as former ogres much reduced to their present attributes. Because of its distinctive folding in half, in epics, the inchworm has the ability to shorten distance or move closer together points on the earth.[78]

To provide background, Sable draws attention to five factors necessary to comprehend the Mi'kmaw cultural universe. In paraphrase, these attributes, best conveyed in their Eastern Algonkian language, are continuous flux and process, shape-shifting realities, interrelationships (never separate, distinct entities), epitomizing images, and hypersensitivity to the geophysics of the Canadian Maritimes. In sum, everything, as macro~microcosm, is mirrored in everything else, seen and unseen in the landscape and cosmos, which is inherently precarious.

In choreography, this dance twice duplicates the cycle of a year. In the first phase, the man in the lead takes up a position in the center, setting the rhythm with a rattle made of a hollow horn -- which was trimmed off, filled with pellets, and plugged up. The dancers form a circle, facing him, and, three times, move to the right. Second, they turn their backs to him and repeat the rotation another three times. Third, they turn their backs to each other, revolving three times. Fourth, still back-to-back, they go around backwards three times.

---

[74] Trudy Sable, Multiple Layers of Meaning in the Mi'kmaw Serpent Dance 1997: 329-340.

[75] Just reading this crucial work was no small feat. Willard Walker recommended it in 2002 at Asheville, NC, but no library I visited across the US had volume 28. Mark Ebert, thankfully, supplied a copy from the University of Alberta in Saskatoon in 2004.

[76] The English translation must follow from the native term, not, as usually happens, have English dominate all discourse. "Slithering" is used here but "crawlying" better conveys the much more dynamic action missing from the gerund alone. The English phrase of "creepy crawly" is unfortunate, highlighting the many problems of translation. The semantic contrast involves a "drag" for crawling, but a "glide" for slithering.

[77] Toad skin can contain toxins that are hallucinogenic or psycho-active, adding to these complexities, See William Wihr, You Toad Sucking Fool 1995.

[78] Thelma Adamson, Folk-Tales of the Coast Salish 1934: 273. Sophie Smith, the narrator, actually called this grandmotherly blind old lady a "Measuring Worm".

In the second phase, the central leader dances through the circle like a snake leaving its den. The dancers follow him in a line as he turns and twists across the field.[79] Three times, the line spirals inwardly around him, tightening up until he leads it to unfold outward and through the field, coiling and uncoiling like a snake shedding its skin. During the last inward spiral, the dancers scatter one by one until only the leader remains in the center.

In all, alternating men and women perform 12 (4 x 3) revolutions to honor and placate the *puwah* (medicines, poisons) of the "snake". They also repeat the maneuver to emulate its writhing to shed its skin, and be reborn. Forward and backward motions mirror each other, achieving overall balance.

Held in the spring, when snakes awaken, the patron of this dance is probably the most powerful of the slitherers. Though the rattlesnake is often mentioned, none occur in the Maritimes.[80] Instead, this being is the *jipijka'm*, the local version of the so-called "horned serpent", an awesome keeper of medicines,[81] whose males and females both have one red and one yellow horn. Though it could take human form, it usually looks like a dragon, crocodile, or alligator.

Moreover, the dance epitomizes many crucial interrelationships. Its seasonal ones extend into the night sky, particularly in terms of the Pleiades or another nearby constellation. On earth, it evokes health-giving medicine, including the plant called golden club, which has a red and yellow stalk, rattling stiff leaves, and a yellow spadix (flower cluster) that looks like a rattle. The horn rattle of the dance leader similarly evokes the horns of two colors. While all the seasons and cycles of a year are represented, spring rebirth of vitality receives special regard.

In its flux and flow, the dance mirrors this ever-dynamic universe, thoroughly infused with interrelated, apportioned, shape-shifting powers who are better able to embody the earth itself because of their proximity to it via their very (f)act of slitherying.

Snaking Walls, Uktena Crystals

The composite horned serpent was very powerful and important for most of the Americas. Groundhog's Mother (*Aganunitsi*) was the name of a Shawnee shaman captured by the Cherokee.[82] Bound to a stake for his final torture, he pleaded to be released to undertake a mortal quest for *Ulvsuti* -- the blazing crystal set into the forehead of the Uktena, the deadly underwater horned panther-snake (akin to *jipijka'm*). After a promise to benefit and cure the Cherokees if he achieved the slim margin for success, he

---

[79] These same maneuvers among other tribes are called by less threatening names such as the Bean, Vine, and Spiral Dance.

[80] Laurence Klauber, Rattlesnakes, Their Habits, Life Histories, and Influence on Mankind 1982.

[81] Throughout the Midwest this is the legendary, crypto-biological, composite animal known as the Piasaw.

[82] Barbara Duncan and Brett Riggs, Cherokee Heritage Trails Guidebook 2003: 153, 317, 347-49.

was released and began his search, moving ever southward through every Appalachian gap in the rough terrain where the monster lurked.

Starting at the northern Great Smoky range, he found only a monster Blacksnake, which he mocked with laughter. At other gaps, he met a gigantic Water Moccasin (Cottonmouth), and, beyond, a giant coiled Greensnake blocking the path and frightening people. Near Andrews at Joanna Bald, a huge lizard basked in the sun. At Blood Mountain (Frog Place, *Walasiyi*), a huge frog filled that gap. At Forked Antler (Newfound Gap, *Duniskwa'lgvyi*) and the enchanted lake at Clingman's Dome (*Atagahi*), he encountered other huge reptiles. At Murphy (*Tlanusi'yi*), he dove into the Hiwassee River to see Turtles, Water Snakes, a pair of immense Sun Perch, and, particularly powerful, a gigantic reddish Leech. At last, he found the Uktena asleep atop Cohutta (*Gahuti*) Mountain near the center of Cherokee territory.

Running down the slope at one breath, he gathered a huge circle of pinecones, dug a deep trench in the middle, and set the pile ablaze. Rushing back up to the sleeping monster, he shot an arrow into its heart, located under the seventh spot down its back. Mortally-wounded, the crystal-blazing snake charged the Shawnee man, who ran downhill and jumped inside the ring of fire beyond the trench. The Uktena rolled down in its death coils, spewing poisonous blood and venom that sizzled in the fire or filled the ditch. After the dead Uktena stopped rolling, the man invited all the birds to feast on it until nothing remained.

Seven days later, the man returned in the dark to find the *Ulvsuti* crystal shining on a lower branch where Raven had left it. The blood in the trench formed a black pool of water, where women afterward dyed cane splints for basketry. Where one drop of fatal blood had struck the man at the back of his head, a snake grew, marking him as the greatest medicine man of all time.

Today, a huge prehistoric carved stone turtle, like that seen during the dive, sits in front of the (combined) police station and museum at Murphy (NC), rescued from rising waters behind a dam. At Fort Mountain State Park (GA), along the under-ridge ledge where the Uktena slept, is a prehistoric stonewall, 855 feet long from east to west, with six-foot rock rings ("coils") set at thirty foot intervals along its south side, providing a panorama of the sky and Piedmont at the southern end of the Appalachians.

Since the birds consumed every shred of the Uktena, the wall is baffling unless it represents a monument to these events or many rock offerings left behind by patrons of the view. The location is ideal for astronomical observations, with the walls and rings providing suitable markers for solar and planetary movements. The equation of wall and snake seems unavoidable, suggesting that other walls, such as those at Hopewell enclosures, may have also represented snakes. In the case of those like Fort Ancient, where there are gaps, these might be places where the vertical folds of the long body remained underground in the manner of typical kid's drawings of a sea serpent where only the upper loops are drawn while the lower ones remain hidden under water. Among such instances, the Serpent Mound of Ohio is merely the most obvious of such snaking parameter walls.

Morphing

Considering only the shape, geography, and outline of this world, however, misses its vital (and threatening) characteristic – dynamic motion rather than inert stasis. This protean – shifting, moving, volatile, precarious, dangerous, cyclical – cosmos of Native America is particularly well illustrated by transmutations unknown to "scientific" biology, if not actively opposed by its rigid classroom teachers.[83] Reports of such beliefs are sporadic at best, and always in danger of being ridiculed away during biased education. Yet the seasonal dominance and high frequency of seemingly different species in the same habitat encourages such native beliefs to continue, reinforced by such obvious changes in nature. They are regarded as natural and typical -- by no means extraordinary states -- because flux and motion are the accepted perspectives on life, just as verbs carry the burden in these native languages.[84]

Entirely distinct from such biology is shape-shifting across "species" as a manifestation of *puwah*, especially by shamans, sorcerers, or witches briefly changing into their animal familiars to carry out a cure, task, or attack. These are temporary spiritually-charged instances of "the deceptiveness of appearances", which Algonquianists call "percept ambiguity", providing a cautious approach to life experiences.[85]

In contrast, ethnobiological intraspecies maturations belong to the ordinary world. Indeed, students learn (and see) in science class that caterpillars turn into butterflies, and tadpoles into frogs, but these are life stages within the same (intra)species. Throughout the world, however, interspecies transference still survives as folk belief of great antiquity. Ovid captured this sense in his <u>Metamorphosis</u>. Aristotle was sure the same bird changed species and plumage to adapt to different summer and winter conditions. English and Scottish folk believed that long-neck barnacles became geese. In Brazil, a hummingbird and a mimicking hawk moth appear so much alike that both were assumed to be life stages of the same species.

Yet American Natives were more wide ranging in their morphings. Thus the Pamunkey of Virginia said that tree frogs turned into shy birds (sora rails, *Porzana carolina*), who add to the mystery because they actually migrate away at night) after the frost and cold arrive.[86] Northeastern tribes displaced to Ohio reported geese changed into

---

[83] Frank Speck and John Witthoft, Some Notable Life-Histories in Zoological Folklore 1947.

[84] Such flux and flow partake of potent precedent vitality when the very first "unrestricted" beings were variously Mist, Fog, Mirage, Shimmer People, Cf. Jerrold Levi, <u>In the Beginning</u> ~ <u>the Navajo Genesis</u> 1998: 171.

[85] Irving Hallowell, Ojibwa Ontology, Behavior, and World View 1969: 70.

[86] "And they [Powhatans] know that the frogs develop from tadpoles ... [and] that the[se] birds have partially webbed feet like the frogs. ... A poetical fancy has associated the disappearance of the myriad croaking frogs from the marshes in the fall with the appearance of the myriads of birds during the season just following; and both filling the same places with their cries [which sound like croaks]. They come about September 20th," Frank Speck,

beavers to restock dams, and snakes became raccoons for the winter. For Great Lakes Menomini, garter snakes turned into chipmunks. Mi'kmaw (Micmac) believed that aged moose stags changed into whales to revitalize in the sea. Among Cherokees of the Carolinas, a fish known to pile stones with its lips on stream bottoms became a lizard (blue-tailed skink) with a bloody red mouth. Michigan Ottawa held that salamanders matured into trout. Chitimacha of Louisiana said hailstones provided the spat that turned into clams, conjoining sky, water, and beach sand.[87] Throughout, the deciding considerations seem to be shared habitat, frequency, and behaviors rather than "scientific" genetics.

While it is tempting to view such shape-shifting as an aspect of a precarious world, this is too simplistic. Instead, this Native world is orderly and much more open to other vitalities. These changes are known and predictable, according to oft-repeated tales in regional folklore. Indeed, today's native artists in the Northwest delight in portraying the shift of wolves into killerwhales and back again, confident that its essence as a social carnivore can travel either on land as packs or in water as pods. It is not the morphing itself that is uncertain, but rather its timing and place, as well as the potential of unexpected attack and turmoil. Sudden complex movement trumps simple stillness, cataclysm jars assumptions and indicates the high degree of volatility of the universe.

Conclusions

Mounds mimic the earth, in all of its aspects, whether creation, conservation, continuity, complexity, or catastrophe. Their foremost representatives are snakes, and other slithering, lunging reptilians. While their outer form mirrors the earth, hill, mountain, volcano, and sky; their insides can evoke hollow heart, womb, spine, nest, den, and fortress. At other times, or even simultaneously, the inside is grave, cave, tube, and passage to the underworld, as well as conduit to new vitality.

Sustained by orderly human rituals and purifying efforts, mounding also acts as atonement for unintended impacts on the earth. Once built up, they provide steadying ballast, bulk, bank, and bulge. More than just places for burials, community projects, or territory markers, mounds provide the means for humans to be bodily involved in a microcosm of the cosmic cycles, while also providing a vital haven from the precarious, unstable, and suddenly-violent world -- given to pulsing, trembling, and occasional writhing turmoil that is not easily predictable or avoidable without some kind of supernatural aid and prophetic warnings.

Chapters on the Ethnology of the Powhatan Tribes of Virginia 1928: 340. These birds are hunted from canoes with a "sora horse" (ironwork torch) at the bow to light-blind them at night so they can be knocked out of their roosts. The activity is called "sorassin" derived from Algonkian –*assin* "torchlight fishing at night".

[87] John Swanton, Indian Tribes of the Lower Mississippi Valley and Adjacent Coast of the Gulf of Mexico 1911: 354.

3 ~ THEORIES, STANCES, AND STORIES

A burial mound is "an 'inverted' grave" providing both interment and "a fitting and a lasting monument [as it] reverses the operation of excavating a receptacle beneath the surface level by heaping the covering of earth above the surface" of the grave.[88] In many instances, an offering will be placed into the ground before mounds and other structures are built up to consecrate and bless the location.

Among the earliest of these inversions seems to be ritual caches, probably made as offerings to the earth and its dwellers. Colored earths, especially red ocher, define these caches as sacred, in both the past and the present. Lived-in spaces also serve as offerings. The earliest dated mounds bury the remains of a prior dwelling with the intent of both memorializing and renewing it in community sentiment. By removing it from view, it is also transported to another world or realm of existence, often that of spirit immortals with their own vitality (Chapter 6).

Sharply contrasting to these ethno-spiritual concerns, American archaeologists specializing on the reductionist analysis of mounds, with Thomas Jefferson and US federal projects leading the way.[89] Sorting out patterns in the locations, types, and diagnostic artifacts added clarity, though datings were long problematic. Instead, geographical patterns were much easier to plot, as was debunking racist cant about the "Mound Builders," said to be a prior ("superior") race that was destroyed by cruel ancestors of native tribes. In time, professional archaeology outlined Americanist continuities; providing reliable materialist insights into the prehistory of the Americas.

We now turn to such key theories, stories, and experiences in the US archaeological record to provide an overview of academic perspectives, focusing on key thinkers across time and space. Excepted and rearranged sections of this chapter were

---

[88] Henry Shetrone, The Mound-Builders 1930: 183.

[89] Much SE archaeology was done under federal auspices during the Depression, with the most chilling episode being the excavation of Irene Mound near Savannah, Georgia, by a crew of African American women who were forbidden to use wheelbarrows because it was unladylike. See Nancy Marie White, Lynne Sullivan, and Rochelle Marrinan, Grit-Tempered ~ Early Women Archaeologists in the Southeastern United States 1999: 92-114, Chapter 5 (Cheryl Claassen). Cf. Joseph Caldwell and Catherine McCann, Irene Mound Site, Chatham County, Georgia 1941.

Equally bizarre are the mound excavations by the southern Plains warriors jailed at St Augustine in the mid-1870s to reform them and expose them to "civilized ways". At the request of Spencer Baird, later second Secretary of the Smithsonian, three mounds were sketched, cleared off, excavated, and finds shipped in barrels to add to early Smithsonian's collections. Put on display in cases, these were erroneously attributed to John Wesley Powell, head of the Bureau of American Ethnology, who had accessioned them, See Richard Henry Pratt, Battlefield and Classroom 1964: 130-1.

recycled in Miller (2015), the half of my original manuscript dealing mostly with the Native Southeast.

Delaware Traditions of Battling Mounds

While Spanish and French writers described mounds in active use in the Southeast, English sources for usage in the Northeast were vague.[90] Under the onslaught of epidemics, disease, and missionaries, most native sages withheld any esoteric knowledge of the mounds to avoid ridicule, insult, martyrdom, and destruction. When some Delawares, already Christians, returned to Ohio in 1772 to reestablish their Moravian missions, they told clergy of their ancestral conflict with the gigantic Tallegwi. "Conquering" these giants on their way to settling their own Atlantic homeland, Lenape thereby retained rights to reoccupy them.

Moravian Rev. John Heckewelder[91] reported this "very powerful nation, who had many large towns [with] regular fortifications and entrenchments ... called themselves Talligewi", since applied to the Allegheny River and Mountains. Described as giants, they buried their warriors in large flat mounds, which dotted the land.

The famous Moravian missionary Rev. David Zeisberger provided the first description and explanation of impressive Ohio Hopewell earthworks in English: "along the Muskingum ... embankments, still to be seen, were thrown up around a whole town [with nearby] mounds, not natural, but made by the hand of man [when natives were] far more numerous". Atop each mound was a hollow where wives and children took refuge, and "great blocks" were stockpiled to roll down the slopes during attack. After a battle, slain men were buried in a pit "and a great mound of earth raised above them, such as may even now [1779-80] be seen bearing in these days great and mighty trees".[92]

The unconverted Delaware majority, in Ohio from the 1750s, were careful to also receive sanctioned permission to settle from the resident Wyandot, who long hunted the region as members of the Huron Nation before they took refuge there from Iroquois assaults, especially the 1649 slaughter on Christian Island.

Thomas Jefferson

Mounds early became an aspect of American character, as they long had been for European themselves, as the mound on the Hill of Tara was linked to Irish Kings.[93] A

---

[90] John Juricek, after a lifetime devoted to Georgia and British Colonial history, sagely remarked to Jay Miller, "The English were blind to mounds", which were, of course, obvious evidence of natives "improving the land" like the barrows built by their own British ancestors.

[91] John Heckewelder, History, Manners, and Customs of the Indian Nations Who Once Inhabited Pennsylvania, and Neighboring States [1819] 1876: 48, 49.

[92] David Zeisberger, History of the Northern American Indian 1910: 30-1.

[93] Tara incorporates a Neolithic tomb called the Mound of the Hostages, adding its venerable age to this seat of the Irish high kings, Simon James, The World of the Celts 1993: 157.

keen intellectual, Thomas Jefferson set a strong course for the popular understanding of the native peoples of the United States and North America, spurred on by nationalist pride. While he wrote voluminously, Jefferson's only published book is modestly titled <u>Notes on the State of Virginia</u>.[94] Its chapter titles were phrased as questions or queries.[95]

Query XI looked at the natives of Virginia, briefly discussing political, cultural, and linguistic differences among the Powhatan, Mannahoacs, Manacans, and their neighbors. But Jefferson expressed the cultural biases of his times, though, sagely, he noted these native lands had been acquired by Euro-Americans not by outright conquest, but by legal proofs of purchase such as treaties. Rather than appreciating keen farming skills of these tribes, however, he repeated the distortion that these people lived "on the spontaneous productions of nature". Seeking evidence of worthy large-scale labor in "monuments", he sought something like a common ditch shared by an entire community for draining farm lands, but instead settled on local "barrows" or earthen mounds.

Curious about these mounds throughout the landscape, Jefferson (by slave labor) excavated one about two miles from his Monticello estate. While much legend and fantasy was and is associated with such mounds, including the apocryphal Mound Builders, he correctly concluded that local natives had built and used them for burials, wisely noting return visits by living Saponi to strengthen his argument. Ahead of his time, he was guided by a sense of stratigraphy – that older layers were naturally below

---

[94] Thomas Jefferson, <u>Notes on the State of Virginia</u> 1785 ~ Paris, 1787~ London. Drafted at the end of the American Revolution (1781) in response to questions raised by French allies, nervous about future US prospects, Jefferson was then the 37-year-old Governor of Virginia.

[95] Its 23 chapters took "notice" of Virginia's boundaries, rivers, mountains, cascades and caverns, mines, vegetation, population, militia, navy, natives (Indiens), counties and townships, charters and constitution, law and justice, colleges and roads, Tory assets, religions, local customs, commerce, European imports, measures and currency, public income, histories, and memorials. Appendices considered a draft constitution, an act for establishing religious freedom, and, in later editions, an examination of the 1774 murder of the "entire" family of Logan, a Mingo (Ohio Iroquois) leader who, with great eloquence and pathos, lamented that he alone was left to mourn for all of his slain kin.

Jefferson quoted Logan's speech in his chapter Query VI while refuting the claim of Count Buffon (Comte Georges Louis Leclerc, 1707-1788) and other French scholars that "vapors" in the defective soil of America caused its inhabitants to degenerate. After commenting on the great size and diversity of American animals, he considered the aboriginal peoples, arguing against certain claims made by these Frenchmen about body stature and ardor. As evidence of insight and ability, he quoted Logan's speech and named the murderer, but subsequent evidence has shown the leader of the murderers to be Daniel Greathouse, whose brother and sister-in-law, in revenge, suffered excruciating tortures to the death.

younger ones, that older was deeper. By this insight, he laid the foundation for future American archaeology, though others were slow to follow his lead.

To understand the origin and distribution of native tribes, moreover, Jefferson thought it was best to look at language, particularly the names for common objects, noun and verb inflections, and principles of regimen and concord (that is, grammar). At the end of his chapter is a chart of known American tribes and their estimated populations for 1759, 1764, and 1768. (Culminating these thoughts, he drafted the guidelines used by Lewis and Clark to collect natural and ethnographic information during their exploration of the newly acquired Louisiana Purchase, which began American expansion into the Middle West as well as providing eventual new homes for Eastern tribes deported from their ancestral homelands.)

Lewis Henry Morgan

Lewis Henry Morgan (1818-1881)[96] -- the Rochester lawyer befriended by Iroquois, father of kinship studies, and American social evolutionist -- assigned mound building to middle Barbarism, along with irrigation farming, domesticated animals, stone and adobe-brick architecture, human sacrifice, and incipient priesthoods, distinguished by distinctive garb. In the fifth section of his classic Ancient Society, published separately as Houses and House-Life of the American Aborigines, the Mound-Builders chapter firmly identifies them as American Indians not as a mysterious prior race. His further explanations, however, err. Supposedly migrating from farming New Mexico Pueblos into the frigid climate of Ohio, "The Mound-Builders in their new area east of the Mississippi, finding it impossible to construct joint-tenement houses of adobe bricks to which they had been accustomed, substituted solid embankments of earth in the place of the first story closed up on the ground, and erected triangular houses upon them covered with earth".[97] Using High Bank (square and circle) in Ohio as his reconstruction, he proposed drying racks scattered within the square and either gardens or councils within the circle, similar to round kivas (estufas, "ovens" in Spanish) of the Southwest Pueblos but here adapted to open-air meetings. Contradictions between houses insulated against the cold and councils in the open are ignored, though he probably intended these uses to be seasonal. He praised their mining of copper and other minerals, while indicating that the lack of ironwork and shift of human sacrifice into slavery kept them from "upper Barbarism".

Morgan's overall concern was tracing, within the sweep of known humanity, the evolution and redistribution of village farming peoples out of Central America into the Southwest and then into the Ohio. Without a correct timeframe, however, he was unaware that mound builders were not maize farmer, but instead relied on local domesticates. His association of mounds with housing is more intriguing, if misplaced,

---

[96] Lewis Henry Morgan, The Indian Journals 1859-62 1959; Ancient Society, or, Researches in the Lines of Human Progress from Savagery through Barbarism to Civilization 1963 [1877]; Houses and House-Life of the American Aborigines 1965 [1881].

[97] Morgan, Houses and House-Life of the American Aborigines 1965: 244.

since some mounds do indeed cover over a burned council, charnel, and temple building, while some earthwork circles bury former palisade rings.[98] Morgan briefly considered conical burial mounds, correctly identifying the so-called "altars" of prior writers as cremation basins and firmly linking the cremation of a chief with the erection of an earthen mound over "his" (sic) remains "as a mark of honor and respect".

Theoretical arguments aside, Morgan gained first hand knowledge of continuing burial mound use, learned from the famous Jesuit Pierre Jean De Smet, in the case of Blackbird, an Omaha leader, buried astride his best horse beneath a high mound beside the Mississippi so he could continue to be visited and remembered.[99]

More personally, Morgan preferred political, social, and economic explanations because, as an upper class Protestant, he was adverse to religious rituals as garish and empty of advanced theology. Though he did call these "natural religions" rather than superstitions, he wrote "all primitive religions are grotesque and to some extent unintelligible".[100]

As an equally practical explanation, William Warren (1984, 180), Ojibway speaker and historian elected to the Minnesota state legislature, identified Midwest mounds "as the remains of [collapsed] former earth lodges of the Dakotas" and other ancestral peoples.[101]

Size Scales

Roger Kennedy[102] reviewed the hope of many US "founding fathers" for a new beginning in the Mississippi (and Ohio) River Valley, then a wide-open frontier. Seeking freedom and appreciation for all races and classes, especially Natives and Africans, the complex array of massive earthworks throughout this region captured their imaginations. As they Americanized, George Washington, Thomas Jefferson, and others had their slaves and gardeners build paired mounds into the landscaping of their estates. In Ohio, politicians such as Thomas Worthington built their mansions atop mounds or positioned them to view earthworks. Albert Gallatin, a Swiss-born Jefferson ally, politician, diplomat, and scholar of native languages, sold window glass for these new mansions from his factory south of Pittsburgh.

While single low mounds were easily attributed to existing tribes, it was the geometry, astronomy, scale, and interconnections of the multi-acre earthworks that suggested that these were monuments of populous and "advanced" civilizations. Local tribes – traumatized, diseased, disowned – hardly seemed capable of such feats. Yet it

---

[98] Bradley Lepper, Ohio Archaeology 2005: 150, 158.

[99] Morgan, The Indian Journals, 1859-62 1959: 91, 144.

[100] Morgan, Ancient Society 1959: 5.

[101] William Warren, History of the Ojibway People. St Paul: Minnesota Historical Society Press 1885 [1984].

[102] Roger Kennedy, Hidden Cities: The Discovery and Loss of Ancient North American Civilization 1994.

became increasingly clear to open-minded European visitors that they had been the builders. With the ability to date and analyze these landforms came the realization that they had been constructed over centuries and millennia, providing the "New World" with a remarkably ancient past.

Simultaneously, in contrast to these scholarly advances, natives were losing their lands and being forced to relocate onto the homelands of other tribes, supposedly for their own good. At the center of these conflicting efforts, ironically, was Thomas Jefferson, who left the White House with many pages of native vocabularies collected by himself and others, including Lewis and Clark, to be analyzed in his retirement, but the locked trunk holding them was stolen from the Potomac dock. Since a few pages of Molala words later washed ashore, the disappointed thieves had tossed the contents into the river.

As noted, Albert Gallatin, Jefferson's Swiss-born Secretary of the Treasury (the first to balance the national budget) followed up on this work and produced an early linguistic map of the eastern United States, using the love of detail famous among the watchmakers of his native Geneva. John Wesley Powell made such careful linguistic mapping an early goal of the Bureau of American Ethnology (BAE), founded in 1879.[103]

BAE Mound Research

Though not part of his original plan for the BAE, Powell was soon directed by a financial stipulation from Congress (due to an Ohio effort) to devote a portion of his annual budget toward the study of the earthen mounds across the Eastern states. Over decades, a growing sense of the complexity of mound types, dates, and associations coincided with the increasing recognition of the linguistic diversity of Native America. It no longer was possible to talk of the mound builders or the Indien language because, for any given time and place, many differences had now been revealed. While stereotypes continued in popular imagination, a better sense of America's past diversity and complexity began to emerge among scholars.[104]

---

[103] Franz Boas, Edward Sapir, Mary Haas, Carl Voegelin, Joseph Greenberg, and Ives Goddard have continued these efforts.

[104] In his masterful summary of Georgia "antiquities" (1999 [1973]), native son Charles Jones (1831-1893), though writing from New York, recognized 6 types: sepulchral tumuli, chieftain mounds (single burial), family or tribal mounds (multiple burials), shell mounds, embankments, and elevations for observation, retreat, and signaling by fire.

Over a century later, Gordon Willey, premier Harvard archeologist, noted in Archeology of the Florida Gulf Coast [1949] 1998: 20-21, the "functional categories of burial mounds, house platform mounds, refuse piles, and the canals, terraces, basins, etc., of the keys below Tampa". After mid-century, seriation became correlated with dates to provide more time-accurate chronologies.

Cyrus Thomas,[105] a naturalist from Illinois who oversaw these mound explorations and excavations, defined three types of "monuments": 1) fixed or local antiquities, 2) movable antiquities, such as relics and remains, and 3) paleographic objects, supposedly ancient writings (another indication of those biased times). The prime example of fixed sites was and is mounds, which he divided into conical tumuli, elongate or wall [rampart], pyramidal, and effigy. Other fixed features listed were refuse heaps [middens], house sites or hut rings, cairns, inclosures (which could have walls and embankments, excavations, canals and ditches, pits and caches), graves and cemeteries, garden beds, hearths, trails, pebble outlines, and mines for copper, flint, and mica – as well as lead, zinc, and colored ores.

Thomas stretched research funds by keeping excavators working year-round, moving them into the South for the winter and North in the summer. Their main goal was to prove whether mounds had been built by a distinct race or by the ancestors of modern Indians. Writers without any native contacts assumed a stereotype of the "restless, roving, unsettled, unhoused, and unagricultural savage, wherever found, as we have learned to consider him in modern times ... judging [their] character ... erroneously by their life after they had been disturbed by the European settlements".[106]

European metals, jewelry, tools, and religious medals found at the top of mounds were intrusive and inconclusive, but those at the bottom of mounds were compelling evidence for the link. Chronicles – left by Spaniards with Soto, by French among the Natchez, and by early Americans such as William Bartram, James Adair, and others – clearly report natives actively using mounds. Without a coherent timeframe, however, age could not be assigned to excavations, continuing confusions.

Understanding that there were varied types and distributions provided cautious controls. While burial mounds were almost always assumed, exceptions were made for the obvious. One (#2 at 38′ x 8′) of the two mounds at McAndrews farm on the Hiawassee River (TN) was identified as a likely signal station.[107] Features such as spiral ramps around mounds, reported as common by Squire and Davis, proved rare – only seen at Rembert,[108] Etowah, and Lamar in Georgia; and Troyville in Louisiana.[109]

---

[105] Cyrus Thomas, Report of the Mound Explorations of the Bureau of Ethnology, [1894] 1985: 28, 29, 33. [reprinting BAE - AR 12, 1890-1, 1894].

[106] Cyrus Thomas, Report on The Mound Explorations of The Bureau of Ethnology 1985: 529, 611.

[107] Thomas, Report 1985: 405.

[108] Rembert (AD 1450-1650), east of Athens, was damaged by floods before being covered by a reservoir; though its spiral ramp might have been due to "cattle grazing", the dated context suggests otherwise, Cf. Joseph Caldwell, The Rembert Mounds, Elbert County, Georgia 1953; Gregory Waselkov and Kathryn Holland Braund, eds., William Bartram on the Southeastern Indians 1995: 73, 252 #83, 269 #6, 298.

[109] Thomas, Report 1985: 300, 315, 588. Today, only Lamar's spiral and Etowah's partial ramp survive under federal protection, though William Bartram described Rembert and Winslow Walker salvaged a bit of Troyville before they were destroyed. Joe Saunders, by remote sensing, has found

Mass graves suggest the magnitude of past trauma. Near Sheboygan (WI), a mound consisted of many historic skeletons above "a mass of rounded bowlders aggregating several wagon loads, below which were some 40 or 50 skeletons in a sitting posture, in a circle, around and facing a very large [two foot] seashell". Similarly, at Dunleith (IL), inside a stone-walled vault under Mound # 16 were buried 11 sitting bodies – consisting of 6 adults, 4 children, and a babe in arms, all facing toward a central shell cup. At the Lindsay Mound near Raleigh (NC), skeletons lay in a circle with heads toward the center like spokes of a wheel, faces to left, with those buried on the west side arranged five layers deep. Another mound in this region held radiating skeletons on their left side, with each head toward the center beside a pot graded by size, bigger for older, according to the age of that person. At Allen County (KY), a stone-lined shaft, 10′ deep and 8′ wide, held layers of slabs between burials at two-foot intervals.[110]

Stone or clay work occurred within some mounds.[111] Under the Rev. T. F. Nelson Mound along the Yadkin River (NC), beehive-shaped stone rings covered seated bodies facing the center, where a boulder dome covered a standing skeleton and cut sheets of mica.[112] Though this mound stood only eighteen inches high, these vaults were set upon

---

significant traces of Troyville mounds still under the ground of modern Jonesville (LA), Cf. Ancient Mounds Heritage Area (owner's manual). Unique to Louisiana (and Europe), the Jonesville Catholic church sits atop one of these, while elsewhere in the South small Baptist churches never come closer than the base of a mound. Family cemeteries, however, frequently cover mound tops, which has incongruously helped preserve them.

[110] Thomas, Report 1985: 42, 51, 94, 111, 116, 582.

[111] Thomas, Report 1985: 81, 196, 673, described coverings of muck in mounds and burials, which might be evocations of the Earth Diver creation epic (Chapter 2), as noted by Robert Hall, An Archaeology of the Soul 1997: 18; or, if the actual cause of the fatality, attributed to drowning by an angered Underwater Panther.

[112] Biloxi dried the body of their chief and stood him (like a statue), with a club in one hand and a pipe in the other, in their temple upon an altar, six feet wide by ten feet long by six inches high, covered by a cane mat woven into red and yellow squares. The temple stood a league from the town and the door was always open, since it had no perpetual fire or attendant. The death of a chief displaced the body of the prior one to join all of the previous chiefs standing in a side room of the temple.

A creeper vine tied the middle of the body to a tall, red-painted pole set up behind it. From its top hung the most famous of the calumet [pipestem with fan of eagle feathers] given him during his career. Everyday, food, such as hominy, was offered to the chief on this altar, as were first fruits of each harvest, which were consumed there by animals or travelers but attributed to the chief himself. His widow, close kin, and retainers visited him occasionally, discussed recent events, and promised his continued care.

a floor dug three feet into the ground, while the central one had been excavated down six feet to accommodate the standing body. On Long Island in the Holston River (TN), Mound #3 held four skeletons, each seated at the corner of a square and facing the middle, where a sundried clay basin, 9 feet long by 4 feet wide by 15 inches deep, held a prone body with a kneeling stone figure at its head.[113]

One of the most elaborate burial tableau occurred at the Kanawha County Poor Farm (WV), where, buried three feet below the top of Mound # 31 (318′ x 25′) within a ten-foot shaft, were a pair of facing prone skeletons, while 10 feet below were two facing sitting skeletons "with their extended legs interlocking at the knees. Their hands, outstretched and slightly elevated, were placed in position to sustain a hemispherical, hollowed, coarse-grained sandstone, burned red and brittle. This was about 2 feet across the top, with a cavity or depression filled with white ashes containing bones fragments (cremains) burned almost to coals. Over it was placed a somewhat wider slab of limestone 3 inches thick, which had a hemispherical or cup-shaped depression of 2 inches in diameter near the center of the under side, but this bore no trace of heat. Two copper bracelets were on the left wrist of one skeleton, a hematite celt and lancehead with the other." At the base of the mound, 25 feet deep, was an altar, measuring 12 by 8 feet, burned brick red and covered by a foot of fine ashes.[114]

A few mounds could be dated by historic events. During the 1800s, an Osage chief died in Missouri while most of his village was away hunting, so his burial was modest until everyone returned and heaped a large mound over his remains. Nickasaw, a Wyandot leader, was buried under a mound at the spot where he was murdered in Summit County (Akron), Ohio. Along the Des Moines River (IA), slain Ioway warriors were buried in low mounds, as were Potawatomi in another section. In 1836, the Sac warrior Black Hawk, sitting up and wearing a uniform given him by Andrew Jackson, was buried nearby under his own mound surrounded by a picket fence.[115]

In all, therefore, evidence from excavations throughout the East and Midwest finding European goods deep inside mounds, chronicles tracing decreasing population and smaller mounds size, and attributions by name and tribe within recent decades – all proved the continuity of native usage, discrediting any claims to a separate and "superior" race of mound builders. The huge scale of these prehistoric remains had been confusing, particularly when compared to the few traumatized survivors of these nations. Another century of scholarship would pass before the full magnitude of epidemic diseases,

---

Biloxi, belonging to the Ohio Valley subset of the Siouan Stock, were correctly Ta'neks a^{n}ya "First People" (shifted through Mobilian Jargon: t > b, n > l), also known to the French as Annochy. Close allies of the Biloxi, the Pascagoula also stood their deceased chiefs in their own temple. See John Swanton, A Dictionary of the Biloxi and Ofo Languages 1912: 7.

[113] Thomas, Report 1985: 334, Figure 207; 335; 359, Figure 239.

[114] Thomas, Report 1985: 432.

[115] Thomas, Report 1985: 658. Subsequently, his grave was robbed and his body subjected to bizarre twists, See Michael Sherfy, Narrating Black Hawk 2005.

slaving, and despair was factored into Americanist understandings of what had horrors happened to native peoples.

Speculations – bulk over beliefs

Mounds, assumed to be inert, are not. Indeed, mounds, mound building, and mound builders, after centuries of speculation, still remain unresolved questions of Americanist research.[116] Despite wholesale destructions, hundreds of thousands of such earthworks, large and small, still dot much of the East, with particular clusterings in the Southeast. Explanations for this impulse toward earth moving, mound building, and imposing bulk have been in the manner of blind men describing an elephant. Each has merit but does not include the whole or even major aspects of it. Such basic data as specific dating have also needed to be constantly revised. Nowhere outside native communities is any recognition given to their primary goal as blessed, ballooning ballast of honored earth banked and vitalized by rhythmic songs and stomps in an unsteady world.

Testing at Watson Brake in northeastern Louisiana has almost doubled the dating of earliest mounds to 5,500 BP. The site itself is not a single mound, but rather 11 mounds with connecting ridges that enclose an oval whose diameter is 280 meters (916 feet long). Gentry mound ("Big A"), the tallest, is 7.5 meters (26 feet) high and the others are between 3 and 4.5 meters high. In reporting these new dates, Science noted:[117]

---

[116] Jon Gibson, Earth Sitting: Architectural Masses at Poverty Point, Northeastern Louisiana 1986: 201-238; Jon Gibson and Philip Carr, Signs of Power, The Rise of Cultural Complexity in the Southeast 2004; Jon Gibson, Navels of the Earth: sendentism in early mound-building cultures in the Lower Mississippi Valley 2006; Robert Hall, An Archaeology of the Soul, North American Indian Belief and Ritual 1997; James Howard, The Southeastern Ceremonial Complex and its Interpretation 1968; Robert Mainfort and Lynne Sullivan, Ancient Earthen Enclosures of the Eastern Woodlands 1998; Robert Mainfort and Richard Walling, Mounds, Embankment, and Ceremonialism in the Midsouth 1996. Roger Kennedy, Hidden Cities, The Discovery and Loss of Ancient North American Civilization 1994; Maureen Korp, The Sacred Geography of the American Mound Builders 1990; William Morgan, Precolumbian Architecture in Eastern North America 1999; John O'Shea, Social Configurations and the Archaeological Study of Mortuary Practices: A Case Study 1981: 39-52; Lynda Norene Shaffer, Native Americans Before 1492, The Moundbuilding Centers of the Eastern Woodlands 1992; Cyrus Thomas, Report on the Mound Explorations of the Bureau of Ethnology 1985 [1894]; Ephraim Squier and Edwin Davis, Ancient Monuments of the Mississippi Valley 1848 [1998, edited by David Meltzer]; James Brown, The Spiro Ceremonial Center An Archaeology of Arkansas Valley Caddoan Culture in Eastern Oklahoma 1996.

[117] Science 1997: 1761.

"Archaeologists once thought mound building was linked to agriculture, which created food surpluses and ... more permanent settlements and more complex societies. But ... there is little evidence of agriculture at places like Poverty Point [so perhaps] these mounds arose as a result of extensive trading networks [but] Trade did not seem to be a factor at Watson Brake, however, as the artifacts found were all made of local materials."

Lastly, Watson Brake had remantling on the north-side mounds, but almost none on the south-side ones, as though these were abandoned or off-limits once the mounds were finished. This walking away from a major construction project to leave raised bulk and banked bulge behind should loom large in any speculation as to why mounds were built initially, and then "abandoned" afterward.

Save mound K, all of the mounds on the north half are multi-stage construction. I would call it addition and not rebuilding. There is evidence of occupation on the intermediate surfaces; so they built and occupied, then added another stage and lived on top of that. In contrast, the south ridges and Mounds E, G, H, were single-stage mounds (perhaps F, we are not sure yet). Also, they lack midden deposits under the mounds, in contrast to the thick middens under the north mounds. There is a light scatter of charcoal under Mound E, which suggests that they planned to build the mound there from the get-go – because the charcoal under Mound A is the same age as charcoal at Mound E.

So, the plan may have existed from the first mound, but remember, they lived at the site for years before the first mound was built. So it was an important place, later marked with mounds.

We have done some survey work near the mounds for years. All we are finding are very ephemeral sites, no large camps around the great mound site, as I expected. Instead it looks like they were living at the mound site – hunting and gathering for food, bringing it directly back to the mounds and subsisting.[118]

From the Archaic into the Woodland period, conical mounds for the dead served as regional ingathering locales, filling the lands along Ohio River tributaries as manifestations of what archaeologists have called the Adena, overlapping with later Hopewell earthworks made in geometric forms. Eventually, platform temple mounds, gracing much of the drainage of the Mississippi River, were again occupied by leaders, living worshipers, and ancestral dead.[119]

By the late 1500s, Spanish and French adventurers actually saw mounds in use, but the English ignored their monumentality in favor of asserting their own claims to making "better" use of the land. Thomas Jefferson thought mounds both important and "American" enough to excavate one (above). Today, scholars still debate – according to intellectual stances, "interests", "problems", and "fads" – how to characterize the role of

---

[118] Joe Saunders, E-mail of 5 December 2006.

[119] Robert Silverberg, The Mound Builders 1986.

mounds in chiefdoms or the import of the urban hub at the mega-site of Cahokia, near modern St Louis at the heart of the continent.[120] Many do this, however, from very Eurocentric understandings, focusing on individual greed and self-interest.

Brief mention of mounds occurs in early colonial histories. Ill-fated[121] John Lawson, writing of the Carolinas in 1708, two centuries after the enslavement of Chicora (below), noted that a mound was built as a "sepulcher" for each of the Santee River "kings," piled higher or lower according to his own "Dignity".[122] Citing a January 1796 flood[123] that crested the Alabama River at 47 feet, Indian Agent Benjamin Hawkins[124] determined that any mound, called in Creek _o-cun-li-ge_, "literally, earth placed," (below) was a "place of safety to the people, in the time of these floods." In the same work, he described an 8-day Green Corn or Busk (Miller 2015) when warriors cleaned the square yard and sprinkled it with fresh white sand, but, with the blinders of an agent of change, he was strangely oblivious to ongoing aspects of mound use.[125]

---

[120] Biloine Whiting Young and Melvin Fowler, Cahokia: The Great American Metropolis 2000.

[121] Lawson was tortured to death by Tuscaroras after he helped to plant a colony of Swiss in North Carolina. Ironically, the manner of his execution is fully described in his ethnographic description of Carolina natives.

[122] John Lawson, A _New_ Voyage to Carolina 1967: 28.

[123] My visits to the Mississippi Delta and reading of Faulkner (below) made this "mound as flood haven" argument all the more plausible, but only in secondary terms of height and size, not in terms of motivating purposes. This seems more of a dividend than a cause, though there are many, many obvious mounds in the flood zone. See Philip Phillips, James Ford, and James Griffin, Archaeological Survey of the Lower Mississippi Alluvial Valley, 1940-1947 1951; Philip Phillips, Archaeological Survey of the Lower Yazoo Basin 1970.

[124] Benjamin Hawkins, A Sketch of the Creek Country in 1798 and 1799 [1848] 1971: 38-39; Letters of Benjamin Hawkins, 1796-1806 1916: 42-43; Cf. Florette Henri, The Southern Indians and Benjamin Hawkins, 1796-1816 1986; Robbie Ethridge, Creek Country, The Creek Indians and Their World 2003.

[125] Benjamin Hawkins, A Sketch of the Creek Country 1848: 75-78.

Largely ignored are political aspects of bringing people together. Today, tribal politicians routinely appear at Busks to gain votes. A century ago, the Green Corn Rebellion (2-3 August 1917), fomented at Busks, set armed Oklahoma tenant farmers (poor young whites, blacks, Seminoles, and Muscogee Creeks) against the Selective Draft Act and US entry into WWI ("rich man's war, poor man's fight"). Bridges were burned, phone lines cut, and skirmishes killed three men. Many belonged to the Working Class Union (WCU), formed in New Orleans but based in Van Buren, Arkansas, because Industrial Workers of the World refused to organize rural tenant farmers.

William Bartram,[126] privately financed to describe, sketch, and collect plant specimens from the newly-British Southeast, relied on native hosts. He duly noted mounds and earthworks as an ancient feature of these landscapes, musing that they were "public works [of massive labor for] ornament and recreation [with] some religious purpose, as great altars and temples [or] look-out towers". Drawing direct analogies between his host's native towns and these sites, he proposed distinct types and functions such that stone mounds were sepulchers for the dead, replaced by earthen ones when stone was not available; that platform "tetragons" were fortress foundations; that conicals were "high places for sacrifice"; and that sunken places served for captive torture sacrifices, with embankments for seats during "games, shews and dances".

Of note, to his inquiries, elderly Cherokees denied any knowledge of or ancestry as to their builders,[127] whom they said were succeeded by a second nation before they themselves arrived in the Appalachians. Yet both Bartram and James Adair described Choctaw funeral practices in which a body was exposed for several months, defleshed, and its bones placed inside a kin-based charnel house. Bartram[128] added that when filled, locals "repair to the bone-house" by family, take up their kin, and march by seniority to "place the coffins in order, forming a pyramid; and, lastly, cover all over with earth, which raises a conical hill or mount". Adair wrote that graves were usually marked by stone piles, or, lacking rocks, by earthen mounds.[129]

Thus, early naturalists like William, and his father John Bartram,[130] and proto-archaeologists like Cyrus Thomas (above), agreed to the continuous use of mounds to cover the dead, much like the Neolithic and later tumuli across much of Europe that marked the graves of warrior heroes.[131] Thomas,[132] after noting the overlap between

---

Courts detained 450 people ⸭ with 266 released, 184 charged, and 150 convicted or pleading guilty, receiving jail and prison terms ranging from 60 days to ten years. Radicalism and the Socialist Party of America lost favor throughout the region, and, nationally, the absent Industrial Workers of the World suffered reprisals and legal suppressions.

[126] Gregory Waselkov and Kathryn Holland Braund, eds., William Bartram on the Southeastern Indians 1995: 73, 84, 131. Until this publication, Bartram's assessment, written in 1788, was only known through an overly-edited 1853 work.

[127] Oklahoma Cherokees know moundbuilders as Red Eye People ~ *Dinikani*, Fierce People ~ *Aninayegi* weighted down by piled earth (Teuton 2012: 61).

[128] Gregory Waselkov and Kathryn Holland Braund, eds., William Bartram on the Southeastern Indians 1995: 129.

[129] James Adair, The History of the American Indians 2005: 212-214 note*.

[130] John and William Bartram, Bartram's America, Selections from the Writings of the Philadelphia Naturalists, Helen Gere Cruickshank, ed. 1957.

[131] R.L.S. Bruce-Mitford, The Sutton Hoo Ship Burial 1964; Martin Carver, Sutton Hoo, Burial Ground of Kings? (1998: 57, 141, 172) tries to correlate each mound with an East Anglia king named by Venerable Bede, prove chemically that their bodies were placed inside (since nothing remains), and document

ancient mound sites and historic Overhill Cherokee towns, quoted James Mooney that such mounds were built during Green Corn ceremonies. The irony is that Mooney was made aware of this connection by Postmaster Terrell of Webster (NC), and only later confirmed it with Cherokee elders such as the man named Tsiskwaya. Even more intriguing, Thomas said Alice Fletcher saw mound building during a secret ritual of the Winnebago (Hochungara, in their own language).[133] Fletcher[134] herself mentioned hearing the song of a famous Omaha warrior while standing beside his "mounded grave" along the Missouri River.

Centuries before, Peter D'Anghera Martyr (1457 - 1526),[135] an Italian at the Spanish court, similarly noted use of a mound by a native orator. While a dinner guest, Francisco Chicorana or Chicora, who had been seized a few years before by an expedition sponsored by Lucas Vasquez de Ayllon, described three festivals among his own coastal Carolina tribes.[136] The third rite involved the reburial of a skeleton in a "tomb [when] the chief priest addresses the surrounding people from the summit of a mound" with a eulogy about the afterlife.

---

the "sand body" stains of criminals hanged nearby at the cwealmstow ("killing place") where Anglo-Saxon Christian kings enforced their laws by executions. In drawing comparisons, Carver noted a religious continuity from mounds at Jelling, Denmark, where Harold Bluetooth built mounds for each of his parents, but, after he converted to Christianity, moved his father's skeleton (King Gorm) from its mound into his new church. His mother remains in her mound, in keeping with the universally female associations of the earth.

[132] Cyrus Thomas, The Cherokees in Pre-Columbian Times, Fact and Theory Papers 4 1890: 32, 43 [1980].

[133] Incidentally, tracing references to such mounding proved particularly convoluted since Cyrus Thomas initially reported only that ongoing mound use had been seen by James Mooney at a Cherokee Green Corn, and by Alice Fletcher among Hochungara (Winnebago) (Cf Jay Miller, Instilling the Earth: Explaining Mounds 2001: 162, #7). Only in his entry on Mounds and Mound-builders in the first Handbook of North American Indians does Thomas explicitly say "According to Miss Fletcher, the Winnebago build miniature mounds in the lodge during certain ceremonies" (Frederick Hodge, Bureau of American Ethnology, Bulletin 30: 1, 951).

[134] Alice Fletcher, A Study of Omaha Indian Music 1994: 31. At Blood Run (Chapter 4), hundreds of mounds dating around AD 1700 demonstrated that the as-yet-unseparated Omaha-Ponka tribe had indeed revived their mound-building traditions.

[135] Peter D'Anghera Martyr, De Orbe Novo ~ The Eight Decades of Pietro d'Anghiera Martire 1970 II: 258, 264. [1912]

[136] Paul Quattlebaum, The Land Called Chicora 1956.

Height itself was always a factor, representing the elevated status of leaders, especially during times of "heightened" concern, such as successions. The later earthen platform mounds, as the "quintessential artifacts of the prehistoric chiefdoms ... represented the 'navel of the world' from which sprang the town's (if not the entire chiefdom's) people sometime in the remote mythical past [and] built these mounds in successive stages, most likely during periodic episodes of rebuilding that occurred when new chiefs were installed as rulers.... A mound likewise served as literal symbol of the chief's elevated status, as his or her private dwellings and other sacred buildings were routinely built on the summit of such earthworks."[137] Such residences, moreover, placed leaders closer to their own ancestors, who came from the sky as famously claimed by the Natchez Suns, while other classes of people came out of the earth. Intermarriage, clanship, and town memberships helped to forge the full multidimensional community relying on on-going vitality.

Kinship is often evoked in explaining mounds, specifically the labor mobilized for their construction. For the much earlier period, archaeologist Martin Byers has referred to the central mound in an Adena-Hopewell enclosure as an "iconic warrant" between living and dead kin.[138] In his review of Florida archaeology, Jerald Milanich[139] insists that, through constant use, especially sequential funeral stages, "Mounds are tied to kinship as corporate monuments of, for, and to clanship; while rituals cleanse and restore the world to balance, normality, and stability". Yet in his study of the Florida Spanish missions,[140] he noted, but did not directly connect, that Guale and Timucuan converts gave up "charnel houses and interment in lineage-maintained mounds" for burial "in the floor of the church nave", a practice discontinued in Europe for centuries. Also, in violation of church dogma, both types of graves included artifact offerings. Both dispositions assured security for these ancestral remains by being placed within a sanctuary defined by weight and height such as mound or sanctified (church) walls. Yet it is as though, with the end of mound building, native leaders took refuge inside buildings, either huge council houses or, later, churches.

---

[137] Steven Hahn, The Invention of the Creek Nation, 1670-1763 2004: 15, 162. Trained by both Charles Hudson and John Juricek, Hahn provides a skilled overview of early Creek history, but does not explore the fascinating bonds of ancient memory that brought Lower Creeks back (1690-1715) to the Macon Plateau where massive earthlodges and mounds at Ocmulgee, Ochese, and Lamar marked a polity that was centuries older. Similarly, when the Yamacraws and Tomochichi were banished, they renewed an ancestral claim to Irene mound near Savannah in time to "welcome" James Oglethorpe and his Georgia settlers.

[138] Martin Byers, Social Structure and the Pragmatic Meaning of Material Culture: Ohio Hopewell as an Ecclesiastical-Communal Cult 1996.

[139] Jerald Milanich, Florida's Indians from Ancient Times to the Present 1998: 48, 71.

[140] Jerald Milanich, Laboring in the Fields of the Lord. Spanish Missions and Southeastern Indians 1999: 138.

Discussing Timucua chiefdoms of North Florida, who did not build temple mounds, John Worth[141] summarized that mounds were ~ are "physical symbols of social rank ... their height a visual reminder ... of distinctions in status [and] of the generational time-depth of noble matrilineages and the hereditary succession of the chiefly office ... constructed ... in episodic stages ... frequently in association with the deaths of chiefs and the succession of heirs to the chiefly office ... a powerful legitimization for chiefly rank and ... an integral part of Mississippian culture."

The most encompassing explanation comes from Iowa's Clark Mallam, a humanist archaeologist who died in the midst of his insightful research into Effigy mounds. Rich in complex symbolism, mounding was atonement by humans for damaging the earth while taking a living from it. More than just burials, community projects, or territory markers, mounds represented life's own "cyclical regularity", a microcosm reborn and reaffirmed with each layer (mantle) of fresh earth.[142] Missing from his theory, however, is awareness of the regularity of song and dance in maintaining the bulge of mounds by inflating and infusing their internal tensions to bank up and charge their vitality.

Regional Examples – Ford to Faulkner

James Ford, in his comparative analysis of Pan-American and worldwide Formative Cultures (4000-1000 BP), called attention to early circular villages mimicked in shell rings of the Southeast and sacred circles of Ohio, with later "retention" shown by Plains camp circles and Amazonian round towns. Over time, construction efforts became more massive, especially after 3200 BP, the date at which Ford divided the Formative Period into Colonial (3000-1200 BC, 5000-3200 BP) and Theocratic (1200-400 BC) divisions, in lieu of the Early, Middle, and Late Eras then in academic favor. The peak came, according to his perplexing commentary, when "At various times after 1200 B.C., the Indians in the three Americas began to waste [sic] untold millions of man hours in the erection of tremendous monuments of earth, adobe brick, and stone that served no practical purpose". He then drew comparisons to Egyptian pyramids and Medieval cathedrals to suggest "a religious base, complete with specialist priest-rulers ... including architects, engineers, sculptors, and artists".[143]

Comparisons have also been drawn between regions across the southern US. Looking at such "constructed eminences", Owen Lindauer and John Blitz analyzed platform mounds in both the Southeast and Southwest.[144] Understandably, their outcome

---

[141] John Worth, The Timucuan Chiefdoms of Spanish Florida ~ Assimilation, Volume 1: 12 1998.

[142] Clark Mallam, Ideology from the Earth: Effigy Mounds in the Midwest 1982; The Iowa Effigy Mound Manifestation: An Interpretative Model 1976.

[143] James Ford, A Comparison of Formative Cultures in the Americas 1969: 5, 42, 46. Robert Hall has called this formulation an "energy sink".

[144] Owen Lindauer and John Blitz, Higher Ground: The Archaeology of North American Platform Mounds 1997.

is concerned with functions, forms, and politics, without appreciation of the native religious system that Ford and modern elders assert was the motivation for these efforts.

For the Southeast, though some platforms occur before AD 800, the majority were built later and served at least four functions: a) elite ~ chiefly residence, b) temple ~ mortuary ~ ancestor shrine, c) council ~ sweat ~ meeting halls, or d) courtyards ~ stages ~ display in the open, often with a huge central upright pole. At multimound sites, each of these functions may well occupy a separate mound top, reached by ramps or stairs up the front. Usually, they are built over earlier occupations, resurfaced over time (often 30-year, one-generation intervals), and then capped by a final seal of colored clay that represents its own enclosed final burial.[145]

In the Southwest, their three functional forms, whose tops were reached by ladders, include a) dance, b) planned, and c) organic mounds. The first was low and open, the second was built upon retaining walls of cell-like rooms filed with rubble, and the third converted prior rooms into a rubble-filled foundation. The last two types had buildings on their summits.[146]

In particular, mounds served as observatories reinforcing elite control of knowledge and reliable predictions. They also provided wider social integration by means of food storage and feasting, invested labor "costs", and interdependence among nodes within a diversity of sites. Pottery sherds from the largest vessels are often found atop mounds, as well as in chiefly homes, indicating their larger food reserves and generosity. Labor "costs", however, seem to have been spread over time, so that building episodes were not as onerous as single-stage (all at once) construction would have been. Mounds marked administrative centers, coordinating community needs, such as irrigation along the Gila and Salt Rivers of Arizona, or farming and raiding cycles in the Southeast.[147] Most importantly, "The repetitive act of covering the symbolically charged older surface with a new episode of construction is a key social dynamic of platform mounds".[148] Such remantling of mounds occurred across the Americas and often used color-coded soils to make absolutely certain that the prior surface was entirely sealed to assure the overall integrity of weight and height. As a torso-like bubble, such thick layering confined internal mound tensions and pressures to assure continued vitality.

For example, the large and small Snodgrass sites were built on a ridge that is now an island in the Guntersville Reservoir of the Tennessee River in far northeast Alabama.[149] The Snodgrass largest mound changed the color of its cap seven times

---

[145] Lindauer and Blitz, Higher Ground 1997: 175. Such sealing by clay caps at Mound 72 and Blood Run assured their survival for centuries.

[146] Lindauer and Blitz, Higher Ground 1997: 177.

[147] Lindauer and Blitz, Higher Ground 1997: 185.

[148] Lindauer and Blitz, Higher Ground 1997: 192.

[149] Richard Krause, Observations on the Excavation of a Mississippian Mound, Robert Mainfort and Richard Walling, eds., Mounds, Embankments, and Ceremonialism in the Midsouth 1996: 54-63; Cf. Corin Pursell, Geographic Distribution and Symbolism of Colored Mound Architecture in the Mississippian Southeast 2004. Another Snodgrass site is located in Missouri.

between AD 1150-1350. The Snodgrass small mound showed alternating layers holding round and square buildings, and mantle caps of red or blue-gray clay.

Instead of viewing such a mound as the tomb of an individual, Richard Krause argued that a mound embodied those aspects of authority based in a corporate identity acting in the public domain. Therefore, a mound is "both a cenotaph and icon, both an empty tomb, a monument honoring an important person or event, and a holy place – a contact point between the sacred and the secular, a tangible visible representation of the continuity that joined the past with the present, which did so despite human mortality and the discontinuity wrought by death."[150]

West of the Mississippi River, the divide between Early / Late Caddo was AD 1250-1300.[151] Early mounds included deep shaft graves and venerated icons, while Late ones, such as Battle Mound, the largest of earthen Caddo monuments, had buildings (temple houses) set into their tops. Between Early and Late, attention shifted from individuals (such as shamans) to buildings (maintained by priests). In southwest Arkansas, the Ferguson site (AD 1300-1500) was vacant of living debris except for the tops of its twin mounds. Its supporting members lived scattered in nearby farmsteads. Mound A was topped by a pair of buildings (10 rebuilt on 5 levels). At each layer, one was round, with thatched walls for summer use; the other was square, with wattle and daub walls for winter. Excavation revealed many construction details because the building materials were carbonized by fire. Each level was burned in the same manner – sand was piled over the fireplace and against outer walls, the roof was removed, and the walls were ignited until flames raged. Then the walls were pushed in, one at a time, and the whole was quickly buried with sand, smothering the fire and raising a huge plume of smoke and steam that must have been seen for miles.[152] Such a smoke plume signaled passage between worlds, realms, or dimensions, alerting the dead and immortals to a shift from physical to spiritual conditions (Chapter 6).

Of note, mounds also feature in novelist William Faulkner's complex portrayals of the human condition set in the South. His ("postage stamp") county's local history begins with its original Chickasaw owners (led by Issetibbeha), but then concentrates on the plantations and homesteaders, both white and black, who replaced them. In the short story "The Fire and the Hearth", during complex marriage negotiations, George Wilkins hides his own "still" inside a freshly excavated trench into "a squat, flat-topped, almost symmetrical mound rising without reason", so he can safely expose the "still" of Lucus Beauchamp, father of his fiancé Nathalie, to make him so vulnerable he will consent to the wedding. Finding a gold piece in the mound, however, sets off an obsessive search

---

[150] Krause, Observations on the Excavation of a Mississippian Mound 1996: 62-63.

[151] Frank Schambach, Mounds, Embankments, and Ceremonialism in Trans-Mississippi South 1996: 36-43.

[152] Schambach, Mounds, Embankments, and Ceremonialism in Trans-Mississippi South 1996: 41.

by Lucus using a connived metal detector that further strains family relations.[153] Notions of stealth, kinship, violation, and treasure hover around this mound setting.

In the Wild Palms, with parallel plots of a physician's tragic love affair and the 1927 Flood of the Delta, a convict rescues a pregnant woman from a tree but their boat is swept away. Finally, a swimming deer leads them to haven on "an acclivity smooth and swift and steep, bizarre, solid and unbelievable; an Indian mound", where the woman immediately gives birth. They share this muddy space with other creatures and many snakes.[154] "The Indian mound on which they land is the earth in the reptilian age, emerging from the waters. Here, in this prehistoric world where the snake predominates, the human female fulfills her childbearing function, and the male assumes the vital responsibility of caring for mother and infant."[155] This mound, writhing with life, new and old, male and female, provides a haven just above treacherously rising waters. Once rescued, the warden adds to this convict's prison time as punishment because his baffling absence and fierce protection of the borrowed rowboat – scrupulously doing his best – created a morass of paperwork.

In the middle volume of the Snopes trilogy, Faulkner[156] mused about the new "tyranny [of] incorrigible and unreconstructable Baptists and Methodists [who] had heired from … usurped and dispossessed … Episcopal and Presbyterian churches and Issetibbeha's old mounds in the low creek bottoms about the country". Like the earliest churches of the "old religions", these mounds represent the antiquity of the land and religion itself, transformed, dated, and mutated but still standing before their believers and heirs.

Knight

Skillfully, in his review of Mississippian religion from the perspective of an archaeologist, Vernon James Knight[157] looked at sacra (artifacts and images displaying the sacred) sorted into three icon families, each one characteristic of a respective cult institution (with its own distinctive rituals and adherents). While others have seen the iconographies of temples, crops, and war in the assortment known as the Southeastern Ceremonial Complex (SECC),[158] Knight saw these images and artifacts as concerned with chiefly authority (chiefs), communal fertility (town), and, mediating between these

---

[153] William Faulkner, Go Down, Moses 1940: 37. By digging into the mound, Lucus "violates the land" and risks punishment, see Edmond Volpe, A Reader's Guide to William Faulkner 1964: 237.

[154] William Faulkner; The Wild Palms 1939: 176. Note the interweaving of fertility, birth, snakes, and vitality.

[155] Edmond Volpe, A Reader's Guide to William Faulkner 1964: 224.

[156] William Faulkner; The Town 1957: 307.

[157] Vernon Knight, The Institutional Organization of Mississippian Religion 1986.

[158] Kent Reilly and James Garber, Ancient Objects and Sacred Realms ~ Interpretations of Mississippian Iconography 2007: 3, 40, renames the SECC as the MIIS = Mississippian Ideological Interaction Sphere.

two, priesthoods (priests). Their associated sacra are, for the first (might) = the warriors, werebeings, weapons, and world portrayals, often in defensive zones or levels, that have been, in the past regarded (too narrowly) as expressions of the Southern or SECC; second (town) = the mounds periodically covered over with new mantles of earth; and, third (priesthood) = temple statuary, especially kneeling, corpse-faced images and figurines [in trance?], at least some of whom were ancestors. For convenience, these three cults can be referred to as mighties, mounds, and ministers.[159]

Accordingly, for Mississippians, "might" is associated with high rank (fusing ages and genders), and so it is inclusively unmarked, while the priesthoods are marked, "clearly having exclusive ritual and supernatural prerogatives distinct from both of the former [and membership] was highly restricted to initiates trained in esoteric arts".[160] As public works, mounds receive constant attention from everyone. In particular, a fresh layer of soil is added periodically, "an act of burial, a mortuary rite for the mound itself rather than for any individual, sometimes complete with funereal furnishings placed upon the old surface".[161] They are built and rebuilt by the labor of all townspeople under the supervision of the other two cults. In a sense, too, they were farmed and planted, allowing for other kinds of growth and rebirth. The proper relationships of this Mississippian matrix, therefore, are expressible either as Mighties (Mounds) Ministers or as $\frac{\text{Mighties} \quad \text{Ministers}}{\text{Mounds}}$, with the mounds always pivotal.

Knight[162] also provided a masterful summary of what the ethnographic literature says about the symbolism of Mississippian platform mounds. Though he wisely notes the obvious difference in scale between those of the past (dozens of feet high) throughout the East and those of the Oklahoma present (about 5 feet high), he sees continuity between the two. Intervening in the 1500s were the catastrophic population losses from both epidemics and massive slaving that "reduced" or wiped out most of the ancient complexity, diversity, and variability of these Mississippians. More recent research and publications help to clarify the meanings and usages of today's mounds.

---

[159] Closer examination, however, calls for realignment among these cults on the basis of theories of linguistic markedness and structuralism. For humanity, semantic and conceptual relationships are inherently threeway (as a matrix) such that they are nested or embedded within each other. The smallest unit is marked or exclusive, fitting within an unmarked or inclusive one, and these together are contained within an overall mediating or enclosive category. Thus for enclosive 'length', the component of 'short' is marked and of 'long' is unmarked. This matrix can be represented as an equation: long (length) short. While Knight suggested a matrix of mights (ministers) mounds, a better one is mights (mounds) ministers, with the two human components balanced against the human-made earthen one, or, more simply, humans/humus.

[160] Knight, The Institutional Organization of Mississippian Religion 1986: 681, 683.

[161] Knight, The Institutional Organization of Mississippian Religion 1986: 676.

[162] Vernon Knight, Symbolism of Mississippian Mounds, Powhatan's Mantle 1989: 279-291.

The earliest reported Mvskoke term (*ēkvn-like* ~ *i:kan leyki*) given for the large mounds means "earth placed, sitting, dwelling," from *ekvnv* = earth, world, with compound extensions into "cave, mountain, hill, earthquake" and *liketv* = "seat, dwelling, residence". The explicit conjoining of "earth" and "earthquake" says volumes about native perceptions of "natural" stability, and thus enforces the sense of "holding steady in place" as banked bulging ballast.[163]

Knight[164] errs when he relegates to his first footnote another term (*ekvn-hvlwuce*) translated as "hillock," literally "little mountain", because "There is no evidence, however, that this term was applied to artificial constructions". Such evidence, however, is definitely insider information among modern native adherents. Moreover, a closer look at this same early dictionary shows a meaning of "high earth".[165] The latest Creek dictionary gives for mound, in technical spelling, *i:kan-leyki* (archaic) = "mound of earth", *łani* = "mound, mons veneris", *tachi* ~ *tači* "ridge of sweepings encircling dance area", and *tacho* ~ *tačo* = "area of the ceremonial grounds by the center fire".[166] In neighboring Caddo, a parallel word means mound, hill, church, because "You look up to pray".[167]

---

[163] Knight, Symbolism of Mississippian Mounds 1989: 280; cf. Jack Martin and Margaret McKane Mauldin, A Dictionary of Creek/Muskogee, with notes on the Florida and Oklahoma Seminole dialects of Creek 2000, 23, 71: i:kana n[oun]. 1. ground, land, earth, 2. world + *leyk-ita* v[erb]. 1. to sit, be situated, exist (of a person, God, land, a town, money in the bank [nota bene], or something about evenly tall, wide, and long ... 2. to settle, live (in a house, a place), reside (of one), [with *ka:k-ita* the dual number (of two)].

[164] Vernon Knight, Symbolism of Mississippian Mounds 1989: 289, #1.

[165] According to Rev. R. M. Loughridge and David Hodge, English and Muskokee Dictionary 1890: 38, 51, 181 [1964]: 'high' is *homahtv*, *hv'lwe*, while their actual listing for 'mound' is *Ekvn-hv'lwuce*, *Rv'ne*, with *rvne* [*łəne*] alone meaning 'mount, mound', and the preferred word used by today's Oklahoma Creek traditionalists.

[166] Jack Martin and Margaret McKane Mauldin, A Dictionary of Creek/Muskogee 2000: 23, 105, 124, 274. Tribal words for mound suggest some varieties are equated with organic life. In addition to the vitality ~ fertility associations of the pubic bulge included in one of the Creek words, Cherokee describe boils as towns built by *tsga'ya* (bug and worm spirits), acting as avenging animals to punish the hurt and harm done by a human to their ubiquitous kin. Its swelling evokes the town mound, while the hard tip was presumably the council house where decisions were made by microbes about the degree of fever, tremor, and pain inflicted on the patient until a shaman could work a counter cure; See James Mooney, Sacred Formulas of the Cherokee 1891: 308, 361.

[167] Jay Miller, Changing Moons: A History of Caddo Religion 1996. While Caddo ancestors built impressive mounds, their Pawnee linguistic relatives revered a constellation of earth-lodge-like hills on the central plains, Cf. Douglas Parks

Knight carefully considered Creek Mvskoke mythology,[168] where both of the Lower Creek "mother towns" of Kasihta (White) and Koweta (Red) mention mounds in their origin epics, serving both for burials and as prayerful offerings. For example, Kasihta warriors find survivors of an enemy town burying their slain in mounds. Later, Kasihta members built large mounds to petition the immortals and to provide a holy platform for taking the all-important Herb Water (*assi*, misknown as Black Drink because of the use of dark roasted holly leaves in the brewing).

Inside of the mounds was a chamber (bubble) that was used for fasting and praying, and, for Koweta, waiting to ambush Cherokee attackers. In general, as outer mounds are likened to navels, inner mounds have complex associations of sanctuary, womb, and den subsumed within a chest or torso. Epics about emergence or "coming out" from mounds include notions of regeneration or resurrection from a womb – the pregnant belly of earth mother.[169] As microcosms, like the earth itself, they are hollow inside and filled with the moving or wind-like air of songs, promising vital order and calm.

As the abode of warriors, they are dangerous dens where attack and death provide the need for rebirth. Inside the mound of Nikwasi on the Little Tennessee (Franklin, NC) live some of the Nunnehi, a race of spirits fond of singing and dancing. They have other town or council houses throughout the Cherokee homeland. During the Colonial era, they offered refuge to those Cherokees who wanted to escape hostilities. Anyone willing to accept their help joined together in silence inside their town council houses for seven days until the roar of thunder and shaking ground signaled their approach. Cherokees who cried out were lost, but the others became invisible and immortal when the townhouse was lifted from its mound up to the top of Lone Peak and turned to stone. Nunnehi remained behind after the Cherokees were forced West. During the Civil War, they again emerged from Nikawsi to protect a handful of Confederates fighting off a Federal attack there.[170]

---

and Waldo Wedel, Pawnee Geography, Historical and Sacred, 1985. Wichita ancestors, also Caddoan speakers, dug out a snake effigy (Chapter 7).

[168] Vernon Knight, Symbolism of Mississippian Mounds 1989: 282.

[169] Today, the use of the word 'heart' for town mounds, moreover, reverberates with their active, pulsing, throbbing, hollow qualities (See Introduction).

[170] James Mooney, Myths of the Cherokee 1982: 335, 337. In 1730, Sir Alexander Cuming dramatically convened a council in the townhouse atop Nikwasi to appoint Moytoy of Tellico as "emperor" of the nation, and delegate seven "chiefs" who visited England to further confirm this "treaty". See Barbara Duncan and Brett Riggs, Cherokee Heritage Trails Guidebook 2003: 153. Today, Nikwasi survives as a heavily-urbanized Franklin town park, purchased by coins collected by school children. Traditions of its Nunnehi help against the Creeks and Yankees continue; See Barbara Duncan, Living Stories of the Cherokee 1998: 99, 201, where Davey Arch mentions it as a refuge for women and children, and Freeman Owle tells of its helpful "little soldiers".

Indeed, regard for focal mounds as "abodes" of the dead, and, especially, as "holy homes" ~ "hollow hills" of resident immortals, recalls the central chamber at such mounds as Craig at the important Mississippian site of Spiro in eastern Oklahoma. Such indwelling life was culturally evoked by references to Ants and Anthills, as at the famous Upper Creek town of Tukabatchee (below, Chapter 6), which has links to Shawnees.[171]

Thus, among Mississippian descendants, "Linguistic and traditional material from Mvskoke, Yuchi, Chickasaw, Choctaw, and Cherokee" sources yields a reasonably coherent picture that "Mounds possess symbolic associations with autochthony, the underworld, birth, fertility, death, burial, the placation of spirits, emergence, purification, and supernatural protection. They are metaphorical mountains, anthills, navels, or womblike 'earth mother' representations".[172] In mythology, hollow mounds serve as nests and dens, as well as passages from the underworld.

Before the publication of the new Creek dictionary, Knight concluded that modern mounds, 4-6 feet high, are known as *tadjo* and "appear to be made up partly of dirt from square ground sweepings and partly of fresh dirt dug up nearby. In each case the new mound covers the remnant of the mound built the previous year. ... These mounds are distinct from other small mounds formed by successive ash piles from the annually renewed sacred fires".[173] In addition, "The low ridge formed around the square ground from repeated sweepings is also called *tadjo* in Mvskoke and Seminole contexts".[174]

Knight found a direct link between Mississippian and historic ritual in the observations of John Howard Payne[175] at the 1835 Tukabatchee Green Corn in Alabama. There, of two mounds, the larger "used as a dance platform during the 'gun dance', had been given a new coat of earth scraped from the adjacent square ground ... stunning testimony documenting Creek mound construction in the nineteenth century, involving the addition of an earth mantle (albeit a thin one) to a genuine Mississippian platform

---

[171] Vernon Knight, Symbolism of Mississippian Mounds 1989: 281; cf. the Pueblo of Zuni in New Mexico calls itself *Halona*, the anthill at the center or earth navel of the world, as measured out by a Spider stretching its legs evenly in all directions, according to their origin saga.

[172] Knight, Symbolism of Mississippian Mounds 1989: 283.

[173] Knight, Symbolism of Mississippian Mounds 1989: 283.

[174] Knight, Symbolism of Mississippian Mounds 1989: 284.

[175] John Howard Payne (9 June 1791 – 1852), from an old Massachusetts family, was the sixth of nine children. Taught elocution, diction, and delivery by his own father, he became an actor, the first American to invade the British stage. He wrote "Home Sweet Home" in 1822 but it was first sung in Covent Garden, England in 1823 as part of the opera "Clari, the Maid of Milan". Back in the US, he was hired to do public relations by the Cherokee on the brink of their removal to Oklahoma, and toured the Southeast. He died while American Consul to Tunis, Africa. See William Anderson, Jane Brown, and Anne Rogers, eds., The Payne-Butrick Papers, Six volumes in two books (1-3, 4-6) 2010.

mound. The ritual context, moreover, is unambiguous. The symbolism is that of world renewal and purification within the framework of communal Green Corn ceremonialism".[176]

Today, at Creek grounds, in ironic contrast to all this past and highly public effort, the actual mound building takes place before, as preparations for, rather than at the actual Green Corn Dance. It occurs in the early morning at a time when almost everyone else is sleeping. In the days or week preceding, fresh willows reroof the four arbors and new upright poles replace any of those greatly weakened during the previous year. At dawn before the all-night dance, the square is scraped clean of weeds and the refuse is raked outward toward the edge to make a ridge (properly the only _tadjo_) setting off the sacred enclosure that is the domain of fasting men. Women only enter it by special invitation from men officials. Once the area is clean, clear, and repacked down, attentions turn to the raised basin in the open center where the sacred fire of crossed logs ⊕ will burn. Its ashes are added to the biggest mound, by no means a "small" ash pile implied by Knight.

Throughout the Americas, the ashes of sacred fires have an especially charged status, as in a Delaware story where twins are sent to ask help from the Sun to kill an underwater monster. Instead of giving them his fire, which was far too hot and dangerous, the Sun provided them with ash "sweeping", which effectively boiled up the lake to kill the serpent.[177]

Reviewing Knight's original source, John Howard Payne[178] himself reported that he first saw the 1835 Tukabatchee Green Corn (see Chapter 6) while standing on a mound "just outside of one of the open corners of the sacred square". He "was afterwards told that this mound was composed of ashes which had been produced many preceding years by such fires as were now blazing in the center; and that ashes of the sort were never permitted to be scattered, but must thus be gathered up, and carefully and religiously preserved."

Thus, one of those two mounds was composed of ashes, as the other was of the scraped up earth noted by Knight. "In the center of this outer square was a very high circular mound ... formed from the earth accumulated yearly by removing the surface of the sacred square thither. At every Green-Corn Festival, the sacred square is strewn with soil yet untrodden; the soil of the year preceding being taken away but preserved as explained above. No stranger's foot is allowed to press the new earth of the sacred square until its consecration by members is complete."[179] Such "new earth" has strong spiritual associations because it opens the way to the underworld, breaking through the all-important surface tension of the land's skin.

---

[176] Knight, Symbolism of Mississippian Mounds 1989: 285.

[177] William Newcomb, Culture and Acculturation of the Delaware Indians 1956: 74. Jim Thompson, the narrator, indicated these "charged" sweepings were from the west side of the Big House [Delaware temple], where old ashes were carried out the west door and specially deposited on the outside. Once these were scattered around the outside edge of the lake, the water boiled and the horned serpent floated up dead.

[178] John Swanton, Green Corn Dance 1932: 179.

[179] Swanton, Green Corn Dance 1932: 177.

Every summer, throughout Oklahoma, as in previous centuries, at the central fireplace of a Creek town (_italwa_, former chiefdom), with great care, the old ashes and upper layer of baked dirt are carried off, a shovelful at a time, by a brigade of men who take it to the east and add it as a topping to the five-foot mound that stands toward the east. Another work group goes in a specific direction to gather special soil, often in a wheelbarrow, to add to the small bump in the northeast that later serves very briefly as a standing place for young man when summoning "the Birds" before men begin the series of Feather Dances.[180] Indeed, these and other dances at the ceremonial ground, all using the distinctively Southeastern dance step called the "stomp", provide the means (Chapter 6) to pump localized songs into the square ground and mounds. In all, at this square, every summer, as decades before, three mounds are remade and blessed, one for the central fireplace, a second for the Birds, and a third replenished mound of ashes.[181]

This ongoing central Oklahoma pattern, however, might be dismissed as a recent import, since prehistorically, except for Caddoans along rivers draining into the lower southwest Mississippi River, mounds are not supposed to occur in the Far West, or so most have assumed. A close look at the ethnography, however, dispels that notion, particularly since mounds, albeit small ones, are still being made during world renewing rituals in northern California and still appear in Salish art (See Chapter 5).

In Knight's equally masterful summary of Southeastern mound archaeology, the initial impulse is traced to offerings of oversized artifacts, especially of chert, shell, and copper, intended for display at and in burials.[182] During the Middle Archaic (BC 4750-3900), "Oversize Bentons, Cache Blades, Turkey Tails, and Double Notch Turkey Tails" had two forms. One was delicately chipped of flint bifaces and the other was "effigy knives of ground and polished siltstone" that had been shattered ('killed'). Both types contrasted in terms of raw material, knapping, and disposal "even when they were buried

---

[180] By analogy based on town plans in John Swanton, <u>Social Organization and Social Usages of the Indians of the Creek Confederacy</u> 1928a (269 Eufaula, 274 Coweta, and, especially, 258 Hillibi), this mound marks the ancient location of the town's hothouse. Thus, while the bird caller seems to stand on a few inches of raised dirt, he symbolically stands on the roof of a high enclosure used for winter, private, and secret meetings. It was just such large communal buildings that incorporated mound functions in recent centuries.

[181] Based on present use, the number of mounds derives from their functions, not from sponsoring by corporate kin groups or other considerations, contra Randolph Widmer, who argued that the number of mounds at a site reflected its number of "lineages" or corporate kin groups; Cf. Randolph Widmer, Explaining Sociopolitical Complexity in the Foraging Adaptations of the Southeastern United States: The Role of Demography, Kinship, and Ecology in Sociopolitical Evolution 2004.

[182] The equation here is clearly chert = land, shell = water, and copper = sky.

in the same cache." [183] Red ocher covered some offerings, often with female graves, but a burial of a dwarf boy included five stacked blades. [184] Insightfully, the effigy form can be compared to the *atassa*, the oversized wooden knives to chop up harm that are carried by two lead women every summer in the Ribbon Dance.

Earth moving and shaping was initially commemorative, sealing off habitation and specialized activity zones with a new, fresh overmantle cap. Often these were large oval embankments, under a ring of low mounds, as at Watson Brake. Over time, one of these mounds came visually to dominate the site, and eventually became paired with another across the open plaza. In all, the five identifiable types of moundings were 1) raised over existing cemeteries to add later burials, as with Copena (derived from copper, galena), 2) raised over charnel huts or mortuary crypts, 3) covering secondary burials and cremations placed on a low earthen platform that is all capped with a dirt dome, 4) raised over the central tomb of a special burial with pots cached along the east side, and 5) raised sequentially over an extended time. [185] Such construction intervals occurred every twenty years, and changed colors highlighted the mound fill and the distinct mantles, often in contrasting hues so the sealing off of the prior surface would be assured and obvious to confine its infused songs.

With the ending of burial mounds, the ethnographically known Woodland ritual complex emerged from the segmenting out of a) world renewal ~ fertility rites such as the Busk, b) adoption ~ succession ~ rebirth rites such as Calumet feathered pipe(stem) ceremonialism, and c) mourning observances such as Lakota Ghost Keeping and other forms of ritualized grief. [186]   Ceremonies moved inside rotunda, halls, and council chambers, sometimes just low protective walls, to further safeguard community vitality.

Backdrop Speck(ulations)

Frank Speck, the great comparative Algonquianist, mused about the role of "mound clusters" as dramatic stages, using the example of the Tutelo Spirit Adoption and Reclothing Ceremony. This rite maintains the spiritual strength and names of the Tutelo nation (Eastern Siouan speakers), banished from the Carolina piedmont and given refuge among Canadian Iroquois. Each of its personal names is renewed a year after the death of the prior holder when someone of the same gender and relative age is garbed and feted

---

[183] Samuel Brookes, Aspects of the Middle Archaic: The Atassa 1997: 62; Cf. Jay Johnson and Samuel Brookes, Benton Points, Turkey Tails, and Cache Blades: Middle Archaic Exchange in the Midsouth 1989.

[184] This dwarf from northwest Alabama was about 17 years old and 40 inches high. Thousands of years later, two achondroplastic dwarves were buried at Moundville, a lone male and a female with a normal adult male. Both were in their forties and about fifty inches high. See Paul Bahn, Written in Bones 2002: 24-26.

[185] Vernon James Knight, Ceremonialism Until 1500, Southeast, Handbook of North American Indians 14: 740 2004.

[186] Robert Hall, An Archaeology of the Soul, North American Indian Belief and Ritual 1997.

during a long night. The renamee, wearing newly made clothes over a string of beads hung diagonally from the left shoulder across the heart, hosts the spirit of the deceased for ten hours until its final departure on the rays of the sunrise. Paced by orderly repetitions of songs, intermissions, and feasts at the start and end, the renamee, drummer, and six singers are attended by deputies, escorts, helpers, and stage hands as well as an audience of mourners, guests, and visitors.

Rattles and water drum provide music during the first set of songs, replaced by split-stick clappers at the actual transfer (embodying) of the name. The renamee with escorts periodically processes and recesses to gift strung beads (72 loops), ribbons, fabric, and other soft goods to the singers, usually tossed (rained down) upon their shoulders. Tobacco offerings are burned in the fire, and, at the end, the clappers and drumstick are also cremated. The drum itself is taken apart to release its potency, returning its pulse to the vitality of the wider world.

Overall, though now "decadent legacies", such "reduced ceremonies [testify to] mass performance of the cult of the dead … being fitted to sacred-shrine precincts of wide and ample ground space … of earthwork structures, elevations, enclosures, and the like which mark so conspicuously the endroits [qualities] of aboriginal settlements in the whole southern area [and survive as] fugitive derelicts of mammoth institutional cults".[187]

Cautions

Today's public sharing of knowledge, especially native astronomy, starkly contrasts with the private possession of esoteric lore, especially cosmology, that was once a defining criterion for elite membership throughout the Americas. The metaphoric, poetic, and obscurest usages given to ordinary Hochungara words in the epic of their Medicine Rite (Chapter 6) serves as a useful reminder as well as a check on misguided research. As one example, Marion Mochon[188] tried to find words for Mississippian farming, commerce, society, polity, and world view by searching through meager dictionaries of five languages variously belonging to the Muskogean (Choctaw, Creek) and Siouian (Osage, Ofo, Biloxi) stocks. Of note, she found many more Muskogean than Siouian examples, and accordingly argued for heavy Muskogean participation in the Mississippian period.

---

[187] Frank Speck, <u>The Tutelo Spirit Adoption Ceremony</u> 1942: 8, 80, 81. Though listed as dormant for more than a century, the last Tutelo speakers lived unrecorded into the later 1900s. This Tutelo rite, which switched to spoken Cayuga Iroquoian except for a few original sentences, is a curious blend of the ritual feeding of the dead, Midewiwin (re)member reincarnation prevalent among tribes of the Great Lakes, and the revivification of hereditary names among towns of the Pacific Northwest.

[188] Marion Mochon, Language, History, and Prehistory: Mississippian Lexico-Reconstruction 1972.

Conversely, a decade later, James Springer and Stanley Witkowski[189] argued, based on sub-branching of the Siouan linguistic stock, especially Central Siouan, a connection with the archaeological complex known as Oneota, whose mound building aspect grew out of earlier Effigy Mounds. At Blood Run (early 1700s, Chapter 4), Siouans (still combined Omaha-Ponka, with some Ioway) built hundreds of mounds.

In all likelihood, however, mounding required esoteric terms, especially by the Mississippian priesthoods.[190] Few of these adepts survived the collapse of these chiefdoms and the decimation of their ranks. These terms would not have been common nor public knowledge. If many members of the communities were not privy to this information, it is even more doubtful that it would have been provided to outsiders. Only a native with an intellectual outlook would have seen the virtue of saving some of this knowledge for posterity. Such was the Osage priest named Saucy Calf, who began the recording of the complex Osage initiation rites (Chapter 6) with Francis LaFlesche, the Omaha-speaking ethnographer, only to die in the suspicious burning of his home.

Geomancers

William Romain[191] reintroduces the term 'geomancers' for the builders of the huge Hopewell earthworks covering acres and miles, and argues for their coordinated planning of these sites, using a standard measuring unit of 1053 feet (321 meters) based on an arm span of 2.1 feet or 25.27 inches. Comparing consistent measurements, he has found "families" of earthwork squares that form a systematically inter-nested series (called an icosatwist). Equally intriguing is the seventy-mile Great Hopewell Road diagonally linking Newark with High Bank at Chillicothe, with an octagon and square set at right angles to each other at either end. While Newark is well preserved, High Bank is an open field where tell-tale compacted earth reveals the subsurface configuration.

Other regularities include placement on the second terrace above a river upon distinctive soils (friable Fox series) near vital resources such as water confluences, ancient trails, and "gifts" from the earth.[192] Among these linkages are the proximity of

---

[189] James Warren Springer and Stanley Witkowski, Siouian Historical Linguistics and Oneota Archaeology, <u>Oneota Studies</u> 1982: 69-83.

[190] Some may have been usual words put to unusual usage; as, for example: ancient Maya used the word 'trees' for the elaborately-carved stone stelae standing in their plazas.

[191] William Romain, <u>Mysteries of the Hopewell</u> 2000: 167, 186.

[192] The most vivid link between these paired earthworks and the Shawnees, whose homeland in colonial times was this section of Ohio, appears in the fieldnotes of Erminie Wheeler Voegelin (Box 32, Folder 290, page 96, quoted from Mark Raymond Harrington), where Shawnee William Skye noted that such locales are paired as grandfather and (grand)mother, such as a flint quarry and a corn field. Shawnee elder Jim Clark described Moundbuilders themselves as four feet tall, with vertical eyes and feet set backwards, wearing fur (not clothes), and able to whoop like little boys (Box 32, Folder

Newark earthworks and gem flint, Tremper and pipestone, Seip and ocher, and McKittrick and salt (though the salt seems to have been open to all willing to dig it out). Each location tapped into a concentrated flow of cosmic *puwah*, which extended from the sun in the sky to the heart in a body, according to a Prairie Potawatomie quote: "Our hearts are only wind and water moving".[193]

Each Hopewell construction is a microcosm of the combined universe in which the circle = earth, square = sky, and a central mound is a mountain mimicking the shape of an actual peak in the local landscape. The axis of each site is aligned to the seasonal path of the sun, moon, or stars. Consistent with native cultural practices, mounds built over charnel houses for the preparation of the dead usually have lunar alignments because of associations of the dead with the night and dark underworld. At the Newark Octagon, the eight phases of the 18.6 year lunar cycle are each indicated by a gap at an angle marked by a gateway mound. Such a feature consists only of soil, and occurs only at linear earthworks like squares and octagons, suggesting continuity for the ethnographic belief that spirits can only travel in straight lines. An octagon's bends were also probably used to track the moon's eight monthly phases (new, waxing crescent, first quarter, waxing gibbous, full, waning gibbous, last quarter, and waning crescent).

Consistent mythic and ritual references recalling these Hopewell sites are the Earth Diver epic (Chapter 2) in which a hero brings up earth from the bottom of the primal sea and the Busk of the Southeast, a world renewal rite historically celebrating the corn (maize) harvest. Since corn was a rare crop at this time period, a bountiful harvest consisted of farmed indigenous plants like sunflower, amaranth, and others. While the actual Earth Diver varied across the Americas and Asia, depending on ecologically appropriate species, Romain suggests that for Hopewell he was shoveler duck or roseate spoonbill, though they could have as easily worked together.[194]

Interesting inclusions in mounds suggest the encouragement of heightened awareness during rituals through the use of tobacco, indicated by hundreds of shattered pipes, and, in at least one instance, a copper sheathed model of a foot-long mushroom that is probably *Amanita muscaria* (fly agaric), famously psychotropic. Of note, the sheen of the copper mimics that of the natural species. Both sheets and bits of shiny mica occur in some burials within mounds, which are usually cremations (cremains), providing shiny surfaces also useful in meditation.

Specific parallels with the modern Busk, celebrated by traditional towns of Creeks now in Oklahoma (Miller 2015) include the event known as "going to water" in which participants purify by washing, preferably in running water but more often today in tubs. Two thousand years before, sites along rivers often include a graded roadway to the shore that would have facilitated this act, such as the Sacra Via at Marietta where the

---

291, Book XII, page 27, 1934). For today's Shawnees, the Creator herself is addressed as Grandmother in prayer and ceremony.

[193] Alanson Skinner. The Mascoutens or Prairie Potawatomi Indians 1924: 221.

[194] These birds appear on the four bulging sides of special Hopewell pottery, suggesting its rounded square form was intended as a microcosm – globose body and square collar, especially when holding water as per the Earth Diver Epic, Cf. Henry Shetrone, The Mound-Builders 1930: 136, 139, Figure 79.

Muskingum joins the Ohio River. They also would have facilitated the rolling of canoes out of and into the water, when these craft were the prime prehistoric transport.[195] River people, such as those of the Pacific Northwest (as well as ancient Egyptians) integrated full size and model boats into many of their rituals, including graded ramps for moving them about on land. Much of this knowledge was lost historically when the importance of watercraft in Ohio was eclipsed by the adoption of horses.

Ontario World

In his review of Ontario mounds, Walter Kenyon[196] noted that, worldwide, mounds belonged to the Neolithic period when crops were being domesticated. This is a useful insight. In other words, once people began actively to work the soil to farm crops, they also raised mounds as another expression of the same interest in vitality. They contain burials, like Westminster Abbey, because they are sacred spaces (honored earth, raised banks of offerings, blessed ballast), closer to the immortals, not because their primary purpose was to be only a cemetery. They were sacred because they were vortices in the cosmos, loci of *puwah* maintained by devoted human ritual to atone for faults and sustain life.

Food fueled the system, both on the table and at the altar. Farming of corn, beans, and squash, however, was only one aspect of the mixed economy of this Great Lakes region. Instead, it was the intensive tending of wild rice plots, complete with tagging and binding over their ripe sheaves just before harvest, that acted as a type of natural farming. That these were aquatic resources makes the elaboration of earthen mounds all the more significant since humans, obviously, live on land not in the water, launching canoes to harvest before cleaning and roasting on shore.

Given usual mound locations on Ontario high points along straight-bank waterways, visibility was a prime consideration in their placement. Colin Renfrew's study of the distribution of megalithic tombs on European islands, including one of the Orkneys, analyzed the remark by V Gordon Childe that the location of these ancient tombs was the same as modern farmsteads. The reason is that both were built on what arable land was available. Such tombs served as both gathering places (emphasis added) and territory markers, in much the same way as the locale of a modern hall, grange, or church fosters community identity and cohesion.

Ritual, in series or by intermittent felt-need, sanctified the mounds and their environs. In Ontario, traces and residues of these rites include cremated bones, grave goods, and skulls (as at Hungry Hall) that have beads set as pupils into caked-in eye sockets, holes in the back to extract brains, or scars on the top from scalping.

In all, "we should look upon mound building as we look upon the performance of a ballet or drama in our own society .... Once the mound was built, of course, it would have served, as does a theatre, as a backdrop for other rituals. For, once again, it is

---

[195] The Ringler Dugout, Bradley Lepper, Ohio Archaeology, With Feature Articles Contributed by Over 20 Archaeologists and Scholars 2005: 260-61.

[196] Walter Kenyon, Mounds of Sacred Earth 1986: 76-81.

through such rituals and ceremonies that human groups are bound together and that individual lives are shaped to accord with ancestral patterns."[197]

Intersecting Parallel Worlds

A recurrent feature of the archaeological record is the covering over of a building or spot by one or more layers of dirt. Often this is repeated periodically – either once a year at the Busk, at the decade, or at the end of a longer cycle (such as the 52 year Mesoamerican calendar) – to increase its size and thereby produce a raised mound.[198] Classic examples range from Watson Brake (5500 BP) to Caddo temples (300 BP). Usually an initial building was burned down, with the first layer heaped on to smother the fire to raise a huge plume of smoke. Fundamental to understanding this action is the role of human intention in keeping the world in motion, and other parallel worlds distinct from each other. Mounds bulge from internal pressure, not solely by packed dirt. In particular they are inflated bubble-like by the songs in rituals and the pumping-like step of the stomp dance that represent order and stability.

Time-space, moreover, is a larger issue, especially from a native perspective. By their very nature, artistic renderings of these parallel worlds appear static. A classic example is the five rings around a central dot ◎[5] used by Yup'ik to represent their Arctic world. A more dynamic and appropriate image is that used for the atom, with the suggestion of whirling particles in orbit about the center. Indeed, these other dimensions, realms, and worlds of Native America seem to be more like separate orbits. In one aspect, however, these ritual acts create separated train tracks, because human efforts deliberately set places and events onto parallel paths and, ritually, keep them there.

How is that done? Apparently, by putting them out of direct sight, either by cremating them or by burying them under a special mantle of earth. Either way, they are transformed in ways that continue to make them useful, vital, and energizing to the human world, but unseen ~ out of direct sight. By contrast, the huge smoke plume is an obvious signal to the universe that such a transformation is occurring, warning and alerting those in other worlds that they are about to be intersected by a building, beings, and souls from the mortal world. As such, burning down, mounding up, and ballasting are more of a launch into eternity than an offering or commemoration from the past or by the present. Repeated cycles of destruction and rebuilding, moreover, allow the built-up and continued use of a favored locale over a length of time. Putting a new surface over a cemetery or burned temple enables new graves or a new temple to occupy the same place repeatedly.

---

[197] Kenyon, Mounds of Sacred Earth 1986: 81.

[198] Vernon James Knight, Ceremonialism Until 1500, Southeast, Volume 14: 734-741 2004.

4 ~ CONTEXTS AND COMPARISONS

Origins

Tribal members, with varying intensity, insist that their people have always been in the Americas. While each and every local native community indeed recounts how and where their ancestors were uniquely created and spiritually attached to their American homelands, a more global perspective adds that the DNA of these ancestral humans came through Asia by way of Siberia and the Bering Strait. These were not natives, nor were they Americans as such.[199] Instead, they were the ancestors of the tribes who homed-in and adapted to the Americas, nourished by local conditions to make these continents their very own through millennia of personal interactions with the species, perceived spirits, and spaces of their special domains.

We turn now to a chronology of such key sites and places, freed from the constraints of strictly archaeological practice, before ending with comparative mounding by Irish, Shilluk, Dobu, and !Kung San that sheds light on Native America. Given the enormity of population losses and cultural trauma in the Americas, it is also important to look at mound use elsewhere in the world for a wider perspective on this pan-human activity. In particular, a link between religion, art, ritual, and mounds through the medium of trance to enhance vitality deserves attention, as suggested for Hopewell shamans (below). Natives relate(d) to their total landscape through constructions, aesthetic "art" works, and visionary states of mind. Mounds – from top, sides, and base – alter perspectives, as does trance. Other facets of our understanding are provided by kindred phenomenon such as rock art – another mark on the land. Intended as observation markers, warning signs, legal claims, and military challenges, such art was "covenant" between place and people in all forms (polyspecies) and intelligences.

The strict archaeological record is unsure about human beginnings in the Americas. Tens of thousands of years ago, these people would have been hunters relying on big game animals (megafauna), such as mammoth, mastodon, and huge bison. Trailing such herds, they needed to be mobile and so lived in skin tents, wore leather clothing, and used hide sacks and containers. This Paleo-American ~ Indien way of life

---

[199]   It is unclear when humans first arrived in the Americas, though a new distinction was briefly made between Paleo-Americans, before 9000 years ago, and Paleo-Indiens afterward. Horses, with a 45 million-year-old fossil record in Wyoming, evolved in the US Plains and, seven million years ago, drifted across the Bering Straits to grasslands of Central Asia. Except for some tribal stories about a tiny breed of horse they knew, this equine became extinct in its homeland about 8,000 years ago. Similarly, the growing popularity of the large, hairy, smelly primate called Bigfoot or Sasquatch (derived from one of its Salish names) finds some support among natives who regard it as a New World ape, though none exist in the scientific record that shows monkeys evolving in both Africa and the Americas but apes in only the "Old World".

survived for generations as people scattered thinly over the Americas, and it continues, aided by modern technology of guns and motors, in Arctic climes.

An obviously continuous ancestral tradition, however, does not stand out until after 15,000 years ago when the Clovis mastodon hunters left behind distinctive spear points. By 10,000 years ago, beautifully made spear points – with a channel flute down the middle to make a tighter hafting and to funnel blood out of wounded bison – mark the complex (kit) known as Folsom. Then, afterwards, things get complicated as late Paleo-Indiens diversified and adapted their Archaic economy to cope with local environmental conditions. The tradition of big game hunting survived longest in the Subarctic, Arctic, and Plains, where modern, smaller bison lived until Euro-Americans slaughtered them in the 1880s, in a deadly combination of trade in hides, bones crushed for fertilizer, sport hunting, poisons, and railroads to speed their demise.[200]

Paleo Caches

As humans settled the Americas, they interacted more with the land, eventually identifying with ("claiming") homelands and territories. In religio-cultural terms, this means that they bonded with the local spirits and their characteristic attributes. Most especially, the leading families forged a special link, and used this knowledge to benefit their larger community through generations.

People would have learned how, where, and why to give thanks, leaving prayers and appropriate offerings behind, usually in caches dug into the ground. Indeed, such pits are a necessary prelude to the building of mounds. Among ethnographic tribes, offerings were usually quite specific and balanced. Delawares once offered corn meal to slain deer, and venison to maize plants just before harvest.[201] Paleo-Indiens are assumed to have followed (and managed) herds, traveling widely from base camps without setting down local roots. Multigenerational bonds would have developed over time between herds and bands, as later occurred in the Plains. Seasonally-shifting, home-base camps would have been established, but nothing substantial or permanently year-round was needed. Megafauna shoulder blades would have been used as hoes to scrape off level surfaces for tent and beds. Necessity left deep imprints on the land. Stone had to be quarried for tools, and plants gathered to supplement big game meat. In a modern reflex of such offerings, Yup'ik Eskimos walk out into the open tundra and bury an offering (tobacco, tea, dried fish) to "feed" the land that feeds them.[202]

In the <u>Popul Vuh</u>, the creation epic of the Quiche Maya, the hero twins, as one of their ordeals, are locked inside a room filled with flint knives, but they win these weapons over by promising that in the future they will feed on game blood and meat as it

---

[200] By weird irony, we have more evidence for extinct mammoths and mastodons than for these millions of slain bison because their bones were shipped east, ground up, and sold as fertilizer, mostly for rose beds. Their tough hides were sliced up to make the belts that ran the machines of Eastern industry.

[201] David Zeisberger, <u>History of the North American Indians</u> 1910: 139.

[202] Ann Fienup-Riordan, <u>Boundaries and Passages</u>, Rule and Ritual in Yup'ik Eskimo Oral Tradition 1994: 58.

is butchered ("you will have the flesh of all animals").[203] The sense is that sharp flints transform from hostile killers into useful, well-fed tools by deciding to cooperate with humans. The blood offering to flint, for these Mayas, is, therefore, delayed until knapping transforms a rock core into chipped-edge tools.

For Clovis, however, there are more direct offerings from 13,000 years ago: caches of bone rods, blades, and points.[204] Unfortunately, most of these were found during construction, damaged and disturbed by machines. The best known caches, with blade count, state, and date of discovery, are Simon (29 artifacts, Idaho, 1961), Anzick (100+, Montana, 1968), Drake (13, Colorado, 1978), Rickey/East Wenatchee (60, Washington, 1987), and Fenn (56, ?, 1902?), which was purchased from a family that was vague about where it was found, but a dry cave seems likely because it is so intact.

How were these caches marked, either to be left undisturbed or found again after they were buried (If they were intended for reuse, as during famines or other hardships)? Usually, both prayers and scattered offerings (tobacco, ocher, sage) leave traces for others to see, either to admire or avoid. By analogy with other landscapes which locals claimed as "private" property in Native America, such as halibut or dentalia beds under Northwest seas, heirs were trained to position their canoe by triangulating between landmarks along the horizon. In other cases, people were guided by the stars, or by blazes on trees and rocks. If these were truly left as offerings, however, no markers would have been needed; the deities already knew what was where. Just to be sure, though, a small mound with a tabooing banner or staff could have warned away everyone except those most desperately in need of stone tools. Among historic tribes, antlers, bones, hides, and offal left at hunting shrines during good times later provided meager starvation foods during hardships.[205]

Anzick blades were covered over with thick red ocher, and other caches also show its traces.[206] While this dense red (iron oxide) powder has been regarded as packing and insulation, its very presence indicates an offering. Because of its ready association with blood and life, red ocher was ~ is much used in ceremonies. In a stark example, Ella Deloria,[207] the Nakota (Sioux) anthropologist and linguist, includes a scene in her novel Waterlily in which a distraught mother prays for her sick baby at a rock. First she smears ocher on its flat surface as though it were a face to "personalize it". As offerings, she positioned an otter skin smeared with ocher atop the rock like a hat and set a stick upright with ten tiny bundles of tobacco dangling from strings. In the same way, across the Dakotas, lonely rocks and trees received applications of ocher to consecrate them as altars where people prayed in times of stress. Ocher, offerings, and prayers made them obviously blessed, and rocks were virtually immortal.

---

[203] Dennis Tedlock, Popul Vuh 1985: 140.

[204] George Frison and Bruce Bradley, The Fenn Cache ~ Clovis Weapons & Tools 1999.

[205] Kerstin Eidlitz, Food and Emergency Food in the Circumpolar Area, Studia Ethnographica Uppsaliensis 32 1969.

[206] Anzick also included remains of a small boy, 12,600 years old whose DNA relate him to Asia.

[207] Ella Deloria, Waterlily 1988: 17, 139.

Providing the impression of a face or eyes gives the offering a more sympathetic and humanized context. Possible early examples of such enfacing are the Malakoff stone heads. Found in gravel pits of Pleistocene (Ice) Age located 60 miles southeast of Dallas, the first was exposed in 1929 sixteen feet below the surface. It was a sandstone concretion 16 by 14 inches, weighing 98 pounds. When a second pit was opened in 1935, another head weighing 63 pounds was found. In 1940, in the second pit, a third head was found, 22 feet down. It was 20 inches long and weighed 135 pounds.[208] Features are minimally carved or gouged into the sandstone, usually just eyes and mouth, as would be expected for an offering. No ocher traces survived, though they would have been likely.[209]

In East Texas in the Llano Estacado ("staked plains" in Spanish) at Mustang Springs, over 60 water wells have been exposed. The site provides evidence of a drought that began 8000 years ago and was severe by BP 6800, when the southern High Plains were "dry, bleak, and windswept". [210] Wells were dug (and had to be) for several hundred years until adequate moisture returned. Similar wells have been found at Blackwater Draw Locality Number 1 (the Clovis type site) and Rattlesnake Springs in New Mexico, as well as Murray Springs in Arizona. They provide further evidence of widespread harsh conditions that contributed to the Pleistocene extinctions of many of the megafauna, leaving smaller modern bison the predominant species on the plains. They also bespeak the need for prayers and offerings to survive these ever-threatening conditions. To live on the land, harsh as it was, people had to dig into and embrace it to satisfy their thirst. Leaving behind the backdirt piles both exposed the life-giving water in the wells and marked their locations with bulges.[211]

Archaic

Over time, in the Americas, specialized Paleo hunters became generalized foragers, living off the land, moving by seasons to harvest (garner) available foods, whether nuts, fresh greens, small game, berries, seeds, or fish. During this Archaic period, camps were widely scattered over a region to make effective and efficient use of its resources as these became available. In some cases, the largest sites indicate a central home base from which families commuted to harvest among regular seasonal camps. To

---

[208] H. Marie Wormington, Ancient Man in North America 1964: 154-155; E. H. Sellards, Stone Images from Henderson County, Texas 1941.

[209] This lack of ochre is telling since many have suggested that these heads were made by workmen as a hoax. On the other hand, the later Olmec heads and other religious use of faces show that this human head tradition is very ancient in the Americas.

[210] David Meltzer, Altithermal Archaeology and Paleoecology at Mustang Springs 1991.

[211] The actual impact or defacement was probably minimal, given that modern natives digging roots and other resources are careful with the dibble to pry them out of the ground instead of digging huge holes to scar the landscape, as most whites would do.

meet storage needs, a variety of cache pits, skin bags, and basketry were developed by women.

In the Southeast of five thousand years ago, a porous fiber-tempered pottery was also invented, probably to transport shellfish.[212] With pottery came a variety of fragile containers, kept safest at home, though baskets and skin bags were still used for travel and transport. Certain places attracted people, because of what was there in the ground or what could be seen far and wide from it. With such in-gathering came public devotion and planning. Mounds and earthworks accumulated via the built-up reuse and overlayering of these special places, where earth and sky, living and dead, seen and unseen, came together in blessing.

By the Archaic period, people were settling down into home territories, applying knowledge to enhance so-called "efficiency" of seasonal resources and abundances. Dalton (BP 9000), which followed the Paleo-Indien era, harvested, thanked, and ate ("exploited" in harsh jargon) pecans. The landscape was tended, but with increasing management of resources, earth shaping and layering also took place. Stepped terraces provided better growing spaces, and scratched ditches brought water into natural plots.

Windover

In the vicinity of the NASA Florida space launch for arcing into the sky is a small dark pond filled with peat. Between BP 7400-8500 (Early Archaic), hundreds of bodies were anchored into its shallow muck, held in place by stakes and heavy limbs. Placed in water in fetal positions, each clearly signaled a return to the womb.

Half of the pond has been excavated, removing 168 burials, evenly divided between males/females and old/young, with age 20 the median.[213] Because of the natural conditions, 91 had preserved brain tissue. Of particular note, only females were buried with hollow bone tubes, often decorated with engraved geometrics. Among ethnographic tribes (Chapters 2, 6), such tubes were symbols of life.

Staking and weighing down the bodies into the peat quagmire,[214] keeping them submerged in bloat, calls attention to the uncertainty of their world. Grave goods were highly varied, with fabrics especially so in seven varieties of weave. Four types of close twining, one of open twining, one of mat twining, and one of plaiting stand in sharp contrast to the few types of later centuries. Clearly, these Early Archaic peoples lived a

---

[212] Kenneth Sassaman, Early Pottery in the Southeast ~ Tradition and Innovation in Cooking Technology 1993.

[213] Glen Doran, ed., Windover ~ Multidisciplinary Investigations of an Early Archaic Florida Cemetery 2002: 11, 12, 18, 106.

[214] Such staking is also European, though reasons there seem more malevolent or criminal, Cf. P. V. Glob, The Bog People ~ Iron-Age Man Preserved 1969. European mounds include burials as well, sometimes, of entire ships, R.L.S. Bruce-Mitford, The Sutton Hoo Ship Burial 1964; as well as the unmarked graves of criminals hanged from a nearby gallows, Cf. Chapter 3, note 37.

fine blend of labor, leisure, and skill.[215] Though the bodies were bundled in fabrics and some hides, and some of the tree limb stakes stood above the water as (decorated ?) markers, these mounded images were not played out on the ground (soil) itself until a few millennia later.[216] Instead, stakes and jellied ooze helped fix ancestors to this uncertain land, unseen but not forgotten. In many ways, this staked-down site, continuously used for 1300 years, foretells the later development of ballasting or weighing-down by mounds. Set in water, it also speaks to on-going vitalities.

Settling Up

Because of their generalized "efficiency," Archaic peoples lived on a rich variety of foods and developed a thorough knowledge of their familiar landscape, including its spiritual aspects. Highlands, caves, confluences, and springs became foci of ritual attention since they symbolized portals into and through the earth. Intensifying foragers identified more intensely with a place and so self-created themselves therein – through the agency of an immortal who became their patron Creator (whether man, woman, both, or neither). Indeed, people, especially astute shamans, began to systematize beliefs, sometimes to the extent of deliberately reversing or otherwise manipulating regional tenets to make them unique to their own society.

---

[215] At the nearby Gauthier Site, being encroached upon by one of Florida's many trailer parks, this 5-6000 year-old community lived around a muck pond (Lake Pointset). Aquatic foods were primary, including many cottonmouths and alligators. They buried 150 members in five clusters, probably kin based, on a low hill characteristic of the region (at a lofty 18 feet above sea level). A third of these burials were lost to prior ditch digging and to an overzealous sheriff's department making sure it was not a modern massacre. Artifacts included stone points, knives, scrapers, and atlatl weights. A pair of side-hair pins were made of incised antler prongs which were pegged through bored holes by raccoon penis bones. All ages were represented in the burials, See Calvin Jones, Excavations of an Archaic Cemetery in Cocoa Beach, Florida 1981.

[216] The lone exception is the L'Anse Amour burial mound dated BP 7500 in Labrador, See Robert McGhee and James Tuck, An Archaic Sequence from the Strait of Belle Isle, Labrador 1975. A twelve-year-old was buried prone and face down under a covering of rocks and dirt. Grave goods included stone and bone points (harpoons), bifaces, red ocher, a bone toggle, a whetstone, a pendant, a whistle, and a walrus tusk. Of note, for my own argument about affirming mounds, the slight body was weighted down under rocks. The excavators suggest that this child was sacrificed to propitiate hunting luck. Among other "advanced" or "complex hunter-gatherers", families enhanced their dead children as a way of gaining higher prestige, See Bryan Hayden, The Pithouses of Keatley Creek, Complex Hunter-Gatherers of the Northwest Plateau 1997: 115, though much of his model of rank is ethnocentrically "greedy".

For example, if most towns in a region had round houses, one group set itself apart by building square homes. If most houses were rectangular, towns varied by aligning the long axis north to south, east to west, or along the shoreline. Thus, among the Iroquois Five Nations, four aligned their longhouses east to west, while the Onondaga, the hub, set theirs north to south,[217] as these directions were perceived. On the ground, these orientations always had more to do with terrain, the direction of waterways, and sun cycles than with points on any compass.[218]

More abstractly, where one community regarded Man as the unmarked generic form, including both males and females (as American English did); the next tribe down the river, speaking another language and observing another ancestral tradition, defined Man as the marked category, the specific subset of generic Woman. Key examples are millennial neighbors such as the Delaware and Iroquois of the Northeast or the Keres and Tewa Pueblos of the Southwest, where the latter in both pairs regard Woman as unmarked, with Man its subset.[219]

Over 3,000 years ago, Late Archaic people began to specialize again, farming local crops like sunflowers and various seed plants as well as building impressive earth works at Poverty Point.[220] Only much later, 1200 years ago, did natives embrace the full corn-beans-squash trinity from central Mexico. Carrying these seeds along overland trade routes were intertribal prophets, crucial for teaching the necessary crop rituals, which were most vital, in native belief, to a good harvest. Some of these traders seem to have taken on mythic qualities, including being deified, by grateful farmers. Religion subsumed everything as a potent first cause because holy goodwill is what assured success, not mere human effort.

---

[217] Edmund Wilson, <u>Apologies to the Iroquois</u> 1960: 58 (Tododaho = He Whose House Blocks the Path), 64 (Onondaga longhouses ran N/S instead of E/W like the others).

[218] Tourists to Hawaii quickly learn to use the contrast between seaward (*makai*) and hillward (*pali*), a place-based awareness common to native languages.

[219] Jay Miller, The Delaware As Woman 1974b; A 'Struckon' Model Of Delaware Culture And The Positioning Of Mediators 1979.

[220] Working without an accurately dated chronology, Shetrone (<u>The Mound-Builders</u> 1930, 379-80) showed the pitfalls of his time by commenting that Poverty Point's six empty mounds were "a welcome relief from the monotony of beautiful pottery forms of other portions of the state," while its famous "baked clay objects, authoritatively regarded as "gambling cones" such as were in use during the past century by the Paiute Indians [p380] in the West [were] all that remains of an aboriginal Monte Carlo, curiously well named if prehistoric gambling led to the same financial state as in modern times." Lacking any local rock, except those brought by pilgrims, these PPO (Poverty Point Objects) were used for stone boiling. While the casino association is spurious, the lure of a regional attraction is probably not by these builders recently christened the Tamaroha.

Farming provided a steady food surplus to be stored in towns, though this diet also included some health hazards. Families still moved with the seasons to take advantage of local produce, but they stored it back at the town for winter use, rather than in camps or cache pits at the harvest area. Local populations increased, fostering more organization. In this way, farming towns developed complex kinship systems based on unilineal descent (through just one parent) into various clans, each of which was associated with a special place where its ancestors began as spirits, plants, animals, rocks, or heroes (of some sort).

Previous periods were characterized by reliance on distinctive tools, weapons, and crafted necessities (finely made to be both diagnostic of its function and its maker's identity). While all manner of materials and techniques were used by these ancestors, only those of stone have usually been preserved (except in the extremes of very wet, very dry, or very cold sites). With farming surplus, creativity focused on pottery, the hallmark of recent centuries, though it was breakable (leaving lots of evidence) and did not transport as well as baskets and skin bags. Pottery was a boon to storage, cooking, and eventual scholarship.

Needless to say, each prior adaptation continued somewhere in the Americas. Big game hunters thrived on the bison (buffalo) herds of the Plains. Archaic foraging developed into a sophisticated tending of the landscape, with fall burnings to clear and nourish the terrain and the selective scattering of seeds to guarantee another local harvest. Such "tenders" lived throughout the West and North of North America and some still do – now driving battered pickup trucks to their "wild seed" plots. Farmers or tillers lived in the East and South, usually with women doing most of the farm work while men continued to hunt in season. Only the Southwestern Pueblos assign field work to men, heavily involved with irrigation ditches, although women do tend kitchen gardens.

Each of these lifeways was adapted to regional climates and, moreover, linked into the vast trade networks that exchanged the meat and furs of hunters for the crops and crafts of farmers. Particular local treasures – such as copper ore, turquoise, shells, minerals, and mica –figured in the trade as exotic luxury goods, often to indicate elite ranks and status. Each was a symbolic token with cosmic import, usually as shells of the water, minerals of the land, and shiny copper of the sky (a link reinforced by meteors).

A curious aspect of this intensifying localization by people – who were truly becoming <u>native</u> Americans – was a corresponding differentiation between ordinary folk and leading families, who traced their own ancestry to even more remote peoples, places, and worlds.[221] Not uncommonly, a leading family "came from" a Star or Sky Being who came to earth with special *puwah*; or their ancestor emerged from the sea or a lake to assume prominence. Sometimes, the human ancestor married a resident spirit to establish the family line. In all cases, leaders were therefore believed to be different, more enhanced ("evolved") than other members of the community, tribe, or region. Of course, they sought intermarriage within other regional elites, interlocking chiefly families to provide stability and security until some natural or social cataclysm forced a re-sorting of their ranks.

---

[221] Mary Helms, <u>Ulysses Sail</u> ~ An Ethnographic Odyssey of Power, Knowledge, and Geographical Distance 1988.

Ultimately, the disaster of European arrival toppled the native societies of these continents, although, with great irony, a few of these leading families survived because alien conquerors deliberately "married" important native women to entrench their own claims to belong in their new homes, as illustrated by the life of El Inka Garcilaso de la Vega (Miller 2015).

A similar irony of contemporary scholarship, noted above, is that many scholars have been attracted to Native American Studies because of the wealth of documentary evidence that exists, ranging from annual and serial federal reports for all reservations and their enrolled members to newspaper accounts, histories, and full scale ethnographies. Yet in many cases, especially in agent and missionary files, documents convey Indiens as white officialdom wanted them to be, but they never, in fact, were. In consequence, the oblivious, single-minded officials created, in writing, Indiens who conformed to the pressures of American culture, and self-righteously criticized those who did not. Thus, we have individuals where we should have communities, and we have material success where there should be spiritual fulfillment. Throughout, we face denials and glimpse distortions that do not match with known conditions of native resistance, long expressed in many ingenious ways. Mighty warriors and Red patriots receive special treatment, sometimes to marginalize and exceptionalize them.

Modern US growth was part of the European world-wide colonial enterprise, with distortion working its insidious way into all aspects of the encounter. As a reverse strategy, aspects of these falsehoods were used by the colonialized as a way of manipulating situations. Thus, love of nature and deep spirituality have become THE native traits, simplifying a much more complex dynamic. At first, newcomers wanted food, materials, and services, particularly (ironically named) goods – gold, slaves, furs, crops, and minerals – along with novelties like tobacco, corn, hammocks, and canoes. With European settlement, native middlemen brought resources from hinterlands, including enslaved humans, to the coastal foreign traders. Acting as traders, slavers, and mercenaries (ethnic soldiers) provided incentives for Iroquois, Chickasaw, Osage, Chinook, and other tribal communities to achieve their brief ascendancy.

Motivating settlement was land hunger, stifled in Europe by the landed elite. Hence, owning land loomed large in the recent history of the Americas. While conquest played its part in beating natives into submission, trailing behind disease, slaving, and discouragement, the actual loss was only made legal by treaties, as Thomas Jefferson knew. But most natives legally "reserved" to themselves a toehold of their former territory as reservations in the United States and reserves in Canada. This was land kept by the Indiens themselves, with the rest exchanged for goods, money, gifts, and services like health care (inadequate yet so necessary because of European trauma and diseases), promised by the national government. Yet even as they were forced off their lands, its significance and monuments, such as mounds, became enshrined in tribal lore, retained by survivors as faint oral history and cherished memory.

After the loss of natural resources, most of the land, and much of their communal integrity, natives were left with only their muscle or labor to exchange, just like any other citizen. In addition, of course, they also had whatever "valuables" were left on their reserves. While these often appeared barren and desolate in the West, hidden reserves of oil, gas, minerals, and gems were sometimes included. Thus, the very few wealthy tribes (Quapaw zinc, Osage oil, Navaho coal, Laguna uranium, Pequot casinos) receive more mention than their frequency would merit. Over all, the capitalist world market has found ways of exploiting every and all known resources, as many surviving mounds provide legitimate park revenues or illicit pothunter sales.

Hocking River Valley of Ohio[222]

The long term study of landscape and mounds along one convenient tributary of the Ohio River provides a context for these expressions of community, near and far, local and displaced. Flowing southeast into the Ohio River, between the Ohio communities of Lancaster and Hockingport, this 80-mile-long river widens at the Plains, now the location of Athens and Ohio University.[223] It has six tributary watersheds, and, physiologically, includes its stem and branches, floodplains, flat terraces, talus slopes, and ridgetops.

Chronologically (with numbers of total sites per era – after the dash, e.g. - 22, ? if unknown, no Paleo-Indian sites listed), this sequence is Archaic (BP 10000-7500 Early - ?, 7500-5000 Middle - 22, 5000-3500 Late - 140), Woodland (BP 3500-2000 Early - 161, 2000-1600 Middle - 161, 1600-1300 Late - 30), Late Prehistoric (BP 1300-550 - 4), Protohistoric (BP 550-400 - ?), and Historic (400> BP - ?). Ohio is famous for its Adena (Early Woodland) and Hopewell (Middle Woodland) artworks.

Site survey revealed a steady increase in population, adoption of pottery as adjunct to the processing of nut meats (BP 3500), a settlement shift (BP 1300) to floodplain farming of corn (maize), and then abandonment (BP 550), under drought acting on maize-caused soil depletion, in favor of the better watered if more vulnerable banks of the Ohio mainstem itself. From earliest times, food reliance was on hunting and nutting, but, with fluctuating nut harvests, people shifted to seed crops (EAC = Eastern Agricultural Complex) along waterways, eventually stepping up their tending of the landscape to begin the planting, weeding, and harvesting of maize. Incipient gardening utilized nutrient-rich patches where abandoned houses had been burned to reduce vermin. Such torching also prevented malicious magic or sorcery by removing vulnerable traces of domestic intimacy and highly personal items.

Beginning about 2500 years ago, mounds on ridgetops, visible to each other, "mimic the natural landscape, thus cognitively associating the interred and the community with the land itself", bundling together sentiments of identity, territory, sedentism, and gardening.[224] The context for this effort was an intense sense of declining productivity and alienation from the land, due to adverse climate. Overwhelmingly a religious expression – as plea, prayer, and atonement – mounds anchored the landscape from that moment onward. As expressions of bulging vitality, mounds also expressed place-based hopes of renewal.

---

[222] An irony is that Hocking probably derives from the Lenapi word 'haaking' meaning "on ~ of the earth".

[223] Elliot Abrams and AnnCorinne Freter, The Emergence of the Moundbuilders 2005.

[224] Abrams and Freter, The Emergence of the Moundbuilders 2005: 93, 178, 184.

The Plains became an "empty" ceremonial center for the dispersed Hocking population.[225] It served as the locale of periodic gatherings to feast, pray, and build monuments, especially mounds and ten earthwork rings (circles)[226] of varying sizes, during the Hopewell (BP 1750-2050) era "as an expression of grieving, honor, and memory of the dead".[227] Variations in the treatment of the deceased (interment, bundle, cremation, excarnation,[228] log tomb, bark blankets, exotic artifact offerings, reburial) are attributed to the separate customs of distinct lineages or family lines.[229] Thus an array of social and family practices co-occurred for each phase.

Accordingly, the apex of life and leadership in the valley came with the efforts in the Plains, followed by a decline that led to the movement downriver to the banks of the Ohio, where new towns were exposed to friend and foe along this major waterway. Despite all the labor to build the mounds and revere their dead, the authors assume the Hockingers were willing to leave their homeland.

A more likely explanation, instead, is that they were willing to expand and diversify their sense of place along the banks of the Ohio itself, further integrating themselves into a regional network. Periodically, they would disperse for members to return to their ancestral mound to conduct ceremonies, but, despite leaving under unfavorable pressures from their local ecology, they were most unlikely to reject continued ties to their home vitalities. Instead of viewing this movement to the Ohio as an abandoning of their homeland, it is better regarded as an expansion of it.

Further, instead of regarding the building of the earthworks at the Plains as a "one off" mark of apogee, a better analogy is the Statue of Liberty (a gift from France). Once assembled on Liberty ~ Bedloe Island, it marked not the end of a political era, but rather a beacon for the future. Mounds, arguably, had a similar long-range purpose as beacon, blessing, bank, and ballasting. They were monuments to place, people, pride, and profits from the land, vital for their own members as well as claims against others.

Most dirt archaeology is not regionally nor systematically focused, but instead now driven by concerns for mitigation of cultural resources in the face of increasing (de)construction and development. Yet each site offers its own insights into the human condition and long-term evolution. It is to some of these significant places that we now turn, each marking major changes along the way to the present, while also showing the continuous stabilizing effects of mounds and earthworks as vital bulk and bulge.

---

[225] Abrams and Freter, The Emergence of the Moundbuilders 2005: 99.

[226] The report says nine but a map clearly shows ten.

[227] Abrams and Freter, The Emergence of the Moundbuilders 2005: 99.

[228] Excarnation involves exposing the body for a period of time, often in a sheltered container, until the flesh softens or fall off, leaving the bones free.

[229] Abrams and Freter, The Emergence of the Moundbuilders 2005: 112-113.

Lower Illinois

Intense, long-term study[230] of the Lower Illinois River, above its confluence with the Missouri and Mississippi, has identified three loci of interments at bluff crest knolls, at flood plain sand ridges, and at villages beside slackwater lakes. Accretion mounds begin about seven thousand years ago, atop bluffs, with the "sequential additions of bodies [of young and middle-aged adults, tools, offerings] and enclosing sediments". On the floodplain, dotted later by huge platform mounds, at lakeside dwellings, young and infirm were buried in middens without offerings, while sand ridges were used for reburials with a high density and variety of offerings. In all, size and location serve to distinguish an exclusive ancestral ~ political cult focused on knolls apart from an inclusive earth ~ fertility one based on floodplain platforms. The former separated out kin units, while the latter integrated whole communities, sustained by such vital mounds.

Bluff crests are double liminal zones (between the earth / sky and valley / uplands), where these Middle Archaic monuments provided an overview of the living by ancestors: "Thus began the mound-building tradition." During mortuary rites, carrying bodies or remains across these pitched surfaces, including raised scaffolding, provided each with both a reintegrative cosmological tour and a route for reaching the afterworld. Orchestrated reburials in the sand ridges clearly show the expected reversal between living and dead because pottery decorated with raptors is always stacked below that with spoonbills, inverting the natural order of these birds.

But the study has analytical missteps. For instance, an inference that Burial 8 in Yokum Mound 4 was a shaman because he was buried with four sets of age-graded antlers is ethnographically flawed. Unlike such past attempts, such analogies must be drawn from the full spectrum of indigenous native traditions, and not be limited to those decimated, traumatized survivals known to history. Widespread patterns better reflect this full diversity. In this context, therefore, deer antlers remain badges of political office, as they do for Iroquois royaner or league chiefs. Shamans, by contrast, are usually associated with bears. Thus, the man at Yokum is much more likely to have been a chief than a healer.

In terms of overall built environment, moreover, these large and small Middle Woodland monuments re-created the cosmos, both vertically and horizontally, as well as providing a forum for the intense negotiation of power relations among the living.

Woodland

Throughout the East, each region had local Woodland manifestations.[231] In the Early Woodland at the Batesville site (circa 200 BC [??] in Tchula Phase (BP 2100-

---

[230] Jane Buikstra and Douglas Charles, Centering the Ancestors: Cemeteries, Mounds, and Sacred Landscapes of the Ancient North American Midcontinent 1999: 208, 212, 216, 218. Dr. Robert Walls provided a timely pdf of this chapter via Notre Dame's "scan~xerox~email~fax~espresso machine".

[231] William Romain, Mysteries of the Hopewell, Astronomers, Geometers, and Magicians of the Eastern Woodlands 2000; A. Martin Byers, Social Structure and the Pragmatic Meaning of Material Culture: Ohio Hopewell as an

2500)), in northern Mississippi, fire-cracked rock concentrated on the top of mound B suggests communal feasting there, a precursor of the elite temples that topped later Mississippian mounds.[232] Such Woodland mound tops received brief, seasonal visits for specialized ritual activity that were much more communal than in later times.[233]

For the Ohio Valley, Adena is an expression of Early (BP 3000) and Hopewell (BP 2400-1500) of Middle Woodland. Current thinking, however, interconnects rather than splits up these Ohio[234] complexes (kits) successively known as Adena, Hopewell, and Fort Ancient. Instead, they are now regarded as an ongoing tradition, with its distinct eras in need of new titles, among peoples that included ancestors of Shawnee.

A careful review of Hopewell studies shows a refocusing to sources and characteristics of mound components, with a preference for extraordinary, labor-intensive soils.[235] In Ohio, academic arguments shifted from place to people, arguing for the mounded landscape as defining local territories rather than as mound shrines providing markers for leading families.[236]

Significant soils (muds) evoked "the Mud Diver myth, or the creation of dry land".[237] Using sod blocks and "allogenetic fills" quarried elsewhere, Illinois Hopewell mounds indicate great effort. Top soil is removed, a layer of clean sand put down, and construction begun. Sod blocks are often placed upside down, forming a core, which is than alternately layered over with wind-blown (loess) and water-borne (gumbo) soils. Some are located on high bluffs approached by high flood waters, others at "relict flood

---

Ecclesiastical-Communal Cult, A View from the Core: A Synthesis of Ohio Hopewell Archaeology 1996; Ray Hively and Robert Horn, Geometry and Astronomy in Prehistoric Ohio 1982; Hopewellian Geometry and Astronomy at High Bank 1984.

[232] Jay Johnson, Gena Aleo, Rodney Stuart, and John Sullivan, The 1966 Excavations at the Batesville Mounds, A Woodland Period Platform Mound Complex in Northwest Mississippi 2002.

[233] James Ford, Greenhouse: A Troyville - Coles Creek Period Site in Avoyelles Parish, Louisiana 1951.

[234] In the protohistoric, the Ohio Valley has been called "empty" or part of a "vacant quarter" due to the relocation or outmigration of its native nations, which must have included the Shawnee on north-side tributaries as well as some of the Siouans on south-side tributaries who fled down to the Mississippi. See Robert Rankin, On Siouan Chronology, ms [1996]; Stephen Williams, The Vacant Quarter and Other Late Events in the Lower Valley 1990: 170-180; The Vacant Quarter Hypothesis and the Yazoo Delta 2001: 191-203.

[235] Douglas Charles and Jane Buikstra, Recreating Hopewell 2006.

[236] Mark Seeman and James Branch, The Mounded Landscapes of Ohio: Hopewell Patterns and Placements 2006: 121.

[237] Ted Sunderhaus and Jack Blosser, Water and Mud and the Recreation of the World 2006: 145.

scour pools" involved in the "formation of bars and islands in the river channel ... as highly dynamic landforms that are remolded and reshaped during floods, and, in essence, they are both partially destroyed and then newly recreated during the same geological flood event ... of the newly rejuvenated floodplain".[238]

Overarching all of these considerations is the leadership of shamans, whose "aerial gaze" in trance accounts for the monumentality of these earth altering efforts. Mounds are "material expression of persons actively engaged in altered states of consciousness ... includ[ing] the tobacco pipe-smoking complex; large scale earthworks; the various bird, bear, and human transformational imagery; and artifacts widely connected with otherworldly power quests".[239]

Adena Cresap

Indeed, the complexity and long term use of mounds was stunningly revealed at one Adena site. To make way for a coal mining plant, the Cresap Mound in West Virginia, constructed over centuries, was excavated and totally removed during 3 months (June-August, 1958).[240] At that time it was a cone, 15 foot high by 70 foot around, slumping from its original 17 feet height and 60 feet diameter. Its radiocarbon dates range from BP 3685 to 2020, covering 1665 years. In all, the final Cresap cone was the fourth mound, covering others built to the west, south, and east sides of the original fireplace of a dwelling. The area to the north is conspicuously devoid of features or of burials. Throughout the Americas, north is often an inauspicious direction on the earth, though not in the sky.[241]

Analysis showed that Cresap was built in a dozen or more stages. First on this spot was a dwelling with a 40-foot diameter. It had a fire pit in the center of a circular clay floor built into the loose gravel subsoil. Second, west of the fire, a shallow burial was set into the floor with low clay embankments on three sides but not at the feet. Third, a cremation basin and two burials were placed into the floor. Fourth, burials were added over time, and then this area was covered by a 5 foot (west) mound. Fifth, midway during overall use, a second grave was dug down into the south part of the first floor and mounded over. Sixth, six more burials were placed in a cremation basin there and capped with a 3 foot (south) mound. Seventh, a log tomb, with a low clay bench, was built into

---

[238] Julieann Van Nest, Rediscovering This Earth: Some Ethnogeological Aspects of the Illinois Valley Hopewell Mounds 2006: 425.

[239] James Brown, The Shamanic Element in Hopewellian Period Ritual 2006, 488.

[240] Don Dragoo, Mounds for the Dead: An Analysis of the Adena Culture 1963: 17-21.

[241] Pueblos regard the North as unlucky, since many towns came from the North in their mythology and returning there would be a sign of defeat. In contrast, Robert Hall (p.c.) has noted that the North Star, because of its fixed stability, was a beacon for native chiefs and leaders.

the east side, and covered by a 5-foot (east) mound. Eighth, eight more bodies were added, including a crematory basin in the dip between the east and south tops.[242]

All three mounds were under the same wooden canopy, which burned and left charcoal over their surfaces.[243] Ninth, these smaller cones were buried under a mound 7 feet high, which then overgrew with a covering of grass sod and humus several inches thick. Tenth, a mantle with ceremonial objects and burials added another foot. Eleventh, a pit was dug into the top peak for a cremation basin, before 15 copper beads and other grave goods were placed under a roof of small logs, the pit filled in, and more earth raised the height to 13 feet. Six inches of humus then grew on the sides. Twelfth, another pit was dug into the top, a fireplace made, and eight bodies arranged around it. Full burials had the heads toward the center, while bone bundles and "trophy" heads (so-called, though the Dobu (below) provide a cautionary perspective on such skulls) were spaced apart. Finally, gravelly earth capped the mound, making it 17 feet high. A few hundred years ago, one last burial was dug into the top of the mound.

For over 1600 years, people used the same place for a set of mounds, each positioned in terms of the central fireplace kindled at the very beginning. Maintaining such continuous orientation, consistent ritual, and serial devotion to a site highlights the regard for place that characterized those entrenched in the Americas until badly scattered by European germs, slaving, and invasions.[244] Though the local populations were not "permanent" residents, they demonstrated another kind of localized stability and vitality.

Kolomoki

A telling example of the use of rocks as caps, fill, ballast, and weights in burial mounds occurs during the Early Woodland (350-750 AD) in present southwestern Georgia. Set along its namesake creek draining into the Chattahoochee River and preserved as a Georgia state park, Kolomoki's ancient dwellings formed a horseshoe-shaped community opening toward the west and facing the high mound on the east.[245] This temple mound (A = 200 by 325 by 56 feet) had twin top platforms, with that on the south three feet higher than that on the north. In the rectangular plaza was a central cone (D), with other mounds set along its edges. These seem to have been paired as burial and platform (staging) mounds. In all known instances, throughout the entire site, the heads of burials were toward the east. Special mortuary pottery, often shaped as effigies, was

---

[242] Notably, this tally of construction stages shows a more-than-suspicious correlation with the same number of burials.

[243] This wooden canopy raises the possibility that some of the remains were exposed on its roof as a type of "air burial".

[244] A direct totemic or clan link with a mound has proven illusive, aside from the later Wisconsin effigies, unlike Isbister, in Scotland's Orkney Islands, which features a 5000 year old Megalithic stone tomb where a prevalence of sea eagle bones indicates a totemic association with the 342 humans buried there, See John Hedges, Tomb of the Eagles: Death and Life in a Stone Age Tribe 1984.

[245] William Sears, Excavations at Kolomoki, Final Report 1956.

distinguished by cutouts (decorative openings along the sides) that made them useless as any kind of containers yet appropriate offerings representing sacred domains.[246]

To the north and the south, beside the east high mound were matching low domes (B, C) about five feet tall. That on the south (B) had numerous postholes, about two feet wide, suggestive of goal or flag posts. That on the north (C) held mixed refuse, suggesting it was built up of special sweepings if not also ashes.

At the center, Mound D, twenty feet high and 100 feet in diameter, was built in stages about AD 30. It was paired with a platform mound (F), measuring 60 by 50 by 6 feet, capping over a platform 30 feet wide with sides of very white clay. D's construction stages seem to have been continuous over some time. First, a fifty-foot diameter space was cleared off. Five individuals were placed in log-lined graves aligned north to south. As these were filled in, eight posts, aligned east to west, were set up to stand above a low round mound that was covered by rocks. One male was buried in a tomb composed of rock slabs and logs on the south edge of this mound. Others were cremated atop this filled-in grave, with debris from a final offering. Two females, each in a slab and log grave, were placed east of the standing-log scaffold.

Second, all of these graves and the round mound were capped by a rectangular one that was 50 by 30 by 5 feet. The log-post ends still protruded, and vessels, sherds, and hanging skulls decorated the east side. A succession of bodies, skulls, and bundled long bones were placed on this platform and set afire. While the flames were raging, rocks and dirt were placed on the remains to redden. At the main burial on the south side, yellow clay was piled over each subsequent interment. Brown earth was piled over the north side. Third, a flat-top mound with a round base covered all of these remains, with a final massive cremation placed at the top. Fourth, red clay, several feet thick, sealing off all the prior stages, produced the final twenty-foot-high dome.

On a smaller scale, a similar burial event in BC 170 resulted in Mound E, whose excavation has been preserved as the on-site museum, paired with platform Mound H. The dimensions of H were the same as F, but its three-foot high platform was of yellow clay. The main burial of Mound E consisted of one individual's cremated remains, conch shell beads, and two copper disks, each with a centered inset pearl. These were placed at the bottom of a squarish, tapering pit, seven-feet deep, that was then filled with rocks. One stone slab was 6 by 3 by 2 feet. Two females, as extended burials, were placed to the east and west beside the opening and a flexed young male was buried off to the side. A low mound covered these burials, capped with rocks. On the top was a human skull wearing a wooden disk covered with copper.[247] At least fifty-four complete pottery

---

[246] Thomas Pluckhahn, The Sacred and the Secular Revisited: The Essential Tensions of Early Village Society in the Southeastern United States 2010. Since the worlds of the living and of the dead are usually reversed, these vessels, "holey" in this world, would be "whole" in the afterworld.

[247] Thomas Pluckhahn (Kolomoki 2003: 62) noted that such skulls have grave goods, and so are probably not trophies. Moreover, the Mound D burials involved a long process, and were not a single event as described by Sears. A diorama inside the museum built within the mound shows the slaying of retainers in the Sears mode.

vessels were lined up along the east side of the mound, then a final thick layer of red clay enclosed the entire area.[248]

More recent work emphasizes corporate, communal effort:

Mound E was a corporate burial facility intended to reinforce group membership rather than an exclusive monument to a single, high-status individual.... Kolomoki demonstrates that such prestige was shared among the members of some collective group – a clan, moiety, or perhaps some type of solidarity along the lines of a women's mortuary society [with] some risk that the shared prestige could be subverted by an individual for his or her own aggrandizement [as] appears to have been the case with the woman interred within the structure on top of Mound B at McKeithan [below].[249]

Moreover, indicating current research interests, sky alignments were traced at this site, as well as basic measurements using the Toltec module (Chapter 7, named for a site in Kansas, not people in Mexico). A "central axis [is marked] by Mounds E, D, A, K ... at an angle of roughly 88 degrees [along with] two east-west pottery caches [which] suggests an orientation toward the rising sun at or around the spring equinox. A line between Mounds F and D is aligned at 63 degrees, the approximate angle of the rising sun at the summer solstice."[250]

In general, within century-long phases, there was "one construction sequence every 20 years", involving perhaps 20 people working for a day or two. Color symbolism was evident. Mounds B, C, D, E, H, and K mixed dark, yellow, brown, and white soils, while all the mounds had a red clay cap. A red film covered the clay vessels cached on the east sides of Mounds D and E. Mounds F and A had a dark core, and a white veneer under the red cap.[251]

In all, along with the use of colored clays in black, brown, yellow, white, and red, Kolomoki mounds were also weighted down with rocks, slabs, and logs. These served both to peg them into the earth, as well as to stabilize and protect these locations. Filling the E pit with huge rocks served both to seal in the cremated remains of a leader, as well as to ballast the entire construction. The capping of rock, topped by the skull, was further sealed in by the outer covering of earth. Inside, moreover, were artifacts and cremains fueling vital renewal.

---

[248] Many of these vessels were stolen in hostilities over the display of human remains in the 1970s, though some have been found at regional swap meets. Plastic skeletons are now exhibited.

[249] Pluckhahn, Kolomoki 2003: 195, 217.

[250] Pluckhahn, Kolomoki 2003: 88.

[251] Pluckhahn, Kolomoki 2003: 88, 194.

McKeithen

At the McKeithen site (300-500 AD) in north Florida, three mounds (two platforms (A, B) and one (C) domed) had distinct functions along a sequence of mortuary activities associated with the Weeden Island Complex (AD 200-900). Mound A was used for temporary burials before defleshing. Atop B was a house or temple (or both) with the key burial into the floor. A charnel house stood on C, while its sides held the burials of 36 people (26 adults, 10 children) and 18 pots.[252] Mound C was formally closed off by a grey-tan cap covering over 40 plain rocks set upon a scorched surface.

The site report was published twice, in 1984 and 1997, with one glaring admission at the start of the reprint: the high status burial on B was a woman not a man, as should have been clear from the very beginning.[253] Though recovering from recent back surgery, William Maples struggled to the top of Mound B to examine what was clearly an important burial, and make detailed notes. In the 1984 report, this buried specialist is called a wounded "gracile male" in his later 30s, yet Maples originally noted a woman as she was subsequently identified in the next edition.

The extended body had the elbows bent upward with the open hands lying near the shoulders. It had been placed into a shallow pit that remained unfilled to allow for more rapid decomposition before some kind of crypt of pine poles was built over it. A stone point was lodged in her left rear pelvis, which had started to heal. Behind her head were red ochre and a disk made from the back of someone else's skull. Near the feet was buried a pottery red turkey vulture head that had lighter side bands with incised designs.

The excavators had the sense that mound A was used to bury, soften, and dismember bodies, with the bones then placed in the C charnel house before burial in the mound itself to await regeneration. The leader in charge of the sequencing lived on B and she was eventually buried there. Since women are universally associated with life and men with death, the misidentification of this key burial becomes more understandable, despite the predominance of evidence. It may well be, however, that she had an honorific male role that was reinforced by both her wound and her wearing of the back of a man's skull.

Wisconsin

Wisconsin, especially the driftless or unglaciated region in its south, saw a remarkable development of burial rituals and mounds.[254] The Old Copper complex (BP

---

[252] Because of the embarrassing misidentified gender, "charnel knowledge" appears as a pun in the title of Chapter 5 within this site report.

[253] Jerald Milanich, Ann Cordell, Vernon Knight, Timothy Kohler, and Brenda Sigler-Lavalle; The McKeithen Weeden Island Culture, The Culture of Northern Florida A.D. 200-900 1984; Archaeology of Northern Florida, A.D. 200-900, The McKeithen Weeden Island Culture 1997: xvi, 109-117, 146.

[254] Robert Birmingham and Leslie Eisenberg, Indian Mounds of Wisconsin 2000: 74, 77, 79, 112, 141; Chandler Rowe, The Effigy Mound Culture of Wisconsin 1956.

6000-3500) used this abundant local mineral for a variety of ordinary tools and weapons, as well as a desired trade item. The Red Ocher complex (BP 3200-2500) used quantities of this sacred pigment on burials and in cemeteries set on knolls or hills, where they served as visible territorial markers. It seems a natural progression from such geological eminences to constructed mounds.

With Archaic efficiency, people scattered over the landscape to gather resources and foods as these became ready by seasons. At certain times, however, better abundances allowed them to gather in – feasting on spawning fish, animal herds, ripe plants, and migrating birds. Between 1000-1400 years ago, near swamps and other fruitful places, they piled dirt in the shapes of animals – the famous Effigy Mounds of the Late Woodland. Around Madison, the state capital, there are over 100 of these groupings, including 1000 distinct mounds. In southeast Wisconsin, effigies are placed near wetlands rich in fowl, fish, game, and wild rice. In addition to domes and linear shapes, the animal forms are species-appropriate to their habitat locales. Thus birds are up on bluffs and serpents are down near the water. Bears and other mammals are in forest settings.[255]

Though no single tribe can be identified with these builders, the mounds are in the homeland of the Chiwere subgroup of the Central Siouans which later split into the historic tribes known as Ioway, Missouria, Oto, and Ho-Chunk (Winnebago). Many (but not all) effigies correspond to known clans found among these tribes, though some are clearly supernatural patrons like underwater panthers because of their long forked tails.[256] Each was probably built by one of a number of kinship-based collectivities of Late Woodland times. Each of these "clans" favored the shape of its own patron. Combined together, they represent the bears, birds, and other creatures that were and are emblems of regional moieties and local clans.[257]

---

[255] Because these Bear mounds are outlines from the side it is readily apparent that many are left views since bears are regarded as "left handed", Cf. Jay Miller, People, Berdaches, And Left-Handed Bears: Human Variation In Native North America 1982.

[256] Such forked tails are an identifying feature of these powerful horned serpents ~ underwater panthers, as seen here, in the Midwest Piasa and the Pawnee Big Doctoring (Chapter 8). They combine horns or antlers with canine claws and fangs, muscled bodies, and long snake-like tails with forked ends to indicate they are aquatic like fish.

[257] In July 2003, I was a guest at the Oto homecoming in Oklahoma and looked particularly for any natural, especially animal, images. While the women wore beautiful dresses decorated in ribbonwork of vine and flower designs, a tribal banner hanging from the speaker's stand showed a circle with images of the seven patri-clans set around its rim. Each could easily have served as the outline of an effigy mound. These clans are now called Beaver, Bear, Buffalo, Pigeon, Hoot Owl, Eagle, and Elk. Snake and Coyote are listed as extinct. Cf. William Whitman, The Oto 1937; Marjorie Schweitzer, Otoe and Missouria 2001: 447-461. In the Chiwere languages, the word for snake is *wakan* (wakã), meaning 'holy' in Lakota, as *wakan tanka* for the 'great holy,

The Effigy Mound complex, or part of it, became the Oneota in the same region when mounds were replaced by graves in cemeteries. In the process, the scatter-out + gather-in economy (that encouraged the building of mounds when people aggregated for natural harvests) shifted to a more settled lifeway devoted to the farming trinity of squash, beans, and maize. Thus, the planting of these separate seeds coincided with individual graves, as mounds were a final, joyful, vital gathering together in death of what had been a widely scattered few among the living.

Troyville: Internal Architecture

Distinctive mounds, by their size, construction, and shape, deserve special consideration, and a few, particularly those in northeast Louisiana were intended to be famously unique attractions. These impressive centers lasted for over five thousand years, as substantiated by Watson Brake (BP 5400), Poverty Point (BP 3300), and Troyville (BP 1300). Each was a ringed enclosure with impressive internal features, such as vast raised ridges or a great towering mound built of two stacked squares topped with a huge cone. Viewed in sequence, they drew distant visitors as pilgrimage sites along the lower Mississippi River. As such, they later vied with that of Mississippian-era Cahokia at the triple confluence of the Missouri and Ohio with the middle Mississippi River (below).

Unlike the domes or platforms so common across the county, Troyville (now Jonesboro, formerly Jonesville, La) was unique. Its 80-foot central mound had a square (180 feet per side) platform about 30 feet tall, another smaller square with steeper-sides about 15 feet tall, and then a steep cone that rose another 35 feet. The very top was eight-feet around. As many as a dozen other mounds (6 of them large) may have been included within the mile-long embankment curving around the Troyville site. The water-filled barrow pits were linked together with the river to provide ready canoe access into the site, as well as a convenient source of fresh fish.

Located in the Tensas Basin, the site is at the confluence of the Ouachita (Washita), Tensas, and Little (Catahoula) Rivers that join to form the Black River, which flows into the Red and then into the Mississippi and Gulf. Because of these three-way flows, the locale across the river is named Trinity. During high floods, some of these rivers run backwards as water reverts into bayous.

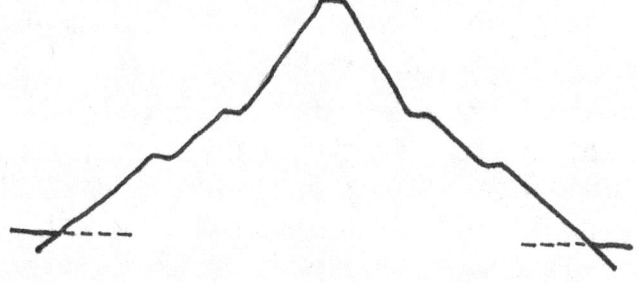

---

mystery, spirit'. In various Algic languages, *manitu* is the word for both spirit and snake.

The cone atop the mound was leveled during the Civil War (of Northern Aggression) to situate a rifle pit there, spreading fill to the north and south to make the base look rectangular. As the settler town grew, the mounds became diverted into fill and then flat spaces. Enough of the great mound remained to provide refuge from the floods of 1912 and 1927 until the remnant was destroyed and added to the abutment of a 1931 bridge, when Winslow Walker arrived on the scene, became intrigued, and returned in 1932 to take notes and photographs of the bottom six feet of the mound.[258] Excavation of the base ended abruptly when the owners of the land, who assumed the diggers were seeking "Natchez treasure", increased their demands for money. Work then shifted to other local mounds with more sympathetic owners.

Trenching of the great mound revealed a bewildering array of colored clays (blue, red, brown, gray, olive), cane mats (still greenish yellow when exposed but soon blackening), stakes, woven domes (24-feet across), wooden boards, slabs, and poles – all put to architectural use. Soil profiles from the south pit show, top to bottom, canes, red clay, sand, light blue clay, sand, blue clay, and blue-gray loam. While the dozen best photos appear in the publication, another hundred have recently been relocated in a DC archive.

Analysis indicated that the great mound was built in stages. Walker concluded that the site was first burned over, to clear a space in the canebrake and trees to build a small mound of river clay carried over in skin bags. Two pecan trees took root and grew on the slope. Human debris and flood silt added to the mound until the surface was burned over, leaving charred stumps. Hickory slabs and poles were put down, then crisscrossed cane bundles, while the surface was still warm, producing slight charring on the undersides of the wood. A small platform was covered in reddish-yellow sand. On the west, a stairway was built of crossways poles as risers to hold in place step treads covered with packed palmetto fronds and grasses. A crushed human skull lay in the imported blue river mud at the base of these stairs.

Subsequent building showed evidence of fire, layers of cane mats several inches thick, and restraining poles held flat by stakes. All of the canes found had been split in half or quartered, bundled and tied with grass twine, and placed in thick layers held together by clay. These bundles were stacked at right angles to add reinforcement. Addition construction phases increased the mound, with a separate ramp built at each of the four corners of the first terrace. Though it was long gone, a spiral route to the very top of the cone was conjectured. Its use as a bonfire beacon was also proposed. Certainly, in this huge floodplain, its great height bespoke great visibility, which would have been heightened by flames and smoke plumes.

As an interesting sidelight, as well as a negative example, the present condition of the Pritchard Landing (Oliphant) Mounds (LA), currently pulling apart in great chunks, indicates why these organic inclusions were necessary to build mounds of lasting shape. Huge leaning trees growing atop these mounds are aiding the fissioning, as did open mining for shells and damaging pothunting. The irony is that the reinforced great mound at Troyville could not survive outside forces, while Pritchard, despite protection from landowners, has not been able to overcome internal ones. At Pritchard, a thick capping to

---

[258] Winslow Walker, The Troyville Mounds, Catahoula Parish, LA 1936.

79

seal off the surface could have forestalled such destruction, but it would not have remained effective once breached by illegal diggers.

Mississippians

As noted, across the Americas, a major reason for earth moving was the construction of mounds (or, on a smaller inverse scale, of cache pits). Best known as the sites for Adena burials and Mississippian temples, other monuments include Anasazi Pueblo passage markers, Tsimshian fort emplacements, and shaped effigies throughout the upper Midwest. Regardless of intent, congruent form was always a significant consideration. The difference between Adena cones, Hopewell ramparts, and Mississippian sloping blocks was probably consistent with beliefs about configurations of their worlds.[259] Moreover, throughout the East, mounds were believed to be chambered and occupied by spirits and the dead. Artificially constructed, mounds were the built equivalent of a "holy home" inside hollow (and hallowed) hills where a particular infrahuman species lived or gathered, as with the Pawnee animal lodges (Chapter 8).[260]

Once thought to arise (literally) a thousand years ago, the earliest dating of square mounds has now doubled. "Platforms imply hierarchy" both in the labor needed to construct them and in the disparity between those a step above or below.[261] They also imply deliberate planting, but not because fields have to be square. Rather, once people were no longer commuting among far camps and replacing regenerating plant parts into the ground, they placed them in lines or rows for convenience of caretaking. In the Southwest, Pueblo farmers spiral their rows out from the center of a field, to boundaries marked by stones buried at the corners. In the Southeast, however, where water was more abundant, these rows stretched along river and stream terraces, creating squarish plots. Unlike the European broadcasting of seeds, natives treated each one with respect. The result was separated hillocks of corn, beans, and squash, in even numbers since they were equated with the breasts of Corn Mother. Such doubling of twos and fours also produced squares by basic principles of geometry.[262] Similarly, because plants "rest" in the ground until they sprout, these fields are like beds, evoking both the English term "flower beds" and the Creek term (*topv* 'bed')[263] for the arbors set around the sides of a square ground.

---

[259] There is also a sense that mounds mimic body parts, with domes suggesting a skull and blocks suggesting a torso or chest.

[260] Vernon Knight, Symbolism of Mississippian Mounds 1989.

[261] Roger Kennedy, Hidden Cities, The Discovery and Loss of Ancient North American Civilization 1994: 67.

[262] While there are many small sites with only a single mound, there is a sense that a ceremonial center had three mounds – consisting of a big and a small platform along with a rounded conical – identified, by tradition, as A, B, and C. As Jay Johnson joked, "Somehow Mississippians always knew to bury in Mound C".

[263] Varied, less technical spellings for 'bed' include *dubba*.

All these mounds, domed or platform, served as centering tysics for dispersed populations. Indeed, since the dead were the only permanent residents of a district, burial mounds provided claim deeds passed through ancestral bloodlines. Though many of these genetic links did not survive European epidemics, likely ethnic continuities can be traced between archaeological sites and modern day entities. While archaeologists have been reluctant to do so in much of the continent; given huge regional displacements, those in the Southeast do so enthusiastically. Their advantage, of course, was the many desperate people who took refuge in the few historic native confederacies which coalesced after the collapse of chiefdoms and the traumas of disease and slavers.

Thus, Ho-chunks (Winnebagos), whose Chiwere Siouan ancestors were among those who built Effigy mounds, were at the northern limit of the Mississippian tradition of chiefdoms and cult of the dead, while others, like Osage and Caddo, were mainstays of the US heartland. In the aftermath of the Mississippian collapse, other confederacies, such as those of the Huron and Iroquois of the Northeast or Creeks of the Southeast, represent regroupings of survivors who had lived around the former borders.

After Mississippian chiefdoms, radical changes had to be devised. Previously, the heads of clans probably met inside temples atop mounds. After severe depopulation, beginning with Spanish-introduced diseases, and British slaving to supply Caribbean plantations, a communal labor force became difficult to muster. Mounds could no longer be built according to complex ritual requirements and few leading families survived to direct the work and worship, yet their obvious surviving bulk provided reassuring ballast, hoped-for blessings, and reserves of vitality during tumultuous times.

Ritual came down from the heights, onto the ground of the town, and around the town fire. The open, public plaza replaced the private temple on the mound, though some councils and elites retreated into rotunda ("hothouses"). Instead of ranked seats in the temple, men sat according to their clans in sunshades on the four sides of a town square. Senior men were in front, and youngsters at the back of the 'bed'. Designs depicting each clan were painted over the front of its section. Town treasures were kept in a small room behind the west arbor where the town chief sat, facing the sunrise. The sacred fire burned in the plaza center, a symbol of the intense purity and vigor of the town, and an avatar of the Sun. In large multi-clan towns, these four seating areas were built like stepped bleachers. Sometimes, covered walkways and arbors formed a stadium around the plaza, with passages at the corners.

Ceremonies honoring the ancestral elite and ceremonial (but not defensive) war were dropped, while timed rites marking the stages of the agricultural year became more important. In the past, six month names were doubled to fill out one year, once in summer and then repeated again for winter. These months were duplicated in each half, making up the entire year, just as each town had two moieties to make the whole. This division was lost when the European calendar of twelve continuous months replaced it.

Four times during the summer, everyone gathered to celebrate stages in the ripening crop, culminating with the Green Corn ceremony just before the harvest to mark the New Year, which divided the twin (half) year. Towns gathered to fast, pray, and dance while the corn was yet alive in their fields. The last rite was held in the fall (around Halloween) when masked dancers consecrated the economic shift from farming to hunting.[264]   During the winter half, some towns used a huge domed rotunda, often called a hothouse, for indoor meetings and ceremonies, until these too became too difficult to repair or be built by survivors (Miller 2015).

Cahokia Hub

Coinciding with a rare supernova that appeared brightly on 4 July 1054 and continued day and night for most of that month, the homes and yards of Old Cahokia were removed and replaced by prefabricated houses and a 50-acre plaza, specially leveled and drained. The result was a "new city of black-earth pyramids, red cedar walls, cypress uprights, yellow thatched roofs, and fragrantly burning tobacco along the Mississippi River in the heart of North America".[265]   After this "Big Bang", New Cahokia became the hub of a religious network fostering trade, gifts (tribute?), and sports, especially the competition known as chunkey. It became the capitol of "Mississippian culture … based on beliefs about ancestors, the stars, maize agriculture, and powerful male and female characters [such as] earth and sky gods, including the Morning and Evening stars".[266]

Mounds, built of alternating layers of light or dark clay, were covered by light-colored sand and a final topping of dark (brownish black) clay. Excavations into the mounds at Emerald, Kunnemann, Horseshoe Lake, Red (#49), and East St. Louis also indicate alternating light and dark or sandy and clayey fills, some of which appear "engineered".[267]   Mound numbers varied with the importance of the location, one for a minor shrine, many for a center. These pyramids served as "elevated stages for special community ceremonies, ritual performances, and feasts probably hosted but not 'owned' by high-ranked leaders".[268]

Building projects, renovations, and adjustments only ceased at the 1450 CE end of this city, leaving an empty quarter along the entire middle Mississippi River. At its height, elites were mobilized by fine-tuning mounds, meetings, and manufacturing, especially of art works; while growing maize and other crops occupied the daily life of most other families. Diplomatic gifts featured reddish flintclay figurines, special flint knives, long-nosed human faces fashioned in shell or copper to be worn as earrings, and Cahokia style chunkey rollers made of stone quarried at Thebes Gap 130 miles downriver on the Mississippi.

As noted, in the genesis epic known as Earth Diver, a speck of dirt expands to become the homeland, expanding outward by magical means, varying from special songs to propulsion devices like chunkey rollers. Javelins, thrown at this disk as it rolled along a runway marked by tiny mounds at each end, helped to pin down outer earth limits. Chunkey spread with the expansion of Cahokia's influence.

---

[264]   John Swanton, Religious Beliefs and Medical Practices of the Creek Indians 1928b: 556 [old men's dance].

[265]   Timothy Pauketat, Cahokia 2009: 9.

[266]   Timothy Pauketat, Cahokia 2009: 8.

[267]   Timothy Pauketat and Susan Alt, Mounds, Memory, and Contested Mississippian History 2003: 165.

[268]   Timothy Pauketat, Cahokia 2009: 18, 22.

Farming and specialty towns filled the surrounding bottomlands, with mortuary zones along the bluffs where scaffolds exposed burials that, with decomposition, were successively bundled and retained in charnel temples until buried in an eventual mound. Some settlements were composed of migrants from far away, living more like peasants on meager diets than those of the lords resident at the downtown core.

All communities had a center post at their heart, serving as their integrative axis and focus. The post and its shadows served to mark the vital passage of time and seasons, while also representing key personages for that locality. A likely parallel is the Northwest totem pole, where this column, along with the spine (backbone) of the acknowledged leader, serves as the conduit for bringing life-force into the community or clan and its lands.[269]

More important neighborhoods also included at least one mound. But, in contrast to the clay core mounds of downtown Cahokia, "other mounds clearly began as mere lenses of fill beneath important buildings .... the earliest "stages" of a particular platform were sometimes only a few centimeters high. These blanket mantles probably would not have been visible from a distance ... several blanket mantles or stage enlargements later, the shape of a platform may have finally become evident. However, it seems reasonable to assert that in these cases, an imposing mound was not the goal of mound construction. Possibly, the goal of construction in these cases was the act of construction itself (and all that this entailed). Presumably, the greater the frequency of communal construction, the greater the integrative effects on a disparate population".[270] Indeed, such continued activity translated into increased vitality for the mound.

At Cahokia and its allied mound centers, mound shapes served many functions. Those with ridgetops were repositories of offerings, honored families (royalty), and carnage that included dozens of sacrificed people, mostly young women. At the center of Mound 72, a pair of reversed males bracketed a huge cape shaped like a falcon and covered in shell beads. The top man faced up, while the lower one, reversed with his feet under the skull above, faced down onto a layer of animal skins. Nearby were almost 200 skeletons arrayed in separate pits, one including men and chunkey equipment. At the Junkyard ridgetop mound, the central burials were three women – pregnant, with newborn, and with child and dog. Though also serving as boundary markers for the town core, these ridgetops emphasized both gender and generation, since they were built every twenty years over a span of 150 years.

Binding these congregations together was a communion in the form of massive meals, especially at the main plaza, where "feasts that took place over the course of a few days would have involved killing, butchering, and carting in as many as thirty-nine hundred deer, the use of up to seventy-nine hundred pots, and enough smoking tobacco to produce more than a million charred tobacco seeds".[271]

---

[269] The symbolic importance of the spinal column as a channel of vitality in human ritual and belief has been slighted, though it builds on our biological status as vertebrates. It appears herein for the San, but applies equally to Tsimshian and other First Nations of the Northwest Coast.

[270] Timothy Pauketat and Susan Alt, Mounds, Memory, and Contested Mississippian History 2003: 165.

[271] Timothy Pauketat, Cahokia 2009: 109.

For Cahokia, political "theater [enhancing legitimacy and authority] seemed to take the form of a grand and repetitive retelling of the age-old story of human creation through festivals, chunkey matches, and mortuary rites".[272]

Above all, Cahokia and other Mississippians relied on communal expressions, with priesthoods both instructing and intimidating the faithful toward the proper route to the afterlife. Humans were sacrificed for the greater good of all. For the elite, mortality led to a long complicated process involving scaffolds, cleaning of flesh and bone, burnings and bundlings, communal storage, and final rest within an earthen mound in the company of certain others. If the 1054 supernova pointed a new way to the afterlife, priesthoods at Cahokia directed its pan-tribal response across ranks, statuses, and distances for centuries, while their espousal of chunkey and other continuing traditions are only now being fully acknowledged.

Charles Towne Landing[273]

In the height of irony, Albemarle Point (SC) encompasses both the 1670 colony of Barbados planters ruthlessly shipping off Indien slaves to die in Caribbean fields and the AD 1450 palisaded temple site with the best evidence for the elite move from mound top to ground level, subsequently followed by arbors built around a plaza. One of its three arbors (13x14, the others 10x12, 10x20) stood within the square where the temple had been, suggesting its use by community leaders related to the historic Cusabo tribes of this region.[274] Santa Elena, a mission founded by Spain in 1565, was near their southern tribal border, as Charleston, a century later, was at their northern one. Spanish missions, massing native life and labor, provided ready targets for native slavers, engaged in a "just war" against Catholics. The labor of their victims provided more profit from Virginia tobacco, lowland rice, and Caribbean sugarcane. Treachery led to revolts by local tribes, such as the Escamacu (1576-79), as well as devastating Carolinian wars against rival native enslavers, such as the Kussah (1671), Westo (Erie, 1680), Winyaw (1681),

---

[272] Timothy Pauketat, Cahokia 2009: 111.

[273] Stanley South, A Ceremonial Center at the Charles Towne Site, South Carolina Institute of Archeology and Anthropology, Notebook II (6-7, June-July) 1970: 3-5; Archeology on Albemarle Point – The Indian Ceremonial Center; Excavation of the Indian Ceremonial Center at the Charles Towne Site, South Carolina Institute of Archeology and Anthropology, Research Manuscript Series 36 1972: 202-248; The Temple at Town Creek Indian Mound State Historic Site, North Carolina. South Carolina Institute of Archeology and Anthropology, Notebook V (5, Sept-Oct) 1973: 145-172.

[274] The Cusaboan Escamacu, neighboring the Spanish, had a round townhouse (temple) whose central fire rested on a huge ash mound; Gene Waddell, Cusabo, Southeast 14: 260 2004. Thus, even while platform mounds were being abandoned, the symbolic stability of this piled microcosm remained in a holy context, as it also did for Cherokees. Indeed, as noted, in recent centuries, council houses (rotunda) took on the vitality of mounds, especially in terms of the central fire of the cohesive community.

Tuscarora (1712), Yamassee (1715), and others. Only recently has this massive commercial slaving and sale by armed native slavers of other native peoples been dealt with in popular history.[275] After cruelly ravaging local populations, British planters turned to Africa, but at much greater expense.

To prepare for the tricentennial of Charleston, Stanley South and Michael Stoner sought out its beginnings along the Ashley River on a point long protected by its concerned land owners. Their excavations (38Ch1a/b) illustrated varieties of planter, settler, slave, and native histories, spanning the human occupation of the Carolinas. During Mississippian times, coterminous with Irene Mound further south, a palisade surrounded a 26-foot-square temple set upon the ground, without any evidence for a platform mound.[276] Later, what their report called three "sheds" (beds, arbors) were marked by post molds set around a central precinct. Within the post barricade were 21 burials – flexed, cremated, or bundled. A set of nested bowls suggested the ritual use of Black Drink [Herb Water], which continues to this day at the annual Green Corn (Busk) Rite of Creeks. With a peak date of AD 1450, during climate change, this transition occurred among coastal tribes at the edge of the fusing Creek Nation, suggesting social collapse at the periphery where disease and slaving later took a heavy toll. Chiefdoms fragmented into tribes that survived, as Cofitacheque, once ruled by a queen, merged into the historic Catawba. Along the Ashley River, the local leader named Kiawah welcomed the Charleston colony of "Barbadian Adventurers" functioning under the 1663 charter to eight Lords Proprietors from the restored Charles II, the last Catholic king of England.

Just to the north, at the mouth of the Santee River, were the ill-fated Sewee (probably Eastern Siouan Catawban speakers), whose men were so sure they could get better prices for their furs across the Atlantic that they loaded up canoes and sailed out, only to be wrecked by a storm. Any survivors were rescued and sold into slavery in the Caribbean.[277] Eventually, tiny remnants of many tribes, known as Settlement Indians (legally if not actually protected from slave raids), took refuge around the relocated Charlestown on Oyster (Battery) Point, where it still prospers, overlooking the island fortress where the US Civil War began in rockets red glare.

Blood Run

The last massive mound site is Blood Run, the largest Oneota town, located 15 miles southeast of Sioux Falls, South Dakota, and 50 miles south of Pipestone quarry in Minnesota. It has been heavily damaged by farming, an older railroad line, and a modern gravel quarry. Historic and ethnohistoric records link it with the Dhegihan-speaking

---

[275] Robbie Ethridge and Sheri Shuck-Hall Ethridge, eds., Mapping the Mississippian Shatter Zone: The Colonial Indian Slave Trade and Regional Instability in the American South 2009.

[276] The Santee National Wildlife Refuge (SC) has the most currently accessible temple mound, especially famous (and archaeologically disturbed) by the Revolutionary War victory there of the Swamp Fox (Francis Marion) against British-built Fort Watson on its top.

[277] John Lawson, A New Voyage to Carolina [1709] 1967: xx.

Omaha-Ponka tribe (before they split), though Chiwere Oto and Iowa were sometimes neighbors. There, renewed mounding resumed after a hiatus of several hundred years:

> "The [1200-acre] site is located on both sides of the Big Sioux River in what is now extreme northwestern Iowa and eastern South Dakota ... occupied between 1500 and 1700 A.D. [with] more than 275 conical earthen mounds. ... An estimated population ... at its height includes six to 10 thousand people [and a] "core area" [of] conical mounds, two effigy mounds, one of which is a 300-foot long "serpent" mound, a 15-acre earthen enclosure, eight Sioux quartzite pitted boulders, and 150-800 stone circles.... mounds have yielded horse bones and one dog burial.... Engraved on the [catlinite] plaques are figures of bison, serpents, lightning, the "birdman" motif and forked eye figures."[278]

Rock Art – Other Markings on the Land

The world over, humans painted, pecked, and sculpted markings on smooth rock surfaces. Later people attribute them to powerful causes, sometimes spiritual, sometimes ancestral, sometimes both. No better example of human reverential relations with the land can be found than such "rock art," which is best described as a system of notation for showing special human relations with the land in all of its dimensions. When natives provide interpretations, they mention the concentration of vitality and *puha* to be available to and for adepts.

Unlike graffiti, done anywhere by anyone, these markings required special privilege and blessings (as Faulkner knew). In some native belief, after the world was made, a Changer (or a team of transformers) went through the landscape preparing the way for humans. Sometimes these changes were deliberate, and sometimes they were inadvertent or clumsy, depending on the characters involved. Two-way rivers and abundant foods were taken away so that humans would be motivated by not having life too easy. In other cases, brambles were provided with berries and trees impregnated with fire so that humans would later benefit.

In the process, the most dangerous inhabitants of the earth – variously called monsters, cannibals, dangers, and demons – were reformed, modified, or petrified. For example, whenever a Changer met monsters, he variously sent them into the earth under a hill (for DunneZa), dismembered the body and flung the pieces in various directions (for Lushootseed), petrified the body on the spot (for Pueblo), or turned the giant into something harmless. Thus, Mosquito was once a huge blood-sucking killer until a Changer killed it and burned its body. From the ashes arose tiny suckers that continue to

---

[278] Dale Henning and Thomas Theissen, eds., Dhegihan and Chiwere Siouans in the Plains: Historical and Archaeological Perspectives 2004, 336. The resumption of mounding around La Crosse is traced in Colin Betts, Protohistoric Oneota Mound Construction: An Early Revitalization Movement 2003, based on his Symbolic, Cognitive, and Technological Dimensions of Orr Phase Oneota Ceramics 2000.

plague the world, although now only as a nuisance rather than a fatal menace (unless teamed with a lethal germ like malaria, yellow fever, or, now, West Nile virus).

To mark each of these sites of transformation, particularly to remind humans of acts done for their benefit, rock art appeared, usually at river rapids, springs, trails, and mountain peaks. Often, these markings indicate the type of being or *puwah* who is fixed there to become available as a spirit partner, as well as providing direct physical contact through touching the image. When a boy or girl had a successful encounter during a vigil, they marked clothing and other artifacts with a disguised sign of its source.

Shamans, however, did even more by marking details of their own visions on outcrops near the site where each happened.[279] Because shamans dealt with great reserves of *puwah*, their marks served to substantiate and harness these flowings. Using red iron oxide (ocher), black carbon, and, rarely, white glaze, the source and direction of the *puwah* was vaguely indicated, as a reminder to the shaman and others who came after him or her that vital *puwah* flowed from that spot. Yet the pictographic representations were never explicit because that would reveal too much and make the *puwah* both too accessible and too ordinary. The colors make seen what is otherwise unseen, and red ocher indicates that which is holy (as in Paleo-caches).

Like an icon painter in the Orthodox Church tradition, the shaman in trance became a channel for the flow of *puwah*. Thus, he or she could also apply marks to other locations to spread powerful influence. In this way, approaches to the town or camp where the shaman lived were marked with signs of his or her *puwah* as counter-protection against enemies or hostile thoughts. More than boundary markers, these paintings served as warding-offs, warning signs, legal claims, and military challenges to any enemy outsiders venturing too near that community intending to harm it.

In general, rock art research indicates the great disparity between cultural perspectives. While researchers, both amateur and academic, have concentrated on the placement of these markings near springs and game trails, supposedly to indicate the location of likely hunting places (where life and death compete),[280] natives emphasize that such markings – whether on rocks, debarked trees, or cave walls – really communicate between these spirits, species, and humans of that place. Like a carved totem pole, which grew out of this same tradition, the marks were a "claim" ~ "deed" ~ "covenant" between place and people in all forms and intelligences. More than "signs from the ancestors", rock art was a kind of aboriginal writing, a signpost preserved at a revered place which was simultaneously a university, cathedral, library, and Eden. These seen designs were used to instruct later generations of well-trained questers, who fasted in proximity to such panels or murals to gain a successful career that was of benefit to themselves and to their people – human and otherwise. They, like mounds, marked intersections of vitality at fixed places.

---

[279] Annie York, Richard Daly, and Chris Arnett, <u>They Write Their Dreams on the Rock Forever</u>: Rock Writings of the Stein River Valley of British Columbia 1994.

[280] Robert Heizer and Martin Baumhoff, <u>Prehistoric Rock Art of Nevada and Eastern California</u> 1962.

Global Comparisons

Mounds occur around the world, where they have been well described by and for certain groups.[281] Looking closely at these varied traditions provides a broader perspective on American practices. For example, Dobu associations between mounds and human remains, especially bones, provide a corrective to Americanist over-emphasis on skulls as war trophies instead of mementos of beloved kindred.

Mounds are universally built up by the natural process of living in the same spot over time (as *tell* ~ Arabic / *tepe* ~ Turkic / *midden* ~ Danish), or deliberately constructed by communal effort to raise people and plants above the landscape. They commonly arise to mark the successive interment of kin at the same location, as burial mounds, as noted in many of the languages of the world: *tumulus* ~ Latin / *anáchoma* ~ Greek / *barrow* ~ English / *kurgan* ~ Turkic / *kofun* ~ Japanese.

The English word "mound" derives from an ancient term for "hand" in the sense of providing protection when held outstretched with palm out, as in Proto-Indo-European *men-*, *man-*, *mar-* ("hand") to Old English *mund* ("hand, hand of protection, protector, guardianship") to Middle English mound, *mund* ("protection, boundary, raised earthen rampart"), along with German *Mündel* ("ward"), *Vormund* ("a guardian"), Old Norse *mund* (Icelandic *mund*, "hand"), and Middle Dutch *mond* ("protection").

Mounds occur in Africa, though they are less widely known than Egyptian pyramids. Like others along the Mediterranean rim, rulers of Morocco, Libya, and Nubia rest within huge burial mounds. Floodplains in Nigeria, Chad, and Cameroon feature "settlement mounds" built up by farmers living in the same location, making garden mounds to grow cassava. Herders moving southward four thousand years ago built domed gravel burial platforms held in place by stone collars and sometimes basalt columns, as at the Jarigole Pillar Site (GbJj1) on the east side of Lake Turkana in Kenya. In western Ugana, enormous earthworks (at Bigo, Ntusi, Mubende, Munsa, Kibengo, Bugoma) enclosing mounds of dung indicate increasing wealth in cattle hundred of years ago. At Bigo, ditches covered 6.5 miles (10.5 km), with walls sometimes ten feet high.

Around the world, leaders were buried within mounds raised by community efforts. At Gyeongju in Korea, formerly known as Kumsong ~ Golden City, 150 mound tombs include rulers of the Silla Kingdom (Old: 578 – 676, Unified: 676-935 CE). In Japan, Emperor Nintoka-ryo (313-99 CE) was notably entombed within an 80-acre keyhole-shaped mound (*mozu kofungun*) at Sakai, Osaka Prefecture. This and other royal mounds are protected by the Japanese Imperial Household Agency, as sanctuaries for

---

[281] Geometric enclosures of huge size occur beyond Ohio and other Hopewell lands, including the newly rediscovered squares and circles of the western Amazon where sites are further enhanced as prehistoric Amazonians built up rich soils (called *terra preta* for 'black soil' and *terra mulata* for 'brown soil' in Portuguese), using broken pottery, household refuse, and cooking debris enriched with charcoal to nourish huge orchards of native trees, as well as gardens of crops like manioc, Cf. Martti Parssinen and Antti Korpisaari, Western Amazonia – Amazonia Occidental, Multidisciplinary Studies on Ancient Expansionistic Movements, Fortifications and Sedentary Life 2003.

spirits of royalty. At Vergina, Greece, a mound marks the burial of King Philip II, murdered in 336 BCE and father of Alexander the Great. Prominent mounds also cover remains as diverse as Genghis Khan and Beowulf. The German "tomb is a raised mound of turf" (Tacitus Chapter 27); the Polish *kopiec* is a memorial mound. At Tara in Ireland, mounds five thousand years old were incorporated into the plan of this seat of the Irish High Kings.

Irish

Mounds housing special inhabitants abound in Celtic folklore. Best known from Ireland, such hallowed hills, called Shidhe, remain the dwelling places of fairies, a prior godly race called the *Tuatha De Danann*. If a human got inside one, he or she was thoroughly enchanted and lost all track of ordinary time. Those few who did emerge described the view, in a manner appropriate to their culture, as ornate palaces.

Like American mounds, the *shidhe* were the focus of periodic rituals, particularly during the four times each year when the "magic mounts" were "open" because the barrier between mortals and immortals thinned. On *Samain* (November 1, which became All Souls for Christians, the day after Halloween), all parts of the world renewed their connections, and, long ago, the Irish high king at Tara symbolically married the earth goddess to assure the prosperity of the country. On *Beltine* (May 1, May Day), cattle were driven between two fires to ward off disease. On *Imbolc* (February 1, now St Bridget's Day), ewe's milk was served to evoke spring renewal. On *Lugnasad* (August 1, harvest), active games and festivals honored Lug of the Long Arm.[282]

After conversion by former slave Saint Patrick, the Irish Catholic Church rededicated these rites to saints and built churches and shrines atop holy places.[283] In such instances, Ireland was following the standard Catholic policy that converted pagan temples into churches, and the Greek grove and *temenos* (places dedicated to outdoor worship) into public shrines. Indeed, the insular Greek reverence for the land has more in common with the Americas than beliefs that later came out of Imperial Rome.

Shilluk

Africa illustrates the special bond among land and leader, especially in terms of fertility, in the institution of "divine kingship". Among Nilotic peoples, such as the Shilluk of the Upper Sudan, the quality of the country is reflected in the health of the king

---

[282] Katharine Scherman, The Flowering of Ireland, Saints, Scholars, and Kings 1981; Alwyn Rees and Brinley Rees, Celtic Heritage ~ Ancient Tradition in Ireland and Wales 1978.

[283] The same happened in North America, where Cherokee town houses were built atop ancient earth mounds, and Catholic monks built a monastery upon a prehistoric mound at Cahokia, Cf. Sally Kitt Chappell, Cahokia – Mirror of the Cosmos 2002. Today, a small catholic church occupies a corner of the space once filled by the great Troyville mound with its 80-foot cone, second only to Monk's Mound in height.

(*reth*). During the great crisis of an unhealthy land with a frail king, he was executed and a vigorous heir installed instead to restore vitality.

These cattle herders and millet gardeners living along the Upper Nile divide the world into earth and sky, with the all-important river mediating between them. Other dualities appear in ceremonial and political contexts. Age, gender, and 100 patriclans organize this society, led by the *reth*. Unities are particularly strong, reinforcing a shared identity traced to the first king, Nyiking, and a high god, *juok*. Nyiking is also sometimes known as *juok piny*, earth spirit or god. In epics, his father was a white bull from heaven and his mother a crocodile: "the totality of riverain beings and phenomena, and offerings are made to her on the river bank, at the grassy spots where the crocodile emerges. She is especially associated with birth and new-born babies".[284]

In other sections of Africa, this gender symbolism is more institutionalized. Among the Swazi, Bantu speakers of South Africa, their divine king is called the Lion. He shares authority with his own mother, who is called Lady Elephant. Every year, Swazi honor their kingship in a ritual that begins with expressions of hate and hostility in song and dance. Following a bull sacrifice and a dance with a vivid green gourd emblematic of past unity, it ends with a flaming pyre of last year's goods that is expected to be put out by rain – the proof of the health, fertility, and wellbeing of the royal pair and the land.[285]

Overall, the divine king is the embodiment of the homeland. He is expected to be fruitful, clever, enlightened, and ruthless. For Shilluks, just after his instillation, the chiefs, "who stick their spears in the ground before him", come forward to swear allegiance and urge what is to be expected of him. His duty is to uphold the social order, and theirs is to advise him on the best way to do this while providing tasty morsels to sustain him.

A *reth* is installed atop the earthen mound[286] in the shrine at Aturwic, invested with emblematic silver bracelets and fanned by stork wings. He descends and is lifted onto the sacred stool, the kingly throne, of wood (not of gold like that of the Ashanti). In a rare eyewitness account, when the king installed in 1943 sat on it for the first time, he "was seized by a trembling fit" as he became engulfed within its vital powers.[287]

---

[284] Godfrey Lienhardt, The Shilluk of the Upper Nile, <u>African Worlds</u> 1954: 146.

[285] Hilda Kuper, The Swazi 1963.

[286] Another Nilotic neighbor is the Nuer, where the Rumjok section of the Luo tribe built an ash and earthen mound, called Ngundeng's Pyramid, before 1901. It was over fifty feet tall and had an impressive ring of ivory tusks around its base. Inspired by their prophet Ngundeng and his son Dwek in honor of the Dinka Sky God named Deng, it was deliberately blown up by British Colonials in 1928, See E. E. Evans-Pritchard, <u>The Nuer</u> 1940: 186, Plate XXV.

[287] Godfrey Lienhardt, The Shilluk of the Upper Nile, <u>African Worlds</u> 1954: 160, 163.

Dobu

As a cross-cultural check on mound use, the Dobu of Melanesia, off the east coast of New Guinea, provide useful comparisons.[288] In place of the plaza in the center of a Creek town, the Dobu have a central mound holding the graves of the local matrilines (*susu*, a word that also means 'milk') composed of mother-daughter series, who share a common ancestress. Croton bushes, with brilliant red leaves, grow over the mound. When someone dies, only the immediate members of the *susu* mourn in that house, while the surviving spouse leaves to kneel outside, never looking at the corpse. After an hour, the dead one is moved onto the outer platform, bathed and adorned. A dirge is sung, while treasures of the deceased are struck by the eldest niece (eZeD) to carry the beat of the tune. Sharing the same matriline, nephews take charge of the corpses of uncles, nieces of aunts. The body is buried in the mound, but the skull and name are inherited by the heir who takes over the house.

Everyone has two names, one inherited and used only among their matriline, and another used by other villagers and by the father. After a death, kin terms change, such that cousins become siblings, moving closer to fill the gap made by the death of an intervening close relation. Valued possessions, claimed by the matriline, include village land, personal name, skull, status, palm and fruit trees, and dicta (magic formulae that control aspects of the world but that became criminalized as sorcery by officers of British colonialism).

Husbands in-marry from other villages, but the couple alternates each year between their respective home fields, bringing along yams and other starts from the planting strains of their own matrilines. As an outsider, he uses only kinship terms for villagers of his spouse, while members of the *susu* use personal names. After the father dies, a child never enters his father's (F) village again. The surviving spouse, if honorable, undergoes a year of mourning at the in-law's village, then leaves it forever.

For this seclusion, a mat enclosure is set up under the house, where the surviving spouse undergoes mourning restrictions for the next year, remaining as grim as possible. A looped, black, bundled rope is worn about the neck. The only food eaten is unripe and coarse. Charcoal coats the body since bathing is forbidden. On the last night, the mourner stays awake and resumes dancing again. This dancing features the skull of the deceased, kept by the sister's children, but the surviving spouse must not look at it.

On the last day, his *susu* brings giant yams to the ex-in-laws, who lead the way to a bathing place. After washing, the mourner's body is anointed with oil, and body ornaments, including herbs in armlets, are put on. Then he or she must leave the village for good, only seeing their own children when they come away to visit. The core of the kin and of the village, therefore, resided in the mounded graveyard at its center.

In contrast to the Americas, in lieu of the harsh idea of a trophy head among Adena burials, the Dobu regard for kin, embodied in skull and name, suggests that kindness and compassion should also apply where appropriate in archaeological interpretations. Euro-ethnocentrism may play a role here, since head taking was also a strong Celtic tradition and scalping for paid bounty was introduced by the Dutch, separating skull from community for personal gain.

---

[288] Reo Fortune, Sorcerers of Dobu [1932] 1963: 3, 12.

!Kung San - Far Flung Trance[289]

Lastly, seeking an explanation as to why Clovis and other mobile hunting peoples would want to anchor themselves to the ground by such flint caches, seeking to "hold on" as it were, modern hunters provide an analogy. Living in stark surroundings, with few possessions, a surprising outlet from the mundane was an emphasis on altered states of mind, fostered by song and dance to renew vitality. Trance, then, is particularly concentrated song and dance leading to catharsis.

Trance among Eskimo (including Canadian Inuit) shamans is a specialist activity, but among the San (misknown as Bushmen) of the Kalahari, it seems to be open to all. But not everyone gains the ability. It is only won by those who make the concerted effort to break through intense emotional pain, fear, and anxiety, often with the help of a seasoned mentor. Though the singers are women and the trance dancers are men, some leeway is allowed for individual inspirations.[290] The central fire (*da'a*, also the inner fire of a person) is lit at sundown, and the dance begins at night, but trancing does not usually occur until midnight.[291]

Among San, the energy-force-sapience-vitality concept (as *puwah*) is called *n/um*, "medicine", and used by adept curers known as its "owners", *n/um k''ausi*. It lies in the pit of the stomach until the human dances in order to heat it up so that it boils up the

---

[289] While dancers can and do enter trance during the long nights of the Busk, the more direct link between trance and mounds is that both provide multilevel experiences, sensory and tactile, while remaining in the very same place.

[290] By comparison, this reverses the roles of the Creek Ribbon Dance, where men sing and women dance.

[291] According to geneticists, San are among the oldest members of the modern human species. Their language has a similar precedent in that it uses so-called "clicks" as meaningful sounds that any human can make but most languages do not use systematically. Cf. Luigi Luca Cavalli-Sforza, <u>Genes, Peoples, and Languages</u> 2000: 137.

For the record, letters used by linguists for these sounds, with corresponding American uses, are

/ dental, tongue sucked from upper teeth, as tsk-tsk in mild reproach

≠ alveolar, tongue sucked against ridge behind upper teeth

! alveopalatal, tongue sucked up the ridge behind upper teeth onto the roof of the mouth to make a popping sound

// lateral, out of the side of the mouth, for horses to giddy up

~ nasal, said through the nose

′ glottal stop, for the pause in oh-ho at the back of the throat

" glottal flap, for a brief closing of the voice box (glottis) in the back of the throat

spinal column ("tube") to explode as vapor in the brain. An owner enters trance (k!ia) while pounding the ground with insistent ("stomp") dancing feet. At this onset, pain is intense, fear of death is real, and sweat (cho) is profuse proof of the boiling up. "The legs tremble, the chest is heaving, the throat is dry."[292]

The owner soon breaks through ("opens up") the pain to become possessed of enormous energy and awareness, sometimes with X-ray vision. After feeling the world spin while he is running around, the healer then begins to cure ("pull" ǂtwe) each person in turn, grasping the patient's sides from the back while moaning and shrieking in a condition called kow-he-dile for the very sound of that wail. Via this contact, the illness transfers into the body of the healer, who is in danger from it until it can be expelled into the void.[293] Full k!ia is like death in that the soul soars from the head to visit God and ancestors to plead for protection of the camp. God provides all n/um, which can be enhanced by training, experience, and herbal medicines, as well as harmed by disrespect, menstrual blood, or ill will.

While the usual curing dance is called Giraffe, other named dances have appeared recently. Of note, during Drum, emphasizing women, those in trance sense a hollow tube three inches wide through the entire upright body. While in tara ("lightning strike", an alternative k!ia trance), these women tremble intensely ("shake off beads sewn on their skin aprons") while feeling hollow.

Curing dances are not held every night, but they do occur after a full day of work. Entering trance, owners can make contact with ancestors and the spirits of other animals and beings, forging lines of communication throughout the universe. By holding on to patients, and themselves being similarly restrained during emotional disorientations, San are able to grasp, literally, their place in the world. By their own trance and personal trembling efforts, moreover, they help set it right and hold it steady. Song and dance play significant parts in these efforts, providing beauty and vital order against the threat of tumult, destruction, and death.

Conclusions

The weight of stone artifacts has ramifications beyond the archaeological record. Weight, color, and design aesthetics carried heavy symbolic meaning. Paleo-Indien caches added color to such offerings, while early Archaic burials at Windover actually pinned bodies to the watery ground. Mounds added their honored earth as ballasting bulk, though scholars were slow to sort out their makers by time, space, and tool kit. Later, in Wisconsin, mounds were given recognizable species shapes and appropriate habitat locations allied with kin groups and clans.

Yet this anchoring also fostered release, in dream, vision, and trance. Northern hunters like the DunneZa believe they must first dream an encounter with the spirit of an animal before they can kill it in the flesh. Vision quests, where a youth met a spirit who provided life-long help, are a Native American hallmark.[294] Given its importance and

---

[292] Richard Lee, The Dobe !Kung 1984: 109.

[293] Richard Katz, Boiling Energy 1982.

[294] Ruth Benedict, The Concept of the Guardian Spirit in North America 1923.

wide frequency, it seems likely that Paleo-Indiens arrived with this tradition of dream, trance, and vision, which became routinized via localized rituals as these were developed by acclimating natives becoming local residents. Facilitating the process, moreover, was a belief that powerful inspiration came from above and could be approached more closely from a high place such as a mound. Placing these links in comparative perspectives, as pan-human aspects, the final sketches of Irish, Shilluk, Dobu, and !Kung practices shed global light on Native American customs.

Mounds proliferated for the same reason as churches do now; everyone wanted a safe haven directly and "personally" linked to vital, life-giving divinity. Unlike right-angled buildings, however, they fit organically into the land itself. Genuine respect for the earth thus had a local focus with an obviously bulging presence. Similarly, mounds took various shapes and configurations as distinctive badges of community. While local ceremonies benefit such an integrated lifeway, they require many visitors to be effective. Size and numbers of mounds was significant; upheld and enforced by the sanctions of neighboring opinion. Each mound's start or new earthen mantle mobilizes community effort, which was shown off and judged by intercommunity feasting and ceremony to legitimate that claim. Larger, more generous communities were entitled by popular opinion to bigger monuments.

This ranking of mounds created links between and among all the regional sites, such that single mound towns gained added stability because they were integrated with multimound centers, sometimes via actual constructed causeways. At least four levels can be assumed, given the universal importance of the number 4 in Native North America. Roughly these would be equivalent, in decreasing significance, to cathedral, church, chapel, and shrine. Surrounding walls or other barriers, like those around both churches and banks, serve to concentrate *puwah* and protect it from outside attack, theft, or siphoning off.

Today, at Creek ceremonies, people remark "they're looking good" both to themselves and to outsiders because the sacred precincts have been beautifully cleaned and cleared, and everyone is dressed in colorful finery. In the home camps, visitors are well fed and made welcome, adding to everyone's enjoyment. Work is done on the basis of ability. Older men, known as "arbor weights, press-downers" (*topv 'mvwetenv*, *topa 'mawitiina*),[295] plan, direct, and advise, while younger men do the heavy and arduous labor. They divide into work teams to hoe and rake the plaza, cut the fresh willows to roof the arbors, and harvest the special medicines needed to make the herb water (misnamed "black drink").

Men work inside the enclosing ring, and women outside in their family camps. Generally, men make direct contributions while women make reverse ones. Men are fasting and thirsting while they clean the ground and take ("touch") medicine; women, inversely, are feeding visitors and exorcising the confines. This is most evident at the dances of men and women. Men celebrate the Feather Dance, devoted to birds and the heavens; while women, elaborately dressed, do the Ribbon Dance, wearing heavy leg rattles, often of turtle shells, holding them to the earth. Men raise river canes decorated with white feathers at the tip; the two lead women hold huge knives carved of wood, used

---

[295] James Hill, Description of Hilabi Round House, Creek Texts by Mary Haas and James Hill, 18, line 5; also Haas and Hill 2015: 67.

to butcher and remove any harm lurking on the grounds. These two women do this by holding the knives (*atassa*) absolutely still so they can more effectively and thoroughly chop in reversed spiritual dimensions.

Moreover, a few constructions were intended to be unique attractions. For northeast Louisiana, such impressive centers lasted for over five thousands of years, as substantiated by Watson Brake, Poverty Point, Troyville, and others. Viewed in sequence, they drew distant visitors to such pilgrimage sites along the crucial lower Mississippi River, partaking of their banked blessings and ballast in a warm climate.

Mississippian Cosmos
drawn by Jack Johnson
permission of F Kent Reilly III

5 ~ OUTSIDE

Mounds occur worldwide, but instances from the Southeastern US have received the most scholarly attention, largely because mounding continues in active use into the present. Erroneously, most academics have the sense that mounds are not culturally as important elsewhere in the Americas, yet a perusal of the regional literature quickly corrects that presumption. These regions also share regard for the precarious uncertainty and instability of the earth, whose skin quavers and shakes. Geophysics is a better guide to understanding mounds than the static, frozen nature asserted by popular impressions of ageless cultures and nations, however soothing they may seem. Rhythmic songs and pulsing dances help "pump up" mounds to enhance their vital qualities.

This chapter turns to the outer form of mounds – their usual piled, bulged, humped, domed, banked, rounded shape – with an outer surface finished in colored plaster or covered in grass. By vertically reoccupying the same hallowed space, mounds vitalize specific places over time. Slope-sided blocks, the familiar SE temple mounds, occur elsewhere with less frequency, though some of the Northwest fort emplacements do fit that shape. In particular, religious and spiritual associations of these other American mounds will next be highlighted to strengthen this connection. Distinct coloring of outer surfaces on a SE mound, especially red or white, is revealed archaeologically, as well as supported by modern elder statements.[296]

We will follow the designated Z-shaped route from the Northwest (Puget Sound, British Columbia, northern California), to the Northeast (Huron, Cayuga, Abenaki) and Plains (Osage, Pawnee, Caddo, Wichita), skipping the Southwest (Miller 2015), before reaching the Southeast (Calusa, Yuchi).

Puget Sound Lushootseeds of Washington State

North along the Pacific coast, my own intimate knowledge, musings, and personal chagrin has now made clear what should have long been obvious in terms of localized mound images. Throughout the Northwest, human-made piles of dirt served as defensive forts or flood protection,[297] but they once seemed not to have the sacred, burial, or spiritual aura of mounds elsewhere. Instead, cultural regard was devoted to arts, crests, and treasures descended from the ancestors, both human and spirit. For Puget Sound, despite my authoring three relevant books, I overlooked any evidence for mounds until I glanced at my own Shamanic Odyssey, with illustrations drawn by my own hand, and groaned. At the base of each one of the protecting planks sheltering a shaman, there is a black half circle that is explicitly said to be the earthen mound serving as the home of a

---

[296] Corin Pursell, Geographic Distribution and Symbolism of Colored Mound Architecture in the Mississippian Southeast 2004.

[297] Jay Miller, First Nations Forts, Refuges, and War Lord Champions Around the Salish Sea 2011.

being called a Little Earth, one of the spirits that is said to "own" the earth.[298] Thus, here is artifactual evidence for a mound as a "holy home" for a powerful earth spirit. If I had not personally traced that mound at the base of each plank diagram, I would have been even slower to see the link. It remains unclear whether these hills or outcrops were specifically built by immortals or by natural forces, though they are probably one and the same (below). In the few instances where this place name has been recorded near Seattle, it refers to a hill that looms over a spring.

The need for such earthy massiveness is supported linguistically. The Lushootseed word for earth is _swatix^wtəd_, indicating outwardly expansive motion, as "something that fully takes care of spreading everything around".[299] Its further extensions mean both forest and these same earth-owning spirit immortals (Little Earths) who live in those hummocks near springs. Thus, the earth, like life, is inherently dynamic, if unstable. To gain stability, the earth, or a portion of it, must be held safely in place in a way that stands out and up from the uncertain landscape. Moreover, it is now clear, mounds are not attested only in Salish rituals and mythology. Archaeologists have indeed found burial mounds at sites just to the north and south.[300]

---

[298] Jay Miller, <u>Shamanic Odyssey</u>, The Lushootseed Salish Journey to the Land of the Dead 1988; <u>Lushootseed Culture and the Shamanic Odyssey</u>, An Anchored Radiance 1999a.

[299] Dawn Bates, Thom Hess, and Vi Hilbert, <u>Lushootseed Dictionary</u> 1994: 245, provides _-ti-_ "spreading" and _-təd_ "implement," with the implication that the earth is constantly expanding, or getting away. For Vi Hilbert, a fluent Lushootseed teacher, the purifying aspects of brushing off with cedar boughs combines with the image of a mother bird protectively "spreading" her wings over her brood to more fully translate _-ti-_ as "take care of, hope for, indicate regard or concern" (Jay Miller and Vi Hilbert, Caring for Control 1993: 238). These morphemes can be traced on pages xvii for s-, p240 for _t'ix^w_ "brush, shake off," p226 for _tix^w_ "bail out a boat," _-ti-_ "spread," p220 for _-təd_ implement suffix, and p246 for _-waw'-_ "take full advantage of." In all, the best translation of this word for earth is "something that fully takes care of spreading everything around."

[300] Kenneth Ames and Herbert Maschner, <u>Peoples of the Northwest Coast</u>, Their Archaeology and Prehistory 1999: 190-191; Keith Carlson, ed., <u>A Sto:lo and Coast Salish Historical Atlas</u> 2001: 36. At an Elder's Lunch near Seattle I was stunned when an old friend mentioned that she knew from her family that they had ancestors buried in these mounds. It is also noteworthy that Northwest earthen forts and mounds (next endnote) were referenced by George Gibbs (1855), the Harvard-trained lawyer whose notes and publications from the mid-1800s had a large part in winning treaty rights to salmon and other resources in the late 1900s.

Rocky Point on Coastal British Columbia

In the Northwest, the largest concentration of surviving cairn mounds is at Rocky Point (DbRv-3) peninsula, protected by a Canadian Forces ammunition depot, between Beecher and Pender Bays at the southernmost tip of Vancouver Island near the city of Victoria.[301] Of the sixty-one (61) archaeological sites of all ages, nineteen (19) have cairns. Eighteen of these sites have a total of only 55, but Rocky Point alone has 382 recorded petroforms, including 323 cairns and 10 mounds, with 240 of these intact. (Mounds here are cairns covered over with more soil.)

Of note, no cairn is located for visibility; none is either placed atop bedrock heights nor along the actual shore. All are set back and somewhat obscured from the sea, though, in reverse, water can be seen from anywhere on this point of land. Since such features express "visible stability and identity", their locations are probably keyed to strategic routes, especially among the cairns. Since adjoining Eemdyk Passage is the safest waterway through this region, it too played a role in site selection because it assured continuing public access without any ostentation. Certainly, etiquette among present-day Salish elites criticizes the obvious and boastful as crass and "low class", valuing discreet subtlety as being appropriately refined. Inside knowledge, acquired skills, generosity, and ancestral lore are most valued. The east side location of Cairn C144 in Area 4, a squarish rock outline with three corner cairns, enforces this argument because it is the most obscured, elaborate, and enigmatic feature on the site.

Rocky Point is now in the homelands of Straits Salish speakers, with two Beecher Bay (Scia'new, Klallam) reserves along its western shores. Straits communities are distinctive because they lived mostly on islands and coasts lacking salmon streams. Instead, they relied on reef nets anchored along fish migration routes to catch, filet, and dry salmon for their winter supplies. If Salishan languages began spreading about 2000 years ago, this linguistic and archaeological correlation of cairns may have merit as a way for Straits speakers to stake a claim to this region.

---

[301] Darcy Mathews, Burial Cairn Taxonomy and the Mortuary Landscape of Rocky Point, BC 2006. A cairn in its most discrete form has a central cyst for burial, an edging of rocks of varying sizes, a fill either of till stones or gabbo bedrock, and an outer rock border, varying in diameter from stones and cobbles to boulders. Coded for 19 variables, a data set of 358 examples yielded six types. Type 1 cairns are oval, till filled, and concave in profile. Type 2 (most common) is oval and rounded. Type 3 is irregular with angular rocks. Type 4 is oval, rounded, and huge. Type 5 is circular and till filled. Type 6 features bedrock boulders in circular shapes. In terms of overall bulk, the smallest types (1.6 square meters (M^3)) are 3, 5, and 6. Increasing in size are Type 2 (3.7 M^3), Type 1 (5.7 M^3), and, largest of all, Type 4 (22.2 M^3). Within this site, cairns cluster in seven areas, with the densest ones (Areas 1, 2, 4) on the east side, while Areas 5, 6, and 7, to the west, beyond wetlands, have smaller features. Based on these distributions, the east side had higher status than did the west one.

In the Northwest, before 1500 year ago, burials were placed in village middens. Then, along the Salish Sea, from 1000-1500 years ago, cairns and mounds proliferated. After BP 1000 began the modern ethnographic custom of burial by rank, with the wealthy placed inside canoes set higher up in trees, and lower ranks nearer the earth. Dead slaves were discarded, often thrown into the sea.

The exception to this Straits claim, though, is the famous Scowlitz site along the Fraser River, now in Sto:lo (Central Salish) homelands, with 18 "house" pits and 42 cairn mounds. Mound 1, the largest, dated to 1290 BP, consisted of a clay cap covering two concentric square petroforms of boulders surrounding a 200-stone cairn built over a cyst holding a flexed adult male accompanied by an abundance of shell and copper jewelry (including 7000 dentalia ~ tusk-shaped shells). While there may be a mismatch of archaeology and language at present Scowlitz, the counterargument is that intermarrying elites throughout the region would share burial customs across multilingual settings.

DunneZa (Beaver) of Interior British Columbia

An apt example of how geology was interpreted as the result of cultural processes, including the crucial importance of song, comes from northwestern Canada. The DunneZa world began as the classic ⊕ image of a cross inside a hoop floating upon the primal waters.[302] Muskrat, as Earth Diver, went down to bring up a speck of earth from the bottom of the sea. This mote was placed at the center of the cross, where it expanded along the Peace (formerly called Beaver) River of northeastern British Columbia.

Earth's population flourished, despite threats from many monsters and other dangers. Years later, a boy was vilified by his step-mother, causing his father to abandon him on an island. There he encountered a Swan (spirit immortal) who advised him to survive by using the *puwah* of the Sun to dry and store the meat of migratory birds. In this manner, the boy (renamed "Swan") thrived until able to avenge himself on his parents.

Thereafter, he went through the world changing monstrous animals which (who) had been eating humans. He locked them underground, often inside hills, to be available as immortal partners for future generations of humans, notably the DunneZa. While he was contending with prototypical animals, he changed his name to Saya (meaning "Sun") to remind everyone that the sun in the sky is the guide to proper orientation, so necessary for a successful life.

By placing these immortal animals within landmarks, many of them mound-like hills, humans could easily know where they are. Enclosing them in earth confined their fury, though they could still shake things up while making themselves available to help those in questing for visionary powers.

In addition to the mounts containing these reformed monsters, throughout this Canadian Plateau region, natives lived during harsh winters in pithouses dug deep into the earth. Entered by a notched log through the roof hatchway, they served as another reminder that mounds were sometimes actual houses with indwelling residents.

---

[302] This DunneZa overview is based on the work of Robin Riddington (see all) and his first wife Tonya Mills.

For Dunne-Za, vitality is expressed in visions, songs, meat, luck, and blood. The functional hub of the world for any DunneZa was ~ is the family camp. Each one, regardless of its duration, represented a tysic that had to have a stand of pristine low "bush" directly to the east so that resident visionaries have unobstructed and untainted access toward the sunrise. A partnership began when an immortal met a human to provide a song and specify the contents to be assembled into a personal mystic bundle. Once combined, such a bundle hung suspended above the eastern or head end of the sleeping area, periodically taken down and unwrapped for ritual use. Its owner must sleep with head at the east, under the bundle, in order to receive the full vital benefits of the Sun at sunrise.

Every partnership also involved a specific set of restrictions or strict taboos. Generally, these were intended to keep separate the immortal and the human so as not to crosswire or intensify *puwah* into a destructive force. Thus, those with Spider *puwah* could not listen to the music of string instruments because these were too much like webbing. If such taboos were violated or breached, even inadvertently, and balance could not be restored, then the human transformed into a wechuge, a monster ogre cannibal from the myth age. He or she then had to be killed and cremated, hopefully before eating others. This particular use of cremation was necessary to destroy the icy heart of the ogre, as well as any trace of the body.

These and other teachings remind the DunneZa that a good life requires moderation and proper orientation, especially to significant trails. As important religious personages, the orbs of Sun and Moon are recognized as daily trail blazers, moving along fixed routes attuned with *puwah*. People live best by recognizing such trails and seeking out important intersections.

Dreaming provides access to some *puwah*, a portion of the potent force in the cosmos attributed to the Sun, whose own power derived from the primordial cross and hoop ⊕ because it too is round, moves east and west each day, shifts from a low in the north at winter to a high in the south at summer, and subsumes all important trails and tracks within a global circuitry. Such astronomical observations, as well as the desire for personal orientation, benefit from standing on hills and other elevated places.

Hunting was a religious act. A good hunter must first dream of the intersection of his own trail with that of a game animal in order to be able to kill it properly. He can only do this by maintaining a proper orientation to the trail of the Sun, which provides an overview of all routes. Remaining attuned to the Sun, therefore, brings health, life, and needed meat.

While both Sun and Moon are called by the same word (*sa*, 'orb'), these planets can be carefully distinguishable as 'day orb' and 'night orb'. Further, in contrast to the Sun, immortal Moon has negative associations linked with ghosts and death, moving along its trail with a retrograde (backwards) motion relative to the stars. While the Sun's trail leads into the future, Moon's leads into the past, like a shadow.

All visionary partners learn to follow the trail of the Sun, but only the most remarkable ones, known as dreamers (prophets, Swans), also learn the trail of the Moon to achieve total orientation and mobility. They are identified with the Swan because its immortal form has the ability to travel beyond the sky dome and yet return to earth intact in the same body. Its wide wings and long body also give it the appearance of a cross + in flight.

Humans attune themselves to trails through song. Personal *puwah* given to a visionary by an immortal is literally called "one's song" in this Athapaskan language. Accompanying drumbeats convey the sound of footfalls along the route; changes in the melodic line are its turns and twists. Dreams and songs provide knowledge of proper trail orientation, rhythms, intersections, and the patterning of the universe. From high points, such as mounded hills, panoramas make all of this more clear.

While orienting themselves in the larger world, DunneZa trace bonds of kinship with each other – either through consubstantiality (shared substance) or affinity (marriage). The social units of this society, assembled from this duality, are technically called <u>personal kindreds</u>, and are both bilateral and egocentric, in lieu of more corporate descent groups such as clans. Everyone (as a personal focus called Ego) traced his or her own web of relatives on both parental sides [F, M] to allow for maximum social flexibility.[303] If local conditions faltered, then help was available from a wide range of relatives.

In their kinship ideology, those people related to you through same-sex relatives are regarded as consubstantials – consanguineals (sharing "blood" in American ideology). Those related through cross-sex relatives were actual or potential inlaws (affines). Generally, consubstantials comprised mother and her sisters [MZ], father and his brothers [FB], then either sisters and daughters for a woman [Z, D] or brothers and sons [B, S] for a man. Affinals, therefore, were mother's brothers [MB], father's sisters [FZ], and the children of sisters or brothers, depending on one's own gender.[304]

Among DunneZa, men had priority and strong *puwah*, but women had their own inherent and awesome *puwah* to give birth to new life. They lived in an orderly world with a sparse population so these kinship considerations could become matters of life and death for a threatened community. Northern hunters explained their own uncertain world in terms of such allotment of *puwah*, often called "luck" in English, as a personal "song" provided by earth-encased spirits to enable the hunter to provide meat. Yet even luck, while aiding hope, remained uncertain.

Medicine Fight

Local politics are expressed in terms of a psychic struggle called a "medicine fight", a contest between the relative *puwah*s of contending visionaries ~ hunters. Each success or failure is judged according to these relative strengths or own lack of vigilance. On a practical and pragmatic level, it serves to justify uncertainties in an environment where even a good hunter would kill game only once in four hunts.

A successful hunter wisely shared his kill with everyone else in the camp, proving a religious basis (obvious *puwah* success) for his accepted authority. In return, others gave him their goodwill and support. This thriving partnership provided his own family with protection, security, and healthy progeny. His prestige and respect became tinged by suspicion, however, as a hunter aged, since an unscrupulous elder might ensure a long life for himself and dear relatives by siphoning off lives (life force) from other families.

---

[303] These single letter kinship abbreviations are defined at Conventions.

[304] Warren Shapiro, The Ethnography of Two-Section Systems 1970.

Every game animal kill proved that a hunter was in control, but every miss was both a personal failure and a religious setback. Vicissitudes of game, climate, and habitat kept everything in flux; there were no consistent winners or losers. The main source of stability was those elders with on-going authority by virtue of their bounty, continued fitness, cogent advice, and respected healthy families.

A medicine fight began when an unsuccessful hunter dreamed of combat between his own animal immortal and another one that was allied with a more successful hunter, usually from a hostile kindred. The dreamer then made a veiled accusation to alert community sentiment; its manner depending on particular circumstances, personalities, political contexts, and general economic conditions.

The accused replied either that a) the dreamer (his accuser) had brought the trouble upon himself and his kin by violating a strict taboo, or b) that he himself intended to fight his accuser to the death by concentrating on achieving a dream of winning a pitched battle between these two guardian spirits in their animal guises.

At the time of the accusation, the fortunes of the accused were almost always superior to those of the accuser. If such success continued, the accused won more admiration. If his success vanished and the accuser provided game, then such "coming from behind" earned the accuser even greater esteem by so effectively mobilizing stronger *puwah* through deliberate dreaming.

Any misfortune was therefore subject to two theories of causation a) the aggressive use of *puwah* by another, or b) the breach of taboo by oneself. Afterwards, a camp closely watched future outcomes to judge by consensus which one was triumphant or at fault. Ultimately, all of these manifestations of *puwah* were due to a heightened ability of willful control ("freedom from risk, luck"). This confident, alert, watchful awareness was and is the most scarce and valued resource known to the DunneZa. It is the cause and basis for routine success. It is the most tangible and useful expression of the bond between a human and an immortal, drawn from the primordial age of epics.

All of it occurs on a known landscape dotted with sources of *puwah*, further enhanced by the Sun and other beings. Though fixed in places like hills, *puwah* is activated and directed through regular actions, songs, and will power which is focused upon an uncertain world that is periodically beset by adversity, conflict, storm, earthquake, or tremor. Though the thin Dunne-Za population did not mobilize to build mounds, their hilly terrain provided the geological means for expressing place-based beliefs about *puwah*, song, and human atonement.

Karuk of Northern California

California, well within an earthquake prone zone, combines hot spots with high ones. During August-September, after the smoke rising from the cremation of the bones of the First Salmon sends a signal to the immortals, Karuk ("upriver" on the Klamath River) stage a series of three world renewal rites, collectively called Fixing the Earth, held, in sequence, at Inaam (Clear Creek, Happy Camp), Panamniik (Orleans), and Katimiin (near Soames Bar).[305]

In traditional belief, after the beginning of the Karuk world, various immortal beings sank into the earth at special places, some leaving mounds. During the ten-day Fixing, a priestly specialist (*Lo'*) visits each of these locales to light fires, pray, make offerings, sweep away refuse, and set aright slumped stones and other landmarks. Keeping his right hand readily empty, and his legs crooked, he seeks to attract "luck", the coveted ability to gain wealth and wellbeing along the entire Klamath River. "The daily travels of the priest, accompanied by archers who shoot at targets [to fix the earth], lead up to the climactic night when the priest stands by the sacred sand pile (*yuxpit*)."[306]

At Orleans and Soames, he was helped by two women, called leader and follower, who reshaped the 18-inch sand pile into a miniature version of Mt. Offield, known and seen by all Karuk as "God's Mountain". They packed firewood to the place and then got river sand for the *yuxpit* at a beach upstream (a boat landing).[307] "Each carries up two loads of sand in tightly woven burden baskets. They step slowly and carefully. There is no prayer. They dump the sand on the ground. The leader models the higher peak, and the follower the shorter one.[308] All night long, the priest stands at this mound and looks up at the twin summits.[309] The next day, the Deerskin Dance or a surrogate is performed [followed by an afternoon War Dance]. Then follows the retreat [seclusion] of the priest for a period of five or ten days."[310]

Overall, this Fixing is believed to prevent famine, disease, and cataclysm.[311] By reconnecting with local immortals, by showing respect for the landscape, and by setting landmarks on firm footings, like the focal mountain, the Karuk world is made steady and reliable for another year, though constant vigilance is needed to maintain vitalities.

Indeed, Stephen Powers,[312] a much traveled 1870s journalist, faithfully called it "the great Dance of Propitiation, at which all the tribe are present, together with deputations from the Yurok, the Hupa, and others ... which signifies, literally 'working the earth' ... to propitiate the spirits of the earth and the forest, in order to prevent disastrous landslides, forest fires, earthquakes, drought, and other calamities".

---

[305] Julian Lang, ed., <u>Ararapikva</u>, Creation Stories of the People, Traditional Karuk Indian Literature from Northwestern California 1994: 25, 27; John P. Harrington, <u>Tobacco among the Karuk Indians of California</u> 1932.

[306] Alfred Kroeber and Edward Gifford, <u>World Renewal</u>: A Cult System of Native Northwest California 1949: 19.

[307] Kroeber and Gifford, <u>World Renewal</u> 1949: 29.

[308] Kroeber and Gifford, <u>World Renewal</u> 1949: 27.

[309] Kroeber and Gifford, <u>World Renewal</u> 1949: 21.

[310] Kroeber and Gifford, <u>World Renewal</u> 1949: 19.

[311] Kroeber and Gifford, <u>World Renewal</u> 1949: 105.

[312] Stephen Powers, <u>Tribes of California</u>, Robert Heizer, ed. [1877] 1976: 28 in Kroeber and Gifford, <u>World Renewal</u> 1949: 8.

Huron of Ontario

In the Northeast, another aspect of mound lore provides a reminder of the kinds of complexity that was lost after epidemics and disruptions took their human toll. It occurs in the <u>Jesuit Relations</u> from New France, particularly for the Huron (Wendat) before their cruel dispersal by the Iroquois in 1649. Originally on Georgian Bay off Lake Huron, burial depended on conditions at death.[313] Stillborns were placed under paths in the hope their souls would enter into a passing woman to be reborn. Mutilated captives, criminals, and witches had their bones dumped into the village middens. Those who drowned or froze to death had offended powerful spirits of water and sky so their bodies were doubly consigned to the village cemetery, where their flesh and innards were cremated and their bones buried.

Every decade, when a village relocated, all of its honored dead were exhumed and, after a night of singing and celebration known as the Feast of the Dead, reburied together in a common ossuary (bone grave) called the "Kettle". Any members who had died violently, however, were regarded as unquiet and so were left in their separate graves under a mound with a hut set on top. This became their final abode. Similarly, those who died very old and very young were too weak to journey to the afterworld and so stayed near the abandoned village, living on the "ghost crops" of the fallowing fields.

Of note, outstanding in all this variety, is the role of the mound in holding down the restless dead, providing further weight to my argument that mounds provide stability as bulk, bulge, bank, and ballast in an unsteady world. The "Kettle" itself provided a succinct symbol of the community as a unified whole over time, but, with its lapsing, the Midewiwin or Shaman's Academy was reformed about 1700 to take on this unifying role for surviving Great Lakes peoples such as Ojibwa.

Cayuga Iroquois

Within the League of the Iroquois, the Five Nations who dispatched the Huron, the Cayuga are known as "those of the great pipe, [but] represent themselves as a tribe by the symbol of a 'mound', literally 'earth' made into a 'lump' … representing a powerful people, that attracted other tribes or nations who desired asylum with the Cayuga, and they came freely, 'trampling the brush down'."[314]

By extension, Frank Speck (Chapter 5) here implied that the size and effort put into such a mound directly indicates the strength, integrity, vitality, and ready resources of its builders, both for themselves and for those who come to them for refuge. This correlation between size and *puwah* was the rule, but it had many deliberately perplexing exceptions that call attention to unique locales, such as eastern Canada.

---

[313] Bruce Trigger, <u>Children of Aataentsic</u>: A History of the Huron People to 1660 1976: 30, 52.

[314] Frank Speck, <u>Midwinter Rites of the Cayuga Longhouse</u> [1949] 1995: 16, native terms omitted; <u>The Iroquois</u>: A Study in Cultural Evolution 1945.

Abenaki of the Maritime Northeast

Among Algonkians of the far Northeast, often known as Abenaki (or Dawnlanders), their rivers, lands, and families were bound together by a special relationship with an ancestral patron (animal spirit) created at a violent moment of transformation when the earth's waters were released in flood.[315] Abenaki (including Pennacook, Saco, Androscoggin, Kennebec, Wawenock, Penobscot) were organized on the basis of who did and did not share this vital bond of spirits, animals, humans, and lands first released by a flood.

In their charter epic, Giant Frog swallowed all the waters, causing a drought when everyone began to die of thirst. People moaned they were as dry as a particular animal – a turtle, beaver, wolf, trout, haddock, etc. Gluskap, the culture hero, killed the Frog, then toppled a birch tree upon its body to force out the water. Running down the trunk and branches as a template, these flooding rivulets formed dendritic river systems with a lake in place of the leaf at the end of each twig. As water reached these ancestors, some of them plunged in to drink, immediately changing into the aquatic animal whose thirst they claimed (showing the power of the spoken word in certain circumstances). Others remained human but took their named animal as the sign or badge (totem) of their ancestral lands, including camps and hunting territory, along a particular stretch of waterway.

Penobscot call this section, _nziibum_ "my river", while nearby Timagami Ojibwa call it _ndakiim_, "my land". Its boundaries were marked by emblems of the family animal itself, a patron totem called by Penobscot either _baohiigan_, "empowerer" or _ntuutem_, "my parent-in-law" ~ alien partner, though the formal relationship was based variously on descent, marriage, or adoption. Inland from the coast, Penobscot patrons (with some of their equivalent English family names in parentheses) were Lobster (Mitchell #1), Crab (Susup), Sculpin, Eel (Neptune), Bear (Mitchell #2), Toad, Insect, Fisher, Whale (Stanislaus), Beaver, Sturgeon (Sockalexis), Wolf (Polis, Susup), Frog, Squirrel (Attean), Raccoon, Wolverine (Lewis), Mermaid, Otter (Saul, Nicola), Lynx (Fransway), Rabbit (Newell), Yellow Perch (Penewit), and Raven. Families were expected to inherit some physical attributes from their animal. For example, among Penobscots, "The members of the Whale family (Stanislaus) are pointed out as large, portly, and dark persons, those of the Rabbit family (Newell) as small, timid, and weak, those of the Bear family (Mitchell #2) as orderly and dignified, and so on."[316]

Highest in rank were Bear and Squirrel, who provided band leaders for all land totems, or Frog and Sturgeon, who provided water band leaders. As elsewhere, Bear was emblematic of the earth, while Squirrel's ability to scurry up and down trees, keeping

---

[315] Frank Speck, The Family Hunting Band as the Basis of Algonkian Social Organization 1915a; The Eastern Algonkian Wabanaki Confederacy 1915b; Game Totems Among the Northeastern Algonkians 1917a; 2. Malecite Version of the Water-Famine and Human Transformation Myth, Malecite Tales 1917b; "Abenaki" Clans – Never 1935.

[316] Frank Speck, "Abenaki" Clans -- Never 1935: 530.

busy lookout, made it an apt sponsor for active leadership. Similarly, Frog once held all the water, while Sturgeon by sheer bulk showed imposing authority.

Among the Wabanaki (Canadian Maritime confederates), tribes themselves had emblems of a game animal depicted as out in front of two humans in a canoe. The Passamaquoddy pair held paddles and followed a pollock fish, Maliseet held poles behind a muskrat, Mik'maw (on either side of a peaked middle gunwale) held paddles behind a deer, and Penobscot held a pole and a paddle behind an otter. While Abenaki placed cultural emphasis on drainages for tracing identity and kinship, the ridges between them were also important because they provided borders, as well as panoramas on high.

Hidatsa of North Dakota[317]

Mounds occupy a small but significant place in Hidatsa rituals, clearly associated with song and with women and berdaches (male-bodied people in female roles and dress). During their Hidebeating (NaxpikE) ceremony, a pledger enacted the torture ordeal inflicted by Long Arm in the sky upon Spring Boy (twin of Lodge Boy). Over the course of their many adventures, these heroes earned other names, with Lodge Boy becoming Big Medicine and Spring Boy also known as Black Medicine and Grandfather, one of the seven deities of the Missouri River.

The Hidebeating, equivalent to the more familiar Plains Sun Dance, was under the auspices of the Moon. Its locale featured an enclosure, center post, and two small mounds. On the first day, the carrying-in of the center post was greeted by the pledger's wife, members of the Holy Women guild, and their attendant berdaches. They tied a bison skull on the top, raised it, and tamped down the earth around the base of the post. The second day, the Long Arm impersonator "erected two small mounds, north of the central post and near the edge of the lodge, from earth already brought in. A bundle of buckbrush was placed upright on each mound. The pledger danced back and forth between the mounds and center post. At the first torture that was later represented in this rite, these mounds were intended to provide the soil to bury the corpse of Spring Boy.

Further, Three Wolf Ceremonies (Wolf Woman, Sunrise Wolf, Sunset Wolf) emerged in the early 1800s (just before horses appeared) to ritually enhance military skills that took the offensive. Each relied on special abilities given by Wolf spirits. A single mound was built for the last dance of the Sunset Wolf Ceremony, enacting the capture, torture, and rescue of a wronged Hidatsa husband named Hungry Wolf. For the last day, Holy Women and berdaches built a small mound outside the town and cleared a bare space all around it. There the last dance took all day as the final song was sung 100 times, with long pauses to revive any fasting dancer who passed out. Holy Women attending to this brave kinsmen received in thanks an offering of robes or goods from a family member to honor his efforts.

The rite is based on a historical incident. When Hungry Wolf tried to rescue his wife from Cheyennes, she callously had him captured. After he was tortured, the Cheyenne camp moved on, leaving him hanging between two posts. Drawn by his suffering, Wolves took pity, rescued him, and taught him this ceremony. In their

---

[317] Alfred Bowers, Hidatsa Social and Ceremonial Organization 1965: 306- 306, 313, Figure 2, 356.

instructions, the Wolves said, "You will have a mound formed to represent yourself and the people will dance around the mound just as they danced around you. … While the men are dancing and running around the mound, the women must stand around waving their robes as though driving the enemy away." Two canes [**tubes**] stuck in the ground represented longevity, in contrast to the two poles that had splayed him for torture. Of particular note, the mound is explicitly equated with his own body.

Osage of Missouri

Any understanding of the religious and symbolic use of mounds within an integrated cultural system, as noted repeatedly, was shattered by epidemics, slaving, and traumatic disruptions. Indeed, even aboriginal transmissions were quite fragile. Throughout the Americas, knowledge, especially esoteric information, was synonymous with healthy long life, but, to be valued, it had to be rare, contested, and protected. The very transmission of linchpin information was supposed to be given only at the last gasp of a mentor. Among Omaha, this meant that the last offering of vital knowledge had an aspect of patricide.

Our best example of a living Mississippian priesthood, though historically located on the Plains, is the Siouan Osage as studied by Francis La Flesche, himself a chief's son and native speaker of related Omaha. The Osage population of 4000, largely spared devastations from epidemics until the 1880s, was governed by priesthoods based in clans, sacred pipes, and the tribe as a whole. The clans were divided into Earth (*honga*) or Sky (tsi-zhu ~ *hcižo*) halves (moieties). Concentrating on clan and tribal initiation rituals, which both prayed for blessings from the Creator (<u>Wakonda</u>) and explained the universe in progressively learned stages, La Flesche deduced there were 170 such rites.[318]

Clan priest initiations generally lasted four days, most of the time spent in alerting all the universe for the finale. [319] After pledging to be inducted and submitting to the

---

[318] Garrick Bailey undertook the herculean task of synthesizing the cosmology of the Osage, the last and most populous Siouan nations to sustain priesthoods directly out of the core Mississippian area, if not from the urban Cahokia center itself. Their cosmology manifested in elaborate rituals of initiation into Osage priesthoods, as recorded by Francis La Flesche. He was the son of an Omaha high chief, non-practicing lawyer, and skilled ethnographer, both on his own and in collaboration with Alice Fletcher, his adoptive mother. His Osage research became tragic when Black Dog, former high chief and source for comparative materials, died a month after Francis began interviews in 1910, and Saucy Calf, the Buffalo Clan priest whose early dictation to Francis filled 140 pages, burned to death in his cabin in 1912 under suspicious circumstances. Within a decade, Osages would be brutally murdered by their corrupt white husbands in order to inherit headrights to huge fortunes from oil pumped out of their unique underground reservation.

[319] Garrick Bailey, <u>The Osage and the Invisible World</u>, From the Works of Francis La Flesche 1995; Carolyn Quintero, <u>Osage Dictionary</u> 2009: 62 cf golden/bald eagles.

threat in the "penalty verses", a candidate had seven years to gather necessary gifts and food for his graduation feast. Both of the tribal priesthood inductions, however, occurred much more rapidly, lasting only a single day, because the unseen universe hung in the balance until both of the great bundles were owned (secured) by priests belonging to the Earth and Sky halves. The other 168 initiations concerned the visible world, inducting a member into a clan priesthood, where each of the 24 clans had seven degrees culminating in the ultimate grade called Sayings of the Ancients.

Osages equated rituals with books since they preserved and transmitted knowledge through a complex interaction of words, actions, images, and objects, intended to puzzle the serious, intrigue the curious, and impress the literal minded. Each ritual combined songs (*wathon*), actions (*we'gaxe*), and recitations (*wi'gie*), repeating many of the same poetic verses, except that the main image of each version derived from that specific clan and degree within its moiety.

A vital identifying phrase specifies "I am a person who has made of X his body" to indicate the clan's "life symbol" through which they approach the Creator. The list of life symbols fills five pages, with examples of X varying from immensities such as the Sun, Water, and Stars to specific animals, plants, objects, weather conditions, colors, and abstractions. The intent is to announce "I am a specific embodiment of my clan". For instance, in the Earth half, Crawfish clan's life symbols are this crustacean and clay that is colored blue, red, yellow, and black; while, in the Sky half, Wolf clan's images are Dog Star, Sun, and Bison tail.

The special embodiment of each clan and priesthood was a sacred bundle. That of a clan, called a "hawk," held a hawk skin, woven mat bag, deerskin bag, buffalo hair bag, buffalo hide rope, eagle leg, human scalp, and buffalo-hide hanging strap. All such items ("life symbols") of the clans were called *waxo'be* (sacred). The hawk, especially as the falcon eye emblem, was a pervasive icon in Mississippian art, indicating a martial context.[320]

Moreover, the two clans referred to as Men of Mystery and Buffalo Bulls were the symbolic keepers of all the clan bundles. For the entire tribe, by moiety, the great bundle's keeper was of the Gentle Ponka clan, while that of the great medicine bundle was Gentle Sky. Osage unity rested on these two great tribal bundle priests (*wawathon*). The Elder Water clan was the symbolic keeper of the peace pipes expressing tribal unity. Among secondary sacra were war standards, rattles, war clubs, sacred bows and arrows, charcoal, and more. In addition, known only to adepts, unconsecrated symbols, called "those carried to excite enthusiasm" (*wazhawa athinbikshe*) and therefore "not real",[321] might be substituted in some rituals. In this way, all degrees of faith and commitment were included, both credulous and not.

---

[320] James Brown explores the Osage political economy in his quest for "The Identity of the Birdman" image and Alice Kehoe cites remarkable parallels between Cahokia artifacts and Osage sacred texts for key rituals, both in Kent Reilly and James Garber, Ancient Objects and Sacred Realms: Interpretations of Mississippian Iconography 2007: 56-106, 246-261.

[321] Bailey, The Osage and the Invisible World 1995: 47.

Each initiation involved a set of officials who served formal or functional roles.[322] Typically, these were the candidate and his wife, a sponsor, an assisting sponsor, priests of all 24 clans sitting at fixed seats, a holy warrior with all 13 possible military honors, a messenger, widows of former priests, and singers. The candidate and sponsor were entitled to formal claims to that clan and degree. The assisting sponsor thoroughly knew the involved ritual in all of its intricacy and precision. The songs were particularly important to bring the universe "to life", with special verses extolling the ability of human ancestors to think – to search with the mind and thereby learn (termed *wathi'gethon*) "to bring things to pass". Songs and recitations were context sensitive, describing a body from head to feet to indicate birth and new beginnings, or from feet to head for growth and maturity. Songs conveyed a sense of beauty, order, and purpose.

As all of life, the original Osages came from the sky (called father) to the earth (called mother), where they met one clan who had always been there and so became known as the Isolated Earth. Between the sky and the underworld, along the surface of the earth, was ~ is the "snare of life", belonging to a sacred spider,[323] holding everything together between birth and death. On this vital snare, the clans divide between Sky and Earth, with Earth further separated into Land and Water branches.

Symbolic thorough-going oppositions between these moieties include

		Sky with male, also		
Left	six	morning star	father
		Earth with female, also		
Right	seven	evening star	mother

Other associations linked

East with	sun	birth	life	red	male
West with	moon	death	harm	black	female

All of these impacted daily life. For example, someone of the Land slept on their right side and first put on the right moccasin, or, if Sky, with head to the left and left shoe first.

After uniting the two moieties on earth, Osage priests reorganized their society three times, each as a "move to a new country". First came an internal reordering begun by Water people of the Earth division. The Isolated Earth priests became responsible for a symbolic "house" where all Osage children were named. The Land (particularly Bear and Puma) priests were given charge of the "house" where war ceremonies were held. War or hunt leadership was assigned to the Bear, Water, Sky, and Isolated Earth clan priests.

Prompt action, however, was impossible because of excessive ceremonialism, so another reordering improved military tactics, though each expedition was still led by a priest. This next "move to a new country" allowed various clans, as needed, to organize

---

[322] Bailey, The Osage and the Invisible World 1995: 76.

[323] Bailey, The Osage and the Invisible World 1995: 241, line 13.

three types of war parties – composed of men either from all the clans, from a few clans in one moiety, or from a single clan.

The third move instituted the civil government by two chiefs, titled *gahi'ge*, from the Ponka clan of the Earth half and the Sky clan of the Sky moiety. To distinguish these as the source of chiefs, they added "gentle" to their name because that was a defining characteristic of such leaders. Each man held vigil until a spirit revealed to him the contents of a "great bundle", either for "medicines" (symbolized by the cormorant, and by man and woman roots) or "long life" (symbolized by the pelican, and tattoos). The other great bundle priests had the pipes, particularly one with a human face carved into its black pipebowl and, hanging from the stem, seven shell beads for the Earth and six copper beads for the Sky. Such emphasis on shell and copper is distinctly Mississippian.

While clan houses were arranged in order around the edges of the town, the two houses of these tribal chiefs were set across the central east to west path of the sun.[324] While each ordinary house had a door facing north or south across this plaza, these chiefly homes had two doors, one on either of the east and west ends.

The goal of all this complex belief was an unbroken line of descendants stretching far into the future since the strongest belief of all was that nothing in the universe ever moved backwards. Today, having deliberately set down or "unloaded" these arduous religious burdens, Osage seek the same intent through Big Moon peyote rituals of the Native American Church, as well as a strong tradition of Catholic ritual.[325]

Pawnee of Nebraska

The Caddoan language family is ancient on the Plains, and includes the Caddo proper to the south, then progressively northward, the Kichai, Wichita, Pawnee, and Arikara. The Wichita, in the hot south, lived in domed grass-thatched houses, but the others in the winter-cold north built massive earth lodge ("mudlodge") villages. Each of the following chapters will feature aspects of Pawnee society and culture because their ritual use of mounds has been well documented, particularly by James Murie, a devoted Skiri Band member keenly interested in preserving his tribal traditions, redeeming his boarding school education to leave a lasting tribal legacy in writing.

In their homeland, Pawnee consisted of four divisions – the three South Bands along the Platte River – Chawi ~ Grand, Pitahawirat ~ Tappage, Kitkshahki ~ Republican – and, fourth, along the Loup River, the Skiri (Skidi) ~ Wolves, inhabiting about fifteen villages of their own. Within the Plains Caddoan languages, Skiri, Arikara, and South Band Pawnee, which preserved more archaic forms, diverged about the same time. Chawi seems to be the parent of Kitkshahki, then Pitahawirat within the South Bands.[326]

The village (totaling about 20) was the basic unit. Each had its own ancestral star, chiefly founder, bundle, fields, and cemetery. Lodges of the same town might be

---

[324] Recall that Onondaga longhouses, where the Iroquois League met formally, were similarly distinguished from those of the other Five Nations, See Edmund Wilson, Apologies to the Iroquois.

[325] John Joseph Mathews, The Osages 1961: 627.

[326] Roger Grange, An Archaeological View of Pawnee Origins 1979: 136.

scattered among those of other villages because allegiance came through matrilines rather than location, and marriage was limited to other members of the town in order to in-focus the bundle and its *puha* (*wa•ruksti•* in Pawnee).

Pawnee economy combined bison, hunted by men from tent (tipi) camps, with crops, farmed by women at villages, especially maize (15 varieties), beans (8 varieties), squash (7 varieties), melons, and sunflowers. Seasonal bison hunts took place after the Spring planting and after Fall harvest, with families returning in Summer to their "mudlodge" in town so women could store the dried meat and work their fields. These homes looked like big grass-covered mounds, with long entry ways to keep out cold blasts, that had to be cleaned and fumigated before families moved in for the Nebraska winter. Thick inner layers of poles and outer ones of sod provided insulation. At the village and along the trail, Pawnee women gathered berries, fruits, seeds, nuts, and tubers, particularly prairie turnip, groundnut, sunroot, plums, riverbank grapes, and chokecherries.

When willows sprouted, heightened rituals conducted by men and female work parties ("bees") greeted the farming season. Fields were hilled, planted, hoed, weeded, and harvested. Three ceremonies marked this bounty – Green Corn, Ripe Corn, and Four Pole, when an earthen ring and tiny mound were shaped by bundle priests. Crops were processed and dried for storage in enormous cache pits, both inside the lodge for easy access and hidden outside for emergencies. Farming beliefs and rituals centered on maize, which ("who") was specifically identified as a symbolic Woman. Therefore, every cornfield was planted with an even number of hillocks to represent her breasts.[327]

Complementing their sky-based system of priests and bundles, Pawnee had earth-based shamanic ~ doctor guilds, including their unique place-based Medicine Lodge. The landscape of all Plains tribes was dotted with buttes and hills which were regarded as the "holy homes" of the spirits of particular species – such a bison, elk, deer, and antelope – which ("who") were each the spirit sponsor of a guild of healers. Those doctors blessed by the same animal formed a separate "guild" named for it (such as a Bear, Deer, Elk, Bison Lodge), and presumably recognized a hill as the "holy home" of that particular species. Twice a year, in spring and the fall, each guild met to sing and dance.

The Pawnee, moreover, recognized a special animal lodge where spirits of many different species gathered and, in special cases, instructed a human visionary in the conduct of an all-encompassing tribal Medicine Lodge. Each of the four Pawnee bands (Chapter 8) had its own version, recruited from the leading doctors of the other cults. Each Medicine Lodge met in the Spring and the Summer to sing and dance before holding their major rite, Big Doctoring (Chapter 8) in the Fall to display their amazingly curative *puwah*s. That of the Skiri lasted a month.[328] During each event, offerings of smoke, corn, and meat were given to each of the known animal lodges. These three "smokings" honored, in order, deity, women, and men.

---

[327] Gene Weltfish, <u>The Lost Universe</u> 1964: 124, 144. To vivify the crops and the earth, the Morning Star sacrifice of a young enemy girl also took place in the Spring. Douglas Parks, Pawnee 2001, Part 1: 515-547.

[328] Douglas Parks and Waldo Wedel, Pawnee Geography, Historical and Sacred 1985.

Named *rahurahwaarukstii'u* ("holy grounds"),[329] fourteen of these animal lodges have recorded names, and most have been correlated with specific geographical places that looked in profile much like the mudlodge homes of ancient Pawnee towns. The insides of both were arranged in the same way, with spirits or humans sitting on the north or south sides of a central fire and east-facing entryway.

The most famous of these sites, shared by other Plains tribes, was Spring Mound ~ Waconda Spring in north central Kansas, developed into a health spa about 1884 by local whites, who also bottled and sold its water. As an artesian spring atop a low mound, the site was famous for spiritual and medicinal help. While Pawnees revered these hollow hills throughout the central Plains, they also built their own massive mudlodges, grown over with grass sod. During rituals, any distinction between hill and lodge was blurred and the lodge interior was cleared out and refurbished to duplicate that believed to be inside a holy hill.

Caddos of the Trans-Mississippi South

Located west of the Mississippi, the Caddos proper were one of the great unsung chiefdoms of the Southeast and North America, better known from their complex archaeological mounds and towns than through their decimated ethnographic past.[330] Settled along interior rivers draining into the middle Gulf coast, Caddos, speaking related languages, were composed of four historic confederacies and other allied tribes. Three of these confederacies were the Kadohadacho along the Red River, mostly in modern Arkansas; the Hasinai in eastern Texas; and the Natchitoches in Louisiana. At the northeastern frontier near enemy Osages, the Cahinnio along the upper Ouachita River lived in a compact town before their remnants joined the Kadohadacho.[331]

In addition to local diversity, overall Caddo complexity included features shared with the Southeast, Plains, Southwest, and Mexico. According to a recent saga of origins, most of the modern nation emerged from Caddo Lake, along the border between present Oklahoma and Louisiana near the center of their overall population distribution. Kadohadacho traced themselves to a cave in a hill called Chakanina ("crying place") where an elderly couple came up from the underworld. The old man carried fire, a pipe, and a drum; the old woman held corn and pumpkin seeds. Other people and animals followed until Wolf closed off this passage, amidst the crying of those left behind.

Among Hasinai, Moon (*niši* ~ *nishi*) – their culture hero who was acting on behalf of a supreme being called Ayo-Caddi-Aymay "father chief above" – appeared on earth after his mother was killed by a giant horned **snake**. His grandmother and virgin aunt

---

[329] Skiri dictionary (Parks and Pratt 2008: 182, 265, 395) lists the singular segments as *hu-raah-waa-ruks-tii*, from land = *huraaru'* + holy = *waa-ruk-sii*. The final syllable seems "to make" it holy.

[330] Daniel Rogers and George Sabo III, Caddo, <u>Southeast</u>, Raymond Fogelson, ed, Handbook of North American Indians 14: 616-631 2004. The lifework of the late Helen Tanner on ethnohistoric Caddo complexity is awaited.

[331] George Sabo, The Caddos, <u>Paths of Our Children</u> 1992; W. W. Newcomb, The Caddo Confederacies, <u>The Indians of Texas</u> 1961.

found a drop of her blood inside an acorn cap and kept it secluded until it developed into a tiny boy the size of a finger. The next day, fully grown, he killed the monster, established regular earthly procedures, and then went into the sky with the two women.

Most Caddos lived in scattered farmsteads along a river, each cluster of houses controlled by the senior woman of an extended family. As intensive farmers, each household expected to have a two-year supply of stored crops on hand, in case there was war or famine. Each community had a central temple, built atop a flat earthen pyramid, as the focus of seasonal and farming rites conducted by their officials. Periodically rekindled afresh, flames from this new sacred fire were used to relight all household hearths within that community.

In keeping with their high population density and wide distribution, which may have numbered a quarter of a million, leaders were graded into an administrative hierarchy of patrilineal offices that blended political, social, and religious responsibilities. At the top of a confederacy was a leader whose title was spelled _shinesi_ by the Spanish. He was a high priest probably addressed as _tsah neeshee_ (Mr. Moon). Districts and communities were headed by a _caddi_ ~ tribal chief, who supervised a staff consisting of various officers called the _canaha_ ~ subchief, _chaya_ ~ lieutenant, and _tamma_ ~ aide. The _tsah neeshee_ lived in a four-sided compound with his own home on one side, a meeting room across the patio, and, on the other two sides, guest rooms for visitors. Near the temple were two small buildings sacred to the _kokoniki_, twin boys who were messenger oracles between the deity and the priest. At least once a year (more often in times of stress), the _tsah neeshee_, surrounded by other officials, consulted with these twins in a darkened temple and, using another voice in trance, announced what had to be done to embrace or avert some impending event.[332]

Caddo prestige was based on their impressive rituals, mound complexes, and trade networks involving salt, fine pottery, Osage orange bow wood (hence, French bois d'arc, bodark), and tanned black velvety hides. Like the Pawnee, also Caddoan speakers, the liturgical role of the priestly chiefs was balanced by that of doctors ~ shamans, some organized into guilds, each empowered by the same spirit to treat specific illnesses. Unfortunately, these guilds have sometimes been mistaken for clans, otherwise unknown among all Caddoans.

Most recently, Caddo worship of Moon provided the basis for much of the symbolism for the peyote rite of the Native American Church, which features a tiny crescent mound along one side of the central fire.[333] Resting at the center of this elevation is the grandfather peyote "button" that is the focus of the seen for the unseen. Again, in miniature, obvious mounds continue into the present in conspicuously religious contexts.

Wichita of Kansas

Another serpent (14RC102), literally in the grass, slides down a hillside about a hundred miles northwest of Wichita, Kansas, the namesake city in the aboriginal homeland of the Caddoan Wichita. Spring fed, these headwaters of the Little Arkansas

---

[332] This linkage of trance, temple, mound, and priest is particularly noteworthy.

[333] See Jay Miller, Changing Moons: A History of Caddo Religion 1996.

remained a lush green when the rest of the prairie dried to brown. While the springs are themselves marked by petroglyphic ~ rock art, the region features four intriguing sites. Three are moated ovals, called council circles (Hayes, Tobias, Thompson), with the remains of a roundish house within each of its four quarters, as well as overall sky orientations and alignments. The fourth one is this dug out snake, which is aligned with the others. The sides of its mouth point toward those three council circles a few miles away. Facing north, the west side of the mouth V also points to the summer solstice (June 21) sunset.

This serpent is not formed as a mound but as a depression known as an intaglio, with the lumpy 160-foot body scooped out along the top of the ridge before bending down the hillside so that the head is at the base. Construction probably involved burning off the hill, staking out the form, then, using hoes, digging out the trough forming the body. The mouth is open around a small round mound, like that between the jaws of the famous Ohio effigy. But the sizes and scales are different: that in Ohio undulates over 1200 feet. Instead, the Kansas serpent is designed for visual impact. Excavated down only 15-20 cm, the removed dirt was placed along the outline to make it seem deeper.

Since both Wichita and Pawnee were Caddoans, direct parallels can be made between this earth figure and the 60-foot model that encircles the inside of the Skiri earth lodge during the Big (Medicine) Doctoring (Chapter 5). Both are water serpents, slithering over land and under rivers of the central prairies. The forked tail of the Pawnee figure indicates that it is much more than a snake, while the analogous open jaws (as forked depressions branching from the ancestral trough) seem a deliberate reversal by Wichita.[334]

Calusa of South Florida

Along the southwest coast of Florida, the Calusa ("fierce people"), a dense population of 10,000 fishers and garnerers ~ harvesters (who fully tended but never farmed), lived among chiefdoms similar to those better known and longer lived along the North Pacific Coast. On both Gulf and Pacific coasts, staple foods were fish and shellfish, supplemented with deer, raccoons, birds, reptiles, plants, and roots.

Neighbors to the north along the Gulf were the Tokobaga, inland were the Mayaimi, and along the Atlantic coast were the Ais, Jeaga, and Tequesta. After these nations, including the larger Alachua and Timucua, were devastated by Spanish missions, foreign diseases, and massive British slave raids; Florida was resettled by Creek refugees who became known as Seminoles (from Spanish cimmaron "feral", return to the wild), who also took in native Floridian survivors.

The Calusa capital was called Calos (Mound Key, Esteros Bay), with 50 subject towns, each governed by an under chief. A high priest, often the brother of the paramount chief, supervised the sacred fire, temple, and rituals. A war captain, often a brother-in-law of the chiefly family, defended the land leading warriors into battle.

For a century and a half after 1600, Catholic missionaries railed against the Calusa temple. About 1700 it enclosed a mounded altar topped by a mat enclosure, and

---

[334] Clark Mallam, The Serpent: A Prehistoric Life-Metaphor in South Central Kansas 1984.

was described as a "very tall and wide house with its door and [roof hole], in the middle a hillock (_cuesta_) or very high flat-topped mound (_mogote_), and on top of it a sort of room (_aposento_) [made] of mats (_esteras_) with latticework seats (_barbacoas_) all closed…. The walls are entirely covered with masks, one worse than the other [sic]." These "many wooden masks, painted in white, red, and black, with noses two yards in length" were worn in seasonal processions "with the women singing certain canticles (_canticos_)." By 1743, the hut (_choza_) held one mask kept "on top of a table (mesa) or altar. And they call it _sipi_ or _sipil_."[335]

The high chief, who sat on a special stool, wore a gold headband and beaded leg garters.[336] Like ancient Egypt, the Calusa high chief married a full sister as his first wife. In formal greeting, he was approached on the knees, with the hands up. His authority rested on the ownership of prime fisheries, nets, stored foods, trading contacts, and secret esoteric information about the world.[337] By his decree, public works – storerooms, canals and mounds for temples or burials – were constructed, mostly with religious intent. Canals provided access, sometimes via canoe processions, to mounds dedicated to a trinity of gods. Indeed, Chief Carlos resisted conversion to Catholicism because, as he explained, knowledge of this triune divinity was a secret of his own royal line.

The highest deity was the creator, the second was the culture hero who fixed most social rules, and the third was concerned with male activities such as war, demanding human sacrifice in order to consume the eyes of victims. Prayers, songs, and rituals honored them. As noted, masks, such as those later found submerged at Key Marco, were worn during a major rite, probably in the Fall, when a procession came down from the temple to bless the town and its lands. Death was accompanied by elaborate treatment of the body in charnel houses, ossuaries, and final burial mounds. Carved sculptures of turtles, barracudas, and other animals, perhaps related to clans, guarded these cemeteries.

As a huge, densely settled population, Calusa were very vulnerable to European diseases, and many succumbed during recurrent epidemics. After Spain ceded Florida to the British in the 1750s, survivors retreated as Catholics to the Caribbean, where they blended into those highly mixed populations. Today, much of their capital center has been destroyed by construction of retirement facilities, though some mounds, sometimes in alternating layers of dark soil and stacked shells, remain in protected areas.[338]

---

[335] John Hann, Missions to the Calusa 1991: 42, 159, 196, 422.

[336] The descent of this office, according to baptizing Catholic priests, continued for six known generations, passing from the founder to his brother, Senequne, to his son, Carlos (died 1567), to his father's sister's son (FZS) Felipe, then finally to another cousin, Pedro. Notably, throughout the Americas, moral character was indicated by the wearing of such restraints, on the head, arms, and legs, as among Yup'ik, Cf. Ann Fienup-Riordan, Boundaries and Passages ~ Rule and Ritual in Yup'ik Eskimo Oral Tradition 1994: 9.

[337] Randolph Widmer, The Evolution of the Calusa 1988.

[338] A modern recreation of such a mound stands in a courtyard outside the fine Calusa exhibits at the University of Florida Museum of Natural History in Gainesville.

Yuchi (Tsoyaha) ~ Lizard Dance

Yuchi celebrate the tumult of the earth in the Lizard Dance, when men carry trembling trees punctuated by noisy blasts.[339] According to its origin legend, three boys were in training to become medicine men. While they were out camping, their trainer warned them away from a tree with a hole in its side. Foolishly, one of the boys tried to chop it down. A gigantic Lizard came out of the hole, and took the boy to feed its young. The other boys fled. The trainer built a fire at their campsite, and a mound on the other side. He made medicine and placed it between the mound and the fire. Then the man and boys sat on the other side of the fire across from the mound. That night, the Lizard came over the mound, tasted the medicine, and died. (In a similar Shawnee story, the ashes from the cooking fire of a menstruating girl are put on the mound, and these are what kill the Lizard.) They cut off its head, killed its young, and left. They tried placing the head atop various trees, but each withered and died until they used a red cedar, which remained healthy and gained red veins from the dripping blood.

During the Lizard Dance, men embody the monster, shaking small trees as they dance in a line. Four men jog outside the ring, firing shotguns to the east. Afterward, everyone "goes to water" to wash. One man then sweeps up the entire ground, removing all traces of the dance because it and its patron are so dangerous.

Among Yuchis, the link between humans, reptiles, mounds, and a tremulous world is directly expressed in the dance that begins their Busk. Of note, Creeks and others of the Southeast say that their own Busk first belonged to the Yuchi, who then shared it with others in the region.

Conclusions

Mounds are not limited or unique to the Southeast. This survey of the Northwest, Northeast, and Plains shows them as "holy homes", havens, burials, and offerings across the continent. Emblematic of the earth itself, Lushootseeds call these inhabitants Little Earths, and look to them for the great *puwah* that enabled shamans to travel safely to the afterworld and return with missing vitalities to cure a patient. Since they went in symbolic canoes, the mounds painted upon empowered planks provided literal ballast for stability. Other spirits, some under hills and mounds, are petitioned for help during quests and rituals. During the all-important Abenaki Flood, humans and animals defined their subsequent identities and emerging hills provided havens. While Osage no longer build mounds, except as tiny peyote altars, their rituals evoke Mississippian times, even to their use of shell and copper. Karuk make their mound from the sands of a boat landing, a protective haven at the end of a sometime turbulent river crossing. With this mound and embedded arrows, they fix for another year a world made unsteady by human faults. But human transgressions again begin the imbalance that outweighs all this yearly good work. Huron placed those who died violently under a mound topped by a small hut,

---

[339] Jason Jackson, Yuchi Ceremonial Life 2003: 213, 237.

reminiscent of that inside the Calusa temple. As protection against the violent outbursts of the earth, Wichitas and other Caddoans petitioned and propitiated special snakes in intaglios or sculptures.

Sky lore is also significant, especially correlations with Sun and Moon. As sky orbs, their motions and shapes often serve to visually set the time for events. Rising and setting along the horizon, their half circle arcs duplicate the mound form. Moreover, as the stars and orbs disappear into the underworld, their movements are believed to be mirrored inside hollow mounds.

IBOFUNGA
OHFVKV / HIGH ABOVE

✸
SUN *hasi* (*hvse*)
birds ~ winds ~ blood
🕊 *fvswa ~ hotvli: ~ ca:tv*

↕

↕
medicine → fire ∩ ← song & dance

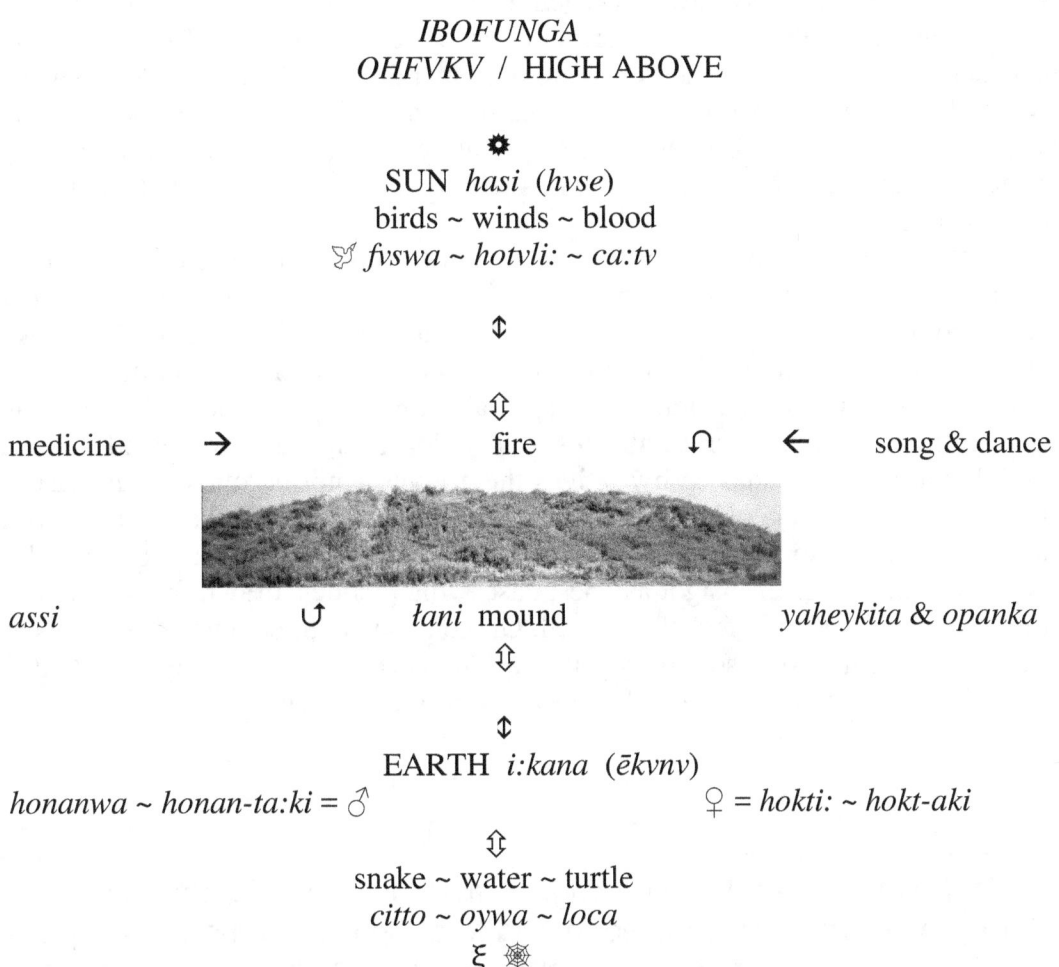

assi   ↻   *łani* mound   *yaheykita & opanka*
↕

↕
EARTH *i:kana* (*ēkvnv*)
honanwa ~ honan-ta:ki = ♂   ♀ = *hokti: ~ hokt-aki*
↕
snake ~ water ~ turtle
citto ~ oywa ~ loca
ξ 🕸

6 ~ INSIDE

What is believed to be inside of mounds, aside from blest soil banked around hollow cavities, adds to their fascination. As a symbolic torso, mounds are especially filled with rhythmic song. For some purposes a mound is like a lung, expanding to breathe with each remantling by human actions (Culture), then contracting under the forces of Nature until reinflated by the prayers and song of the next ritual gathering. Often, reptile, insect, bird, and animal associations with singing are particularly strong, involving turtle, locust, ant, snake, alligator, frog, bee, insects, owl, hawk, falcon, or other birds.[340] These non-human dwellers include the "slitherings" which ("who") live close to the earth and have their own powerful songs. Though not treated in this chapter, they also include spider, toad, and other animals mentioned when the Mi'kmaw term was reviewed (Chapter 2). Mounds themselves serve as their holy homes, nests, shells, dens, wombs, tubes, ducts, and tunnels. As such, they are stable havens, where people were protected within the coils of the mound, sheltered in its embrace, whether living atop or buried inside.

Some mounds also harbor the remains of the honored dead, variously as cremains (cremations), bone bundles, and full skeletons. The use of fire inside these mounds evokes both the domed homes of many regions, as well as the pit oven for cooking. To help understand the role of cremation, in particular, a number of comparisons will be made to Native California practices, especially the Cry ceremony. The aim is not to suggest direct analogies across all these far regions, but rather to consider the range of possible variations as attested by natives themselves – not by outsider theorists.[341] Too often, ethnographic analogies are based in suburban America, rather than native life and thought. Comparisons of activities across Native America, throughout this book, are assumed to have greater insight as "best cases" than models drawn from other continents or proposed by academic fads.[342] Indeed, Oregon "Klamath believed that the ashes of the dead revivified the soil" so strongly that a purifying doctrine of the 1870 Ghost Dance was "whites were to burn up and disappear without even leaving ashes".[343]

---

[340] Each species has its own song, some more powerful than others, as with frogs who are often believed to sing forth Spring weather. Song provided by a Turtle spirit offers special protection, like its carapace. Species not only have songs of their own, but their spirit bosses can confer songs on worthy humans. In a Creek story, a turtle was given a song to heal its smashed shell.

[341] Jay Miller, Ashes Ethereal: Cremation in the Americas 2001a.

[342] See Introduction, Note 32, on Eurobias, mound monopoly by archaeologists, and the false comfort of a static world.

[343] Cora Du Bois, The 1870 Ghost Dance 2007: 23, 337, # 22, quoting Leslie Spier.

Denizens

Hollow / Hallow

Some human communities also lived in homes that seemed to be inside the earth and set into hills.[344] The "kiva" of the Southwest developed out of a pithouse dug into the ground and covered over by a stacked-timber dome holding up a flat-topped roof. Central California tribes used a "warm house" for religious gatherings, as well as meetings. There, inside the very first one, Yuki believe humans were sung into life from sticks that were arranged on the floor. The huge, sod-covered "earthlodge" of the Plains sheltered several families, as well as their favorite horses in later times. The Plateau dwelling (pithouse = s?istn) was dug deep into the earth for warmth and domed over with soil. The "hothouse" of the Southeast ranged between two sizes, smaller for a winter family home and larger as a community council house. In addition to these domed, roundish forms, squarish semisubterranean houses covered over with dirt were used by Alaskan Eskimos as a men's club and by Quechans ~ Yumas of the Colorado River for wealthy families.

Harold Driver[345] noticed that such homes often had tunnel entrances, strongly suggesting an Arctic origin, as a cold-trap adaptation against frigid conditions. He also observed that this form of an earth-covered dome was shared by the sweatlodge, spread across the Americas and Scandinavia, as well as deeply embedded in native beliefs.[346]

In all, natives would have been very familiar with domed shelters serving as sweatlodges, which cleansed and purified with steam vapor and songs, working from the inside of the body outward to produce sweat. They were as much clinic as oven. Mudlodges and other enlarged homes throughout Americas provided roofs used for a variety of activities, from working outside in the sunshine to watching rituals and the night sky. Their inside provided warmth, shelter, and storage.

Louisiana Choctaw

Among those who stayed behind in the southern section of their homeland,[347] creation epics combined mound, birth canal, humans, grasshoppers (locusts), ants, and

---

[344] Harold Driver, <u>Indians of North America</u> 1965: 112, 114,119, 126.

[345] Driver, <u>Indians of North America</u> 1965: 126, 128-130.

[346] Ivan Alexis Lopatin, Origin Of The Native American Steam Bath 1960; Moreover, some mounds are built over existing buildings, such as an original stone sweathouse, See Frank Seltzer and Jesse Jennings, <u>Peachtree Mound and Village Site</u>, Cherokee County, North Carolina 1941: 24. The flint nodules shown, however, would have burst under heat and so were not likely to be sweatlodge stones.

[347] Of particular note in terms of tribal unity, a Choctaw priesthood (*Unkala*) centered at the temple in the ancient town called *Taska-tchuka* ~ Warriors House on the banks of Cushtusha Creek in Neshoba ~ Wolf County, Mississippi. Chanting in a special language, *Unkala* once led funeral processions to that temple after *Iksa Anumpule* ~ clan speakers prepared

deity to convey a sense of common if threatened kinship among beings who emerged from an underworld. A fascinating subtext warns of the dangers of completely centralized communal effort. Here is a summary account.

> Soon after he made the earth, the creator formed yellow clay into humans and grasshoppers deep inside a cavern. These came through a long passageway to emerge at the top of a high hill or mound named *Nane chaba*. From there, they scattered in all directions. This upward movement continued from beneath the earth until waiting humans killed the mother of all the grasshoppers. No more were born, yet, up on the earth, humans inadvertently still trampled many grasshoppers to death. Alarmed that they would all be outnumbered and killed off by the ever-emerging humans, they prayed to the creator, who blocked off the passage. He changed the remaining underground humans into ants so they can still "come forth from holes in the ground" but not overwhelm other species.[348]

These yellow grasshoppers have only a single mother, unlike more viable humans. Given their size, they were ineffective when trying to pool their defenses until saved by divine intervention. As industrious, communal earth-dwellers, ants serve as the model for tribal life, as among Southwestern Pueblos, particularly Zuni. Grasshoppers are equally numerous, sharing a plant diet with farmers, along with an all-mother in keeping with Southeastern matrilineal traditions. As yellowish locusts, moreover, their song is quite distinctive.

Birds

In a fictionalized overview of Mississippian theology, the high priest of Coosa centered his lecture on birds (fellow bipeds) with symbolic import – "The world of birds mirrors the world of men",[349] animated by song. Subsuming all considerations, however, was gender because "Woman is to man as the sun is to the moon, as corn is to venison, as red is to white, as disorder is to order, as the Underworld is to the Upperworld; even as **snake** is to falcon". Left and right are also associated with female and male. Mortal humans must circle to the right (counterclockwise) in their dances, showing their left side towards the central fire, as well as during other activities, because the ever-jealous Sun turns herself toward the left (clockwise). Only the Sun chief, himself her child, can circle to the left.

---

the bones of great warriors for burial therein. See John FH Claiborne, Mississippi 1880 I: 518, quoted in Albert Gatschet, A Migration Legend of the Creek Indians 1884 I: 37, 105-6.

[348] David Bushnell, Myths of the Louisiana Choctaw 1910: 526-535, 526; Cf. Bushnell, The Choctaw of Bayou Lacomb 1909.

[349] Charles Hudson, Conversations with the High Priest of Coosa, Lamar Archaeology 1990: 222-30. It was later expanded into book form with the same title in 2003.

Birds provide character and attributes. The peregrine *falcon* is the warrior of swift attack. *Woodpeckers*, red-bellied or ivory-billed, are bold and aggressive. Their pounding on trees, deep in the eerie forest, evokes the pounding of war clubs. *Turkey* struts and puffs up to intimidate, wearing a scalp at the wattle. *Kingfishers* are multitalented. They fly, hunt in water, and nest, not in trees, but in a burrow in the face of a steep bank. By diving into water, it can thwart a falcon attack and stay alive. *Crows* are deceiving but humorous. The horned *owl* of the night is a familiar of witches and others intent on harm. *Redbird* is a favorite of the Sun because of its bright coloring and is treated like a daughter. *Martins* fly south at the time of the Busk because they do not like to see people ritually scratched. Allied with the orderly Upperworld, birds and their nests protect their eggs and fledglings as mound and temple guard the treasures of the past and future. As singing bipeds, they share vital characteristics with humans.

Great Lakes HoChungara (Winnebago)

Among nations of the Midwest, the traditions of the Ho-chunk (called Winnebago by neighboring Algonkians), whose homeland was Wisconsin, shed further light on the mystery of snakes, turmoil, and the earth.[350] Centuries before, Effigy Mounds[351] across the driftless region of southern Wisconsin were probably built by their ancestors among the Chiwere Siouans.[352] Their sacred epic describing creation by Earthmaker was once fully known (told and sung) only by initiates inside of the Medicine or Mystic Lodge, both a building and a guild membership.[353] Its initiation of new members enacted this creation of the world, again retelling it during memorials for deceased members.[354]

---

[350] Ho-chunk are particularly well known, thanks to the 1908-1913 research, followed by lifelong publications (see all) by Paul Radin (1883-1959).

[351] William Hurley, An Analysis of Effigy Mound Complexes in Wisconsin 1975.

[352] Martha Royce Blaine, The Ioway Indians 1979; William Whitman, The Oto 1937.

[353] Through amazing circumstances, Jasper Blowsnake, who lived among the half of the tribe forced to Nebraska, described this "Mystic Lodge" after his conversion to the peyote religion, brought to the Ho-chunk by John Rave. In their zeal to convert others, three old men were convinced to give Paul Radin an account of Ho-chunk creation, though they had to leave Nebraska before doing so to avoid revenge from local spirits.

Thus, across the Mississippi River, in the top floor of a small hotel in Sioux City, Iowa, precisely at midnight, these men began the saga and finished it five hours later. By the next afternoon, every Ho-chunk knew what had happened and many pressed for a public reading of the text. Previously, only elite members of the lodge knew its details. Bowing to this pressure, the native text was soon read to a stunned audience. Much anger focused on the old men, but John Rave gave them firm support until Radin left for New York with the untranslated text.

Four other mythic cycles followed creation, with various protagonists engaged in complex activities to make the world as it is today. Paul Radin, their recorder, saw these different cycles of Trickster, Hare, Red Horn, and Twins as a temporal series defining the psychological growth of the individual and tribe, each gaining and giving character virtues to those who came after.

Trickster lived during a primordial, unformed cosmos of vaporous (shimmering) beings. Many of his traits were (or foreshadowed) human ones, often in the negative, but his total being was never specified. From the beginning, although he is a chief, all of his actions were contrary to modern ideals. Some of his adventures were prophetic, others were parodies, yet all contributed to an increasing orderliness in the world.

Hare (or Rabbit), born of a spirit father and human mother, was raised by his grandmother, the Earth. In his cycle, humans made their initial appearance. They gained advantages as he matured and learned about parts of his body through a series of misadventures. Through his actions, few of them laudatory, various customs and institutions began, such as the use of tobacco, slain bear thanking rituals, and menstruation observances, along with the special creation of the Medicine Rite. By means of initiation into this guild, members became immortal. The image of and for this reincarnation, of especial note, was that of a **snake** shedding its skin.[355] Indeed, "skin-shedding" is the translation of the poetic phrase used in this rite to express immortality conferred through successive rebirths at guild initiations.

Red Horn was heroic, living in a well-differentiated world with a wide range of defined characters, including humans, monsters, and giants. A majestic figure, his death

---

Jasper Blowsnake, regarded as the most knowledgeable member of the Medicine Lodge, converted the next year. He agreed to recite the Ho-chunk words of the rite, though warning that someone would die from this forced telling. Radin wrote the text in longhand (this was before tape recorders), working six hours a day for two months, though these words did not have their ordinary meanings. As the recitation ended, Radin received a telegram that his own father was gravely ill, and died a few days later.

Jasper blamed himself, refused further work for several years, but finally decided that telling the Medicine Rite to Radin was indeed "his mission in life". For the first month, Jasper corrected the prior dictation, while the translation itself took six hours a day for another two and a half months. Lodge members remained bitter at Jasper for half a year, but the peyote believers extolled his courage for performing a dangerous and heroic act. His continued health also worked in his favor. Had he become ill, it would have been interpreted as spiritual retribution for revealing great secrets.

[354] This guild of shamans was like the Mide priests of the nearby Ojibwa who belonged to the Midewiwin (Grand Lodge, Shaman's Academy) of Great Lakes nations. It was recast about 1700 in the aftermath of severe depopulation and the demise of the elaborate Feasts of the Dead ("Kettle"), when ancestral bones were redeposited in a communal ossuary (Chapter 7).

[355] Paul Radin, The Road of Life and Death 1945: 112, 154, 264, 337n31.

was avenged by his sons, who revived him, then rid the earth of giants, and received war bundles from Thunderbirds as a reward. These gifts provided great benefit for humans, who came into their own during this cycle.[356]

Twins (Flesh and Stump) behaved as bravado juveniles, with a promise of new beginnings. Their contrasting temperaments caused trouble, until they learned a final lesson from Earthmaker that curbed their unbridled enthusiasms. After killing one of the four animals (anchoring upright snakes, Chapter 1) holding up the earth, they were terrorized by a giant Turkey to learn fear. Thus, the twins benefited from prior characters to mature as fully formed individuals. Since they had at least one adventure with Red Horn, they were doubly tied into the Hochungara mythic past.

By the end of all these cycles, this world included four underworlds – led from bottom to top, by Turtle, Trickster, Earthmaker, and Rabbit – and a sky supported by four island weights. These anchors ("island quiet makers") are located at its corners, including one near Effigy Mounds National Park, along the Iowa shore of the Mississippi. There, in addition to a collapsed Longtail mural on a cliff face and piled earthen mounds in the shape of lines and dots, a row of heaped hummocks in the shape of side-view bears and stretched-wing birds march up the hillside.

Pawnee

The association of earth lodges with mounded hills has already been noted (Chapter 7) for the northern Plains, but, as expected, Pawnee move earth as well as revere their natural landscape and its features. At the Four Pole Rite held to mark spring planting, priests use a compass of string with a pointed stick at each end to trace a circle on the ground, along with a 3-foot round fireplace in the center. A low embankment was built over the big circle, and the dirt from digging out the fireplace was placed as a mound outside its east entrance, "four holes about a foot deep [were dug] in the semicardinal [diagonal] positions within the circle to receive the posts that would be planted later. All around the inside of the circular embankment saplings were set up in the ground, forming a screen that shaded the participants as they sat during the ceremony".[357]

Moreover, Pawnee cosmology also dramatizes enormous snake imagery. The culmination of the ritual year of the animal guilds was a grand Medicine display variously known as the 20 Day, 30 Day, Grand Magic, or Big Doctoring.[358]   In

---

[356]   Red Horn and others are featured in the wall paintings of a rock shelter in Wisconsin, see Robert Salzer and Grace Rajnovich, The Gottscall Rockshelter: An Archaeological Mystery 2001.

[357]   Gene Weltfish, The Lost Universe, Pawnee Life and Culture 1965: 259.

[358]   James Murie, a Skiri band Pawnee who was sent off to government boarding school in Pennsylvania, used his education to record and preserve the traditions and language of his people. He worked closely with several early anthropologists and oversaw the set of dioramas featuring major Pawnee ceremonies on display for a century at the Field Museum in Chicago, but now in storage.

preparation, a huge lodge was vacated by its residents and several imposing figures were constructed.[359]

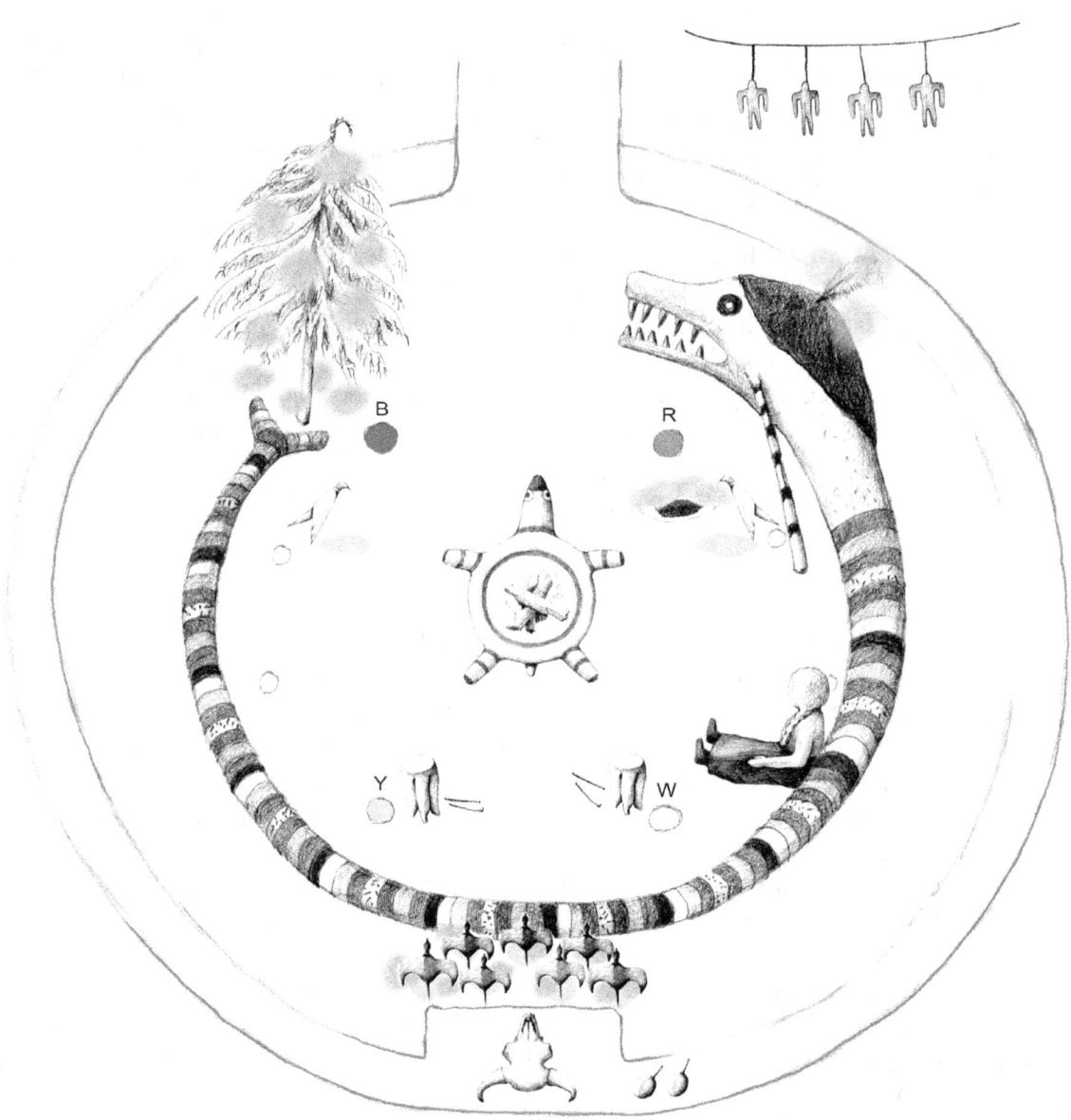

On the crown of the [serpent's] head is a large erect plume of down feathers [its body] is formed of bowed willows, plastered over with mud. The tail is at the north side of the door and is forked like that of a fish.... A tree was cut and brought in with a ceremony almost identical with that found in the sun dances of other tribes. The Skiri ~ Skidi plant the tree (a cedar) in the forked tail of the monster, the others put it (a cottonwood) at the altar. A life-sized woman is

---

[359] Weltfish, The Lost Universe 1965: 174.

built on a clay-covered frame, dressed in regular costume, and set up [seated] on the south side of the lodge. A large figure of a man is cut from rawhide and placed [hung] upon a pole above the lodge. Numerous small human figures are cut from rawhide, strung upon cords and stretched about overhead in the lodge. All these objects are highly symbolic: thus, the fire is the sun; the mud woman, the moon; the large rawhide image, the morning star; the many small images, stars.

At the end the animal powers and images are taken down and carried to a stream or lake. Here they are heaped up in the water something like a beaver's house and the mud woman placed on top.[360]

Separate compartments were built along the sides of the lodge for each guild. In 1867, these booths were occupied, on the south half, by Deer led by Old Bull, Black-tailed Deer led by Old Lady Tsitawa, Buffalo led by Wonderful Old Bull, and another Buffalo led by Leading Buffalo. On the north side were the booths of Bear led by Sitting Hawk and Angry Horse, of Coyote, of Fishhawk, and of Eagle.[361]

Epic

According to its founding epic, one night a Pawnee man dreamed that a giant serpent arose from a river and spoke to him. When he awoke, he set off to find this place. Going east, he saw it along the Wonderful River (Missouri). As he stood on the bank, the same being arose. Its head had hairs and feelers of many colors. Without speaking, it dove down, and the man jumped in after it. At the bottom, he entered a huge lodge where animals sat around the sides [both described in text and once depicted in a diorama at the Field Museum in Chicago].

The fireplace was a turtle. Near the east door were two ponds, with two big geese [mallards in the diorama] nearby. A woman sat on the west side. At the west altar were an owl and a beaver. Beside the altar were loons [geese in the diorama] who flapped their wings to make a noise that reminds the deities of their promise to help humans. The water serpent, resting on the south, spoke for all the other animals. One by one, each instructed the man in its own mysteries, as had been ordained by the Creator Tirawahat ("heavenly expanse").

After he returned home, this man built an identical lodge of willows and lived inside it. Each night, the serpent came in dreams with further instructions and songs. He made a curved model of its long body inside the lodge, and was taught how to catch eagles from inside a pit trap and to use these feathers as a plume on its head.

---

[360] James Murie, Pawnee Indian Societies 1914: 602-3. Clark Wissler, the volume editor, provided a footnote (#1) recalling that Blackfoot, Dakota, Arikara, Hidatsa, and Mandan ritually disposed of tipis painted with animal images by submerging them, Cf. James Murie, Ceremonies of the Pawnee 1981: 167-176.

[361] Weltfish, The Lost Universe 1965: 331.

In time, the man was sent to an island in the Platte River (near Fremont, Nebraska), where sparks rising above it. Nearby fish seemed to have fire in their mouths. He heard singing and drumming. Drowsy, he went to sleep and awoke inside the animal lodge that was within the island. He saw beaver, owl, otter, ermine, bear, bison, wolf, cougar, wildcat, and many birds. Over many days, each taught him its mystery. Then a deer took him to dry land, and onto a hill where a place had been prepared to set up a duplicate medicine building. This was the first lodge to be on land.

On this special hilltop, animals had stripped off the grass; badgers had dug out postholes; beavers had cut, peeled, and trimmed trees; and bears and cougars had carried them up. In other words, each had fulfilled an assigned task knowing that it contributed to the entire finished building. Everything inside the underwater medicine lodge was duplicated on the hilltop. Then the man went home to Pumpkin Vine Village to invite the chiefs, who agreed to move everyone to settle around the new lodge. Before they left, the man's earlier lodge was taken apart and reassembled in the river [as an offering].

Every night, animals took the man around the country, teaching him herbs, plants, and cures. When he was ready, he invited a few men to join him, teaching them to become doctors. When they went out, each wore a body coating of blue clay, and eagle down on the head. Two men became messengers, one wore a magpie skin and the other that of a muskrat, since these species served the animal doctors.

The new village was west of the lodge, which became their house model. Thereafter, a domed Skiri earth lodge had an entryway facing east, and a sacred area (called _waharu_ representing the garden of the Evening Star) on the west side. This altar, jutting out from the surrounding platform, held a bison skull facing the door. Any holy bundles owned by the householders hung overhead. Bed compartments, divided by willow screens, filled the north and south sides. Each bed consisted of piled layers of willow stick mats, rush mats, and tanned bison skins. Older children slept nearest the altar, then aunts and uncles, then the parents, and then the elderly nearest the entrance. When the bigger lodges hosted ceremonies, all of this bedding was removed from the platforms and the floor was cleared.

Rite

Skiri ceremonies were either public – devoted to the sky deities and tribal bundles under the direction of priests; or private – sponsored by doctoring guilds with earthly concerns. Such doctors, evoking animal helpers, wore a woolly bison robe, bear claw necklace, and beaver skin cap.[362] A bandoleer of strung beads or seeds, worn across the

---

[362] Beavers invoke mounds, probably because of their domed lodges. The most dramatic curing rite of the Comanche, nomadic Numic speakers from the Great Basin, is the Beaver Ceremony ("Big Doctoring") set inside a huge tipi with a tall cottonwood tree at the center, a fireplace to its east, and, to the north and south, two elongated "beaver ponds" full of water and edged with willows. Outside each pool was a tiny effigy mound shaped like a beaver facing westward. See Ernest Wallace and E Adamson Hoebel, The Comanches, Lords of the South Plains 1952: 175, 177, who suggest this unusually elaborated rite among pastoralists was inspired by Pawnees.

chest, had dangling amulets, such as the claws and tails of a wildcat, badger, bear. Other talismans included bear ears, tiny smoking pipes, or downy feathers. Another medical insignia, like the emblematic MD's black bag, was a bundle made of the whole tanned skin of the patron animal, holding roots, paints, white clay, deer tails, eagle bones and claws, human remains, and a bison maw stone, containing its soul. Such bags were passed down through males, either father to son or mentor to student.

All doctors, as members of different spirit animal lodges, possessed three abilities. As appropriate to their species patron, these were healing, slights of hand (theatrical magic) as tangible proof of abilities, and *pikawiu*,[363] a hypnotic-like control over a patient or victim. Derived from "right hand, rightwise", it could also be "thrown" or "shot" into an enemy, rendering him or her immobile until a more powerful doctor broke its "spell".

Cures involved the sucking out of some harmful item and taking prescribed medicines, made from roots and herbs, as teas or powders. The offending probe was sucked out and burned up in the fire. The doctor was gifted ("paid") with bison robes, parfleches (hide envelopes) filled with dried meat, sacks of corn, and braided mats formed of dried pumpkin strips.

During a yearly cycle, booth members gathered for rituals in the Winter, the Spring, and the first thunder of Summer. No *pikawiu*, however, was to be done at these three events. It was reserved only for the fourth one, the great doctoring held for several months in the Fall, when they all renewed their *puwahs*. Before each event, for four days, the doctor fasted, beside his or her bundle, away from the village. Then they bathed in the river and went into the lodge.

The Big Doctoring Diorama[364] of the Skiri, once displayed in the Field Museum, represents the doctors starting on one of their outer circuits of the lodge. Inside, the various figures are in place but not the separate booths, each occupied by the devotees of a patron animal species. It represents the second lodge of the epic, built on a hilltop with the help of the animal patrons. (A first lodge was built of willows by the founder, according to a vision he saw of the underwater lodge.)

Unlike the separate animal lodges which were joined by "paying" for an apprenticeship under a member, the Doctors Guild recruited by means of an audition or test of abilities so as to impress judges with some spectacular feat. Usually, these candidates were the most senior members of each animal lodge, who earned a place as adepts among their peers.

On the first morning of the Big Doctoring, participants cut willows and cottonwoods along the riverbanks, after one leader gave thanks to the Heavens and another thanked the Earth for their use. These branches were used to build the inner booths. Throughout that month, not only did the individual doctor booths vie with each other in shooting, fainting, and amazing, but they also contested as North versus South sides. Nightly displays were planned as four acts, such as making a duck made of mud come alive, locating a hidden horse tail, shooting an arrow into the chest of a young man,

---

[363] <u>Skiri Dictionary</u> (Parks and Pratt 2008: 260, 460) lists *piihkawi'u'* = right arm, right side, on right.

[364] Annual Ceremony of the Pawnee Medicine Men, Ralph Linton 1923: 1-20, based on notes by George Dorsey and James Murie.

and swallowing a whole deer head, complete with antlers.[365] Another reported feat involved cutting open the belly of a volunteer, eating part of his liver, and then making him whole again. The aim was to be as impressive as possible.

The second day, they built the serpent, each doctor performing a separate task toward finishing the whole body. The sixty-foot, curved framework was made of ashwood (willow?) boughs lashed together with sinews, covered by grass bundles tied on to overlap and by a mud-coating that was smoothed out and painted in repeated bands of seven colors = blue, orange, green, brown, white, yellow, red.[366] One special bull hide, dyed black, covered the top of the head, with a downy eagle plume standing in its center. (During the spring hunt, two bows and four arrows were crafted and dedicated for selected doctors to use to kill four bison, two pairs of a male bull and female cow, consecrated to this use.) Pointed ashwood stakes filled the inside of the huge mouth like sharp fangs. Stretching backwards from this opening were feelers (like those of catfish) made of long, painted, willow rods. The end of the tail was forked, like a fish, to indicate its aquatic abode.

On the third day, the turtle fireplace (Sun) and the woman (Moon) were made. A deep hole was dug out, then a turtle-shaped rim was modeled of clay. The seated woman was formed of a willow framework that was then covered in bundled grass and plastered over with mud. The face was carefully molded, and the eyes set with pumpkin seeds having black dots burned into the centers as pupils. The scalp of one of the bison cow hides was attached to the top of her head, then two braids of human hair were fastened to its sides, each hanging down to her knees. The full cow hide served as her dress. When these figures were finished, the doctors divided up, some taking *puwah* from the male and some from the female. Indeed, the oppositions of man/woman, land/water, sky/earth, and others pervade all of Pawnee culture and its rituals.

The fourth day, the cedar tree was cut down. The men formed a circle around it, prayed, gave it robes and other presents, and transferred its life elsewhere. Only then did they cut it down, using *pikawiu* on each other as it fell. Singing, they carried it back to the lodge. Outside the village, they were met by another group of doctors, who tried to drive them back with *pikawiu*. Eventually those carrying the tree won out. At the edge of the village, the tree was put down. Villagers threw offerings to it, and went home. All of these gifts reverted to the doctors, who finished their trek. Inside the lodge, the tree was set in a hole prepared between the forks of the serpent tail, then covered over with white eagle down.

Toward the end of these preparations, the loon [geese] skins with their wings pegged open were set up along the west side. The space between them (as ponds) was sprinkled with water and then a layer of downy feathers, which stuck. The leader of the lodge looked up, told Sky Father that the (messenger) loons were in place, and loudly prayed for rain. Then he looked down, and, in a whisper, told Earth Mother the same, praying for a good harvest. Next he went outside to ask everything in the universe to empower the loons and, thereby, allow them to vitalize humans.

---

[365] Weltfish, The Lost Universe 1965: 358, 362.

[366] This seven-color sequence duplicates that on each of the eight support poles holding up the roof of the lodge. The (clear) gap between each series may represent the eighth post.

That night, the images of the star and sky deities were cut from the other pair of special hides. The Morning Star (father) figure was cut out from the bull hide, and the nine humanoid images of the other heavenly deities, including the Evening Star (mother), were cut from the other cowhide. Just before its namesake rose, the Morning Star figure was hung from the end of a long pole sticking far above the smokehole. The other nine figures were hung at the tops of the four main posts or from a cord drooping across the under-roof of the lodge.

The following (fifth) dawn, the doctors, dressed as their animal patrons, marched, in order of their abilities, around the outside and then into the lodge. After four such circuits, they came inside to sit down for a feast. That night, in procession, they visited every lodge owning a sacred bundle and danced for it. Upon their return, certain doctors were sent back to revisit every lodge and diagnose those who were sick. When they returned, other doctors with patrons appropriate to cure that particular illness were sent to each patient.

The sixth morning women were asked to gather firewood. After they delivered their loads, they were feasted and told of mysteries. That afternoon, the doctors marched four times through the village, dressed as their patron animals and performing magic, often swallowing long rods. That night they built a bonfire inside the turtle and invited the public to see *pikawiu*. Such grand displays recurred every night for a few months.

Outdoor events featured "clowns" (known as *kitsahuruksu*) who were heavily-mud-plastered men acting as people who survived scalping. These actual "scalped" victims led a terrifying existence because they were regarded as dead though remaining among the living.[367] The "clowns" wore bizarre masks made of cornhusks, rawhide, wood, or feathers. Their antics were both funny and mocking, blending necessary humor with somber seriousness. Life was a mix of emotions, and so were rituals.

A new doctor was initiated during the Fall rite. In preparation, his family had assembled many gifts to be taken into the lodge to secure a mentor. He went up to the chosen doctor, blessing and soothing that man with his own raised hands. Then he pleaded that he was a poor man who wanted to learn mysteries, giving the adept all of the assembled gifts, along with a filled pipe ready to smoke. If the candidate were accepted, the doctor took the pipe and led him into his booth. The man's wife also "slept" with the mentor to learn mysteries, which were usually engendered in pairs.

On the final day of the doctoring, each man again dressed in a manner appropriate to his own animal patron. The sides faced off as Bears of the North or clownish Buffalos (Bison) of the South, feuding ~jostling their way to the end. The Buffalo clowns wore war gear that was made of cornhusks, humorous because it was so flimsy and incongruous that it would have been useless in any real battle. The Bears wore crowns of cedar boughs. The constructed figures served as dramatic props in this finale. One Bison engaged in conversations and byplay with the huge seated woman (Moon). Later, to avoid a Bear attack, a Buffalo rushed into the mouth of the serpent, breaking all of its teeth. By the end, the Buffalos had made the Bears as harmless as puppies.[368]

Then they all marched once around the outside of the lodge, led by two men each carrying a spread-out loon skin from the altar. They returned inside to crowd around the

---

[367] Weltfish, <u>The Lost Universe</u> 1965: 370-372.

[368] Weltfish, <u>The Lost Universe</u> 1965: 376-8.

fireplace, stamping their feet to awaken the turtle. After marching outside again and shooting their *pikawiu*, they rushed inside – singing, shouting animal cries, and, in all, making such a great commotion that ashes flew up through the smokehole.[369] Finally, exhausted, they rested until night.

After dark, they again used *pikawiu* inside, shooting talismans into each other so that doctors were collapsing onto the floor until 2 a.m., while other villagers looked on in awe. Finally, they adjourned and took the booths apart. While still shooting at each other, they carried the pieces into the river, along with the whole serpent and woman figures, arranging them as they had stood in the lodge. Just before the image of the woman was put in, a devout woman took off all her clothes and jewelry to place them with the image. In Skiri belief, the entire setup was next used by creatures of the water for their own Big Doctoring.

Back in the lodge, the doctors smoked for their animal patrons and sprinkled water all over the floor, to release any lingering forces by evaporation. After a last feast, the members dispersed to their own homes. Two of the main leaders stayed behind to take down the west altar and bundle up its contents. Finally, the resident families returned to resume ordinary life in the lodge until the next seasonal rite.

During their long Fall meeting, therefore, they challenged, "attacked", and competed against each other to highlight their own abilities and those of their guild. The earth's own tumult was portrayed during this Big Doctoring by the model of a huge water serpent; antics of men portraying scalped clowns; the stamping, shouting, and noisy feats of the doctors; and, particularly, their mystic combat among themselves, taking turns feigning deaths and revivals throughout. Of note, while ordinary Pawnees called this Fall gathering the "big doctoring" or "grand show", the doctors themselves referred to it as "true doctoring", because it gave form and substance to their vital powers inside a large house that looked like a hollow mound.[370]

Burning to Interlayer Parallel Worlds

As recalled by the ash plume during these final acts, an ancient and recurrent feature of the archaeological record is the incinerating and covering over of building remains by one or more layers of soil, renewed and repeated periodically, as a burial, memorial, or commemoration of and at that place.

[371] By this means, a special place was repeatedly reoccupied at increasingly higher elevations.

In Vernon Knight's masterful summary of Southeastern mound archaeology (Chapter 3), the layering impulse is traced to the covering up [and sending off] of offerings. Over time, one of these mounds rose to visually dominate the site, and

---

[369] This is an ethnographic parallel to the prehistoric burning of a Caddo temple on a mound.

[370] Douglas Parks and Waldo Wedel, Pawnee Geography 1985: 166.

[371] Cyrus Thomas, Report On The Mound Explorations of the Bureau of Ethnology 1985: 207, 561, 568, 664. [1894]

eventually become paired with another across the plaza. Such construction intervals occurred about every twenty-five years, and alternating colors served to highlight contrasts in mound fill and overmantles, making the sealing off of a prior surface both assured and obvious.[372] As noted, this thorough enveloping assured that the integrity of the mound would be maintained by the internal pressure of the compressed songs it held. Such human effort deliberately set places and events onto parallel other-world orbits and kept them there, either by cremating them or by burying them under an earth seal while continuing to make them useful and energizing in the human world. The Creeks systematically burned [to cleanse and purify] discarded personal clothing, utensils, and building materials, and cyclically burned up used-up fields and structures so that new, shared cycles of vitality would begin.[373]

Of particular concern was the manner of signaling so that this transfer could be done safely. Giving thanks and showing respect serve to obligate immortals to mortals, who exist in separate parallel worlds – except for moments of crux, approach, or overlap during rituals when their intervening barrier becomes "thin". At the Yuchi Green Corn of today, men never step across benches in the arbors so as not to jostle or displace visiting ancestors sitting there invisibly but observant. Before their Bead and Ribbon Dances, deceased kin and others were invited into the square by throwing beads into the air.[374]

In the past, the huge plume arising from a smoldering temple would be even more obvious as a visible axis mundi linking layers. Sent high into the air, its whiteness would be seen by "witnesses" such as birds acting as messengers between these worlds, as well as immortals themselves. The effect was to let them know that bulk ~ body was being transmitted into their own world, and thus avoid possible harm and irritation during the displacement. Since qualities, times, and conditions were usually reversed between these parallel worlds, the burnt building would be whole in its new abode, while any mortal remains took active human form. Similarly, broken pots became whole, and burnt offerings appeared intact. Noises reversed such that whispers became shouts, yawns became speech, and yells became caresses. The pan-being values of sharing and respect were upheld, in public, cosmic, and obvious ways.

An overlooked aspect of this reversal, moreover, may have been that the multiple layers formed by successive rebuilding of the temple at that location fused into a single building representing the ideal form that had been renewed at each relayering. Understanding these public, ritual acts requires a grasp of native cosmology and needful pan-being reciprocity and respect between parallel orbits or existences. Most easily passing between them are songs, prayers, offerings, blessings, and "witnesses" such as emblematic birds, snakes, tobacco, and fire. Thus, burning down temples served both to fuel the mound and transmute them beyond mortal time and space, as cremation did for bodies.

---

[372] Vernon James Knight, Ceremonialism Until 1500, Southeast Volume 14: 734-741 2004.

[373] Jean Hill Chaudhuri and Joyotpaul Chaudhuri, A Sacred Path - The Way of the Muscogee Creeks 2001: 114.

[374] Jason Jackson, Yuchi Ceremonial Life 2003: 254.

Cremation

Across the breadth of the Americas, cremation had many expressions, including final ingestion. In South America, cremated remains (cremains) were added to a drink because it is "better to be inside a warm friend than inside the cold earth". In most places, burning was a means of making the dead transportable, and sending bodies quickly and cleanly into the afterworld. It was a supremely cultural act that avoided the unpleasant consequences of natural decomposition. In the Northwest, the Hamatsa of the Kwakwaka'wakw and the Xgyet of the Tsimshian are metaphors for chiefly consumption of the possessions of their followers in order to enhance the prestige of their noble house by giving generously to others, both living and dead. Incidentally, the name of the patron of this consumption (consumer, cannibal) cult among the Kwakiutlans has now been carefully translated to mean an increasing perfection into the human state because "you are what you eat".[375]

Adena

Paleo-Indian cremations, dated at over 9000 BP, have been found in Washington (Marmes site) and Wisconsin (Ranier). Given the mobility of these hunters, such burning of the remains shows care by their loved ones immediately after death. The only human remains found at Poverty Point are also a cremation, from the Late Archaic. In the Woodland era, cremation was one of the features of Adena, though inhumations also occurred. After a careful study of such cremains, Raymond Baby concluded,[376]

> The deceased was removed to a sacred structure or "fenced" area and the body dismembered. The torso and disarticulated segments [head, legs] were then placed in a clay basin and cremated. Interment of the calcined remains was made on the floor of the structure and enclosed by small stone or log tombs.

Earth was piled over these to form a series of mounds, that grew incrementally like that at Cresap (Chapter 4), until they were sealed off by a clay capping. Of note, the torso was burned as a unit, releasing its breath and songs directly into the fire, a cosmic nexus.

Lingits (Tlingits)

In the cool, rainy northern Pacific coast, the matrilineal Tsimshian, Haida, and Lingit once cremated virtually all of their honored dead. This was believed to accord them a place by a warm fire in the afterlife. It also hastened the removal of the bodily remains, and facilitated the transfer of hereditary name-titles to living successors.

---

[375] Susanne Hilton and John Rath, Objections to Franz Boas's referring to eating people in the translation of the Kwakwala terms *baXwbakwalnuXwsiwe* and *hamats!a* 1983: 98-106.

[376] Raymond Baby, Hopewell Cremation Practices 1954: 7.

Among Ḻingits, a person is conceived to be composed of layers from a vitalizing "mind" located in the heart at the center of the body, then outward to bones, flesh, and outer skin, along with spirits or souls. The most ideal person was said to be dry, hard, and heavy – best represented by a humane and moral member of the nobility who dispensed cultural expertise in return for labor, food, and help provided by others.

The great if tragic irony of a successful Ḻlingit life, however, was that a noble reached his or her apex just after death, particularly after cremation produced all the ideal attributes. He or she was transmogrified into "heat, light, smoke, charcoal, and ashes" as fire consumed one life in order to rekindle another.[377] Timing was crucial. A slave slated to accompany the deceased had to be killed in such a way as to duplicate the manner of the deceased's own death, such as by drowning or accident, before their bodies were cremated together. A slave could escape this fate, however, by hiding out until the funeral was over and the crucial moment had passed.[378]

People and events at the funeral represented the seen for the unseen. The handling of the body reflected the fate of its soul(s). Ḻlingit society was divided between matri-moieites of Raven and Eagle (~ Wolf). When a Raven noble died, her kin and house went into deep mourning while Eagles of the other side washed and prepared the body for cremation, conducting all the necessary rites with great care. At Forty Days, the mourning Raven moiety hosted the Eagle other side, signaling the safe release of a soul. Later, the Raven mourners generously thanked the Eagles for all their efforts. Generally, throughout the funeral, the Ravens represented the inner aspects of the deceased person, and the Eagles the outer ones. In addition, members of the father's Eagle matriline and house in the other moiety had the added responsibility of specifically representing the dead in the afterworld. This double "otherness" made the dead that much more real during ritual.[379]

When a Ḻlingit body reclined on the pyre, the soul spirit more easily arose to travel in stages from the cemetery,[380] into the forest, and up a mountainside where it entered the second land of the dead to take up residence in its ancestral house. According to an explicit statement, those who had been cremated gained the virtue of staying near the fire,[381] warmed and ready to receive offerings sent by the living through mortal fires.[382] "In the house of the spirits the essences of the food, clothing, and other objects

---

[377] Sergei Kan, Symbolic Immortality 1989: 114; Jay Miller, Tsimshian Culture 1997: 44.

[378] Kan, Symbolic Immortality 1989: 136.

[379] Kan, Symbolic Immortality 1989: 126, 136, 153.

[380] Kan, Symbolic Immortality 1989: 127.

[381] Kan, Symbolic Immortality 1989: 112.

[382] Of considerable note, this custom was reported in the first detailed, balanced, and coherent Americanist ethnography (written by clergy at that), Rev. Ivan Veniaminov, Notes on the Islands of the Unalaska District 1984: 398, first published in 1840 to describe and compare Aleuts and Indians (Kolosh), particularly Ḻlingits.

burned by the living descended through the smokehole upon the spirits sitting around this ancestral fireplace".[383]

Indeed, the Llingit word-root _gaan_ is compounded into words meaning "burn ~ cremate ~ shine".[384] "Located in the center of the house, which itself was the center of the human-occupied space, the fire was firmly associated with humanity and social life and was opposed to the peripheral domains of the rain-soaked forest and the sea."[385] The bodies of shamans and battle-slain warriors were not cremated. Shamans instead were encased and left on some lonely rocky point to become the object of questing for shamanic power, especially by a nephew (ZS, sister's son). Warriors killed in battle went into the sky to join the Northern Lights, where their life was spartan but well attended by slaves and enemies they had slain.[386]

A year after the awkward body had been burned, it was replaced by a monumental pole (tube) or other great artwork. A mortuary potlatch was held to install a successor to the same name, persona, and position as the deceased. Thereby, ritual served to continue society and confirmed its eternal character as yet another person was given to a name so that, as nearby Gitksan say, "only the skin changes". Yet such transfer also involves an element of personal "will" since one Gitksan grandmother who felt neglected by her family threatened to be reincarnated outside of her matriline and, when really piqued, into some undeserving Anglo baby.[387]

California

Cremation was ~ is characteristic of native southern California. The best regional overview of ethnographic practices remains Kroeber's 1925 monumental Handbook of the Indians of California.[388] Throughout California, the usual reason given for cremation or partial cremation was ease in transporting back home someone who had died at some distance because "All California Indians have strong sentiments on this point; old people will express satisfaction at the prospect of being buried adjacent to the house in which they were born".[389] Nearby, Tohono O'odam (Papago) of southern Arizona add that cremating a body killed in battle also prevented its use in sorcery by enemies, who had some control over it by virtue of taking its life.[390]

---

[383] Kan, Symbolic Immortality 1989: 113.

[384] Kan, Symbolic Immortality 1989: 112.

[385] Kan, Symbolic Immortality 1989: 112.

[386] Kan, Symbolic Immortality 1989: 120-121.

[387] John Adams, The Gitksan Potlatch: Population Flux, Resource Ownership, and Reciprocity 1973: 32.

[388] The quick-fix 1978 California Handbook 8 has many flaws, though it does provide current tribal ethnonyms, as well as a useful index entry for "recremation" under death practices of Lake Miwok and Pomo, Robert Heizer, ed., California 1978: 268, 776, 297.

[389] Alfred Kroeber, Handbook of the Indians of California 1925: 499.

[390] Ruth Underhill, Social Organization of the Papago Indians 1939: 190.

In northeastern California, Modoc cremated their dead at one of the spots associated with a patriline,[391] with everyone but shamans attending. Possessions and beads were placed on the pyre, but these goods, along with any slaves intended for immolation, could be appropriated by anyone present in return for due compensation.[392] Mourners and others sat during the burning, apparently to avoid interfering with the rising smoke. Later, the house was burned down if the deceased had been such emotionally close kin as a child or a spouse because of a "desire to eliminate any reminder of the dead person, and thus to ease mourning".[393]

Pomo

In central California, "The Pomo were opposed to burial because they believed that the ghost of the dead person would continue to haunt the spot",[394] so they cremated – along with beads, robes, and baskets – on a pyre set in a trench, with the body face down, head to the south, allowing the spirit to more easily lift itself to journey to the afterworld.[395] Of note,[396] for Pomos, the essence of a person – variously called breath, soul, or knowledge – was contained in the heart (_kam_). During the burning, mourners were so distraught in grief that family friends had to keep a careful tally for them of all gifts and offerings, such as beads, so these lamenting hosts could later be able to give proper thanks to donors.[397]

The close male relative who used a long pole to keep the body in densest flames became polluted for a few years afterwards and was forbidden meat, hunting, and gambling to emphasize this too-close association with human meat and the seriousness of the duty, in contrast to the levity expected while playing games of chance.[398]

All possessions were burned so as not to lure back the ghost with the potential of harming the living, even inadvertently.[399] The next day, a close male (F, S) gathered up the cooled cremains, put them in a basket, buried it nearby, and then obliterated any evidence of the pyre.[400] Mourning continued for a year, with women visiting the deceased's favorite haunts to sing and sprinkle acorn meal (_pinole_).

A year later at a rite called _Lonewis_, the cremains were dug up and reburned along with donated gifts, in a version (below) of the famous Californian "Cry" that Pomo

---

[391] Verne Ray, <u>Primitive Pragmatists</u>, The Modoc Indians of Northern California 1963: 113.

[392] Ray, <u>Primitive Pragmatists</u> 1963: 116.

[393] Ray, <u>Primitive Pragmatists</u> 1963: 119.

[394] Edwin Loeb, <u>Pomo Folkways</u> 1926: 290.

[395] Loeb, <u>Pomo Folkways</u> 1926: 287.

[396] Loeb, <u>Pomo Folkways</u> 1926: 290, 296.

[397] Loeb, <u>Pomo Folkways</u> 1926: 286.

[398] Loeb, <u>Pomo Folkways</u> 1926: 292.

[399] Loeb, <u>Pomo Folkways</u> 1926: 291.

[400] Loeb, <u>Pomo Folkways</u> 1926: 289.

shared with the Maidu.[401] Even after the Pomo began burying, they burned offerings for the dead upon the grave for a year or so afterward.[402]

Maidu

While other Maidu buried their dead, those of the hill (Konkow) and southern (Nisinan) provinces cremated. The Hill Maidu mourning anniversary was the northernmost example of the Cry, the rite celebrated throughout the lower half of native California in the Fall to remember and resupply the distinguished dead.[403]

For each Cry, a round brush fence was set up around the community's burning ground, open to the west and sometimes also the east. A director oversaw the whole rite, but the functional sponsors were bereaved families who paid the director in return for a special necklace given to mark their own mourning. The pattern and sequence of beads, by colors and counts within this loop, was specific to that ground. After use in five such Cries, a necklace was redeemed by return payment from the director, who finally cremated it. Of note, a poor family could participate in this ceremony by receiving payment instead of giving it, highlighting the prestige that came from generosity by elites across the Americas.

When a ground was ready, its director sent out to each intended guest a string of knots, to be untied one by one each successive day so all visitors arrived on the same date. The first night, family mourners came to the old enclosure about sundown to keen (wail) and to sprinkle acorn meal as an offering. The second day, the enclosure was repaired and poles up to 20 feet tall were prepared to hold offerings that had been amassed for a year or more.[404] A widow should have spent the past year making many baskets to be burned. By evening, each mourning family had a dozen poles filled from top to bottom, set up as north / south pairs across the fire. Bulky items were placed around their bases.

For those notable deceased, effigies were made of stuffed and decorated wildcat skins, arranged to look like standing humans, then staked near the entrance and "fed" during the night. Within each such effigy (literally called a "spirit within") resided the ghost of that person for the duration of the Cry.

As an old man lit the central fire, bargaining began to rescue offerings in return for an exchange, barter, or purchase. Such rescuing must be understood in the same way as the gifts given to guests at a memorial potlatch, where it is clear that for hosts these "others" are both their guests and their own dead. Each substituted for the other, but with the living bodies being the more obvious, the seen for the unseen. While the spirit of the artifact went to the beyond, its physical expression stayed among the living who acted on behalf of the dead.

---

[401] Loeb, <u>Pomo Folkways</u> 1926: 288.

[402] Loeb, <u>Pomo Folkways</u> 1926: 294.

[403] Kroeber, <u>Handbook of the Indians of California</u> 1925: 429-432, 859-861.

[404] Robert Heizer, <u>California</u> 1978: 383, Figure 10.

When negotiations quieted, the director spoke about the intent, purpose, and procedure of the Cry, as Kroeber wryly noted,[405] "carefully instructing the people in what they perfectly well know how to do" in upholding high moral standards. For the rest of the night, in distinct groupings composed of mourning families, everyone wailed, keened, and sang. Their speakers periodically expressed pity and concern for these ancestral dead and placed bits of food into the fire to "feed" them.

At dawn, the tall poles were emptied and everything piled onto the fire while the elders mournfully keened for their loved ones. Effigies were "walked" into the fire to be set ablaze. Mourners continuously exhaled forceful breaths, presumably to blow away harm. At first light, emotional intensity peaked and old widows had to be restrained from throwing themselves onto the pyre. Everyone was totally exhausted with grief, prostrate from their lamentations.

In the morning, after the fire died down and everyone rested, the director urged all to eat, gamble, and have fun for a day or more in order to end their gathering on a happy note. Throughout southern California, this Cry overlapped with the Toloache (datura) cult, and, in the Sierra Nevadas, with that called Kuksu, which featured an elaborate "big head" dancer and other spirit embodiments.

Yokuts

In a declaration that resonates with native understanding of this and all cremations, Yoimut [406] emphasized the immediacy of fire. She was the last speaker of Chunut Yokuts, a subtribe who once lived on the northeastern shore of Lake Tulare. To honor her late father, her mother saved money for a year to buy a good suit for her deceased husband for sixteen dollars in Visalia. She also bought a fine hat, shoes, socks, and underwear, as well as assembling fine baskets and his own keepsakes. A tule framework was made, dressed up in these clothes, and the face was painted before everything was burned up at the Lonewis. Yoimut thought White (Anglo) people were less thoughtful because, while they also buy clothes and coffins for their deceased kin, everything is put in the ground to rot away. Instead, her people burn the clothes to keep them new, "so our dead person always had good clothes to wear" in the afterlife.

Luiseño

Among the so-called Mission Indians, the Luiseño of San Juan Capistrano (Juaneño) had hereditary officials in charge of all cremations. They shared a Polynesian-like epic of creation (Chapter 1) from the primordial union of Sky and Earth culminating in the appearance of Wiyot, whose fearful *puwah* resulted in his being poisoned, then cremated to protect his body from desecration. Though to no avail, since Coyote rushed into the flaming pyre, grabbed a bit of his flesh, and ate it.[407] Today, the consumption of

---

[405] Kroeber, <u>Handbook of the Indians of California</u> 1925: 860.

[406] Frank Latta, <u>Handbook of Yokuts Indians</u> 1977: 667, 675, 682 [1949].

[407] Kroeber, <u>Handbook of the Indians of California</u> 1925: 637.

a bit of cooked flesh by a loved one remains an aspect of southern California cremations.[408]

Similarly, in southern California, at a later time, in consequence of Coyote's cannibal act, Chungishnish – the founder of the datura ~ jimsonweed ~ toloache cult – finished the world by changing the first people into present species, spirits, or sacra before making modern humans from molded earth and giving them cultures, laws, and the ceremonial enclosure (*wankech*).

Kamia

Kamia of the Imperial Valley trace their culture to a hermaphrodite with two sons who moved south along the Colorado River into this valley, but most of the Kamia ancestors fled from them in terror because of their frightful appearance. One brave woman, however, stayed and married a son, producing twins who provided corn and bean seeds, bows, arrows, and war clubs passed out according to patrilineages, as well as their mourning ceremonies.[409]

As death approached, a person's soul could be seen leaving his or her body, going south of Black Butte (Wiespa) in Lower California, where it glided on the wind waiting to rejoin its twin spirit. This ghost arose from the body at the moment of death, but lingered nearby for four days, visiting everywhere that person had lived.

As the body was cremated, this spirit returned to gather up the burnt clothes, rub charcoal on its eyes to enhance them, and go south, where it was escorted by deceased relatives and rejoined its other soul to reconstitute that person, who lived, died, and was reborn to be cremated four times. After each death the shape of the returning "body" changed until, after the fourth death, it became a black beetle or other insect which came back to the Kamia country. "If the heart did not burn, it was buried in the pit with the ashes, to enliven and emerge as a young owl."[410]

Maricopa

Among Yuman-speaking tribes of the Southwest, Maricopa[411] required cremation for all who entered their afterworld, otherwise he or she smelled too badly.[412] Should a Maricopa happen to be buried, his or her ghost stayed only on the north side of a "deadline", wandering around carrying their coffin box on their head, sometimes putting it down for a seat. After death, twins and the deformed, sent to a separate town, were

---

[408] Kroeber, Handbook of the Indians of California 1925: 740, Plate 69.

[409] Edward Gifford, The Kamia of Imperial Valley 1931: 79.

[410] Gifford, The Kamia of Imperial Valley 1931: 71, 72.

[411] Leslie Spier, Yuman Tribes of the Gila River 1933: 296, 299, 302, 308.

[412] To further offset this olfactory concern, the pyre used aromatic mesquite, whose intense heat as "the ultimate in fragrant fuels" was extolled by Aldo Leopold, A Sand County Almanac 1978: 153.

reborn to visit the living for a time. An adult could be reborn up to four times, ending the last existence as a bit of charcoal lying in the desert.

Maricopa recognize that each person had four spiritual aspects which transformed at death into a soul that goes to the afterworld, a ghost that becomes a whirlwind, a heart that becomes a horned owl, and pulses that become screech owls. The crucial importance of the heart is indicated by a belief that it is the last part of a body to burn.

The pyre was strongly made by first setting a big post into the ground until it stood a yard tall. Four logs were laid down beside it to the west, with a smaller post set on the outside to hold these four in place. Logs were then piled up to three feet, even in height with the top of the big post, and dry arrowweed was stuffed as kindling between the layers.

The corpse was carried from the house with four halts en route. The last was on the ground beside the south side of the pyre. During each pause, a speaker addressed the mourners. Finally, a man climbed onto the north side of the pyre, the corpse was handed up, and he briefly placed it prone with head to the east, before turning it onto its right side to face north. Its feet were unwrapped from the shroud and wedged between logs, the left one to the north and right to the south. This was to anchor the body before it was covered by gifts of clothing and blankets. During the blaze, an old man with a long pole kept the body hidden within burning wood. Everyone fasted, and heard orations at the middle and the end of the cremation. If a dead man had been a musician, his favorite songs were sung throughout his burning.

Afterward, four holes, two on the north and two on the south, were dug and the ashes divided among them. The fire tender first divided the remains from south to north, and then west to east. While the ethnography is otherwise silent, these four deposits probably relate to the four souls.

The deceased's home and all possessions were burned or buried. After mourning for four days, family and officials returned to routine tasks. If the deceased were exceptional, a mourning ceremony (Cry) was held a few days later. Unlike neighboring tribes, it was not annual nor did it involve effigies, though some did include staged versions of great moments (battles, songs, orations) from a distinguished life.

Conclusions

The insides of mounds were more than mere empty hollows; they sing. They also provided safe haven, as sound chamber, womb, nest, and den. In some instances, however, it also became an oven, and charged repository for whatever remained. Pawnee priests, using ancient technology, outlined enclosures with a compass made of a string tightened between sharp sticks. After being freshly made, bare mounds became worn by erosion channels and other typical features of the earth itself. Once grassed-over and stabilized, mounds became obvious permanent markers on the landscape. Their blessed insides sometimes included the dead and (c)remains, acting like seeds to revivify the land, with many species. Prime among these species were snakes, insects, reptiles, and birds, with the ability both to sing and to provide humans with songs.

Cremation created a quick and sweet release of the souls from their mortal remains. Their very insubstantiality, however, was sometimes countered by the monumentality of mounds that came to hold their ashes. Offerings and other reminders added further substance. In most cases, this rendering of the corpse served to ease and enhance the transmission of a name and persona to its next holder, a successor who thereby became more secure or certain in their distinctly new identity.

The Hochungara best characterize this native world, in all of its instability. After repeated attempts, it was only made habitable for free-ranging animals when four island earth weights, brother water serpents, implanted themselves tail first at the four directional corners. They all now face east and the sun, to stretch, steady, and hold the earth. Rocks (women) add bulk, weight, height, and ballast.

Snakes play vital roles, representing the earth itself for Pawnee doctors. Their "skin shedding" provides the poetic phrase for immortality. Closely allied with women, and the Moon woman of the Skiri, these reptiles can either steady or shake the earth. Human care, attention, dance, and song play vital roles in influencing each of these outcomes to be orderly, though mounting human faults take a heavy toll that always threatens to upset the earth.

7 ~ OVER ABOVE

Relying on their vital bulge and charged bulk, mounds represent the unseen, or provide the means for expressing it. Symbolically beneath each one, like a bull's-eye, is the universal ⊕ crossed hoop, representing the earth her(its)self. Their tops provide lookouts and flood refuge, as well as a way of looking up as an observatory. In particular, mounds can be mirrors of the dark night, in convoluted inside-out ways. Thus, the roof inside a Pawnee mudlodge was hung with human-shaped stars to become the sky. This is the same darkness as the parallel conditions under the earth, in the afterworld, and up in the night sky. Night was potent with *puwah*. For instance, "In Osage belief Night was the mother of Day, and rather widely the night sky was perceived to be the equivalent of the dark interior of the earth as the primal Mother."[413]

Ethnographic materials emphasize the role of mounds as observatories, a way of connecting with the universe, providing a fixed point above rooftops for plotting the movements of the sun, moon, planets, comets, and stars. Certainly, by reaching upward they direct attention toward the sky, like modern telescopes set on clear mountain tops. Given the ideology tracing elite origins and political offices from Star beings in the sky, along with the pivotal importance of kinship, a fascination with light beams and movements in the sky is to be expected. Moreover, as memory aids, shadow-casting uprights (gnomon), berms, and other additions to the surface of the earth helped to keep track of the sky movements. Massive earthworks began over 6000 years ago in the Middle Archaic, but people had obviously been watching the sky far longer.

Indeed, though unreported in publications, ritual participants are expected to take the broadest view possible as they pray for "the whole world". During the Busk, fasters watch the daily movement of the Sun in the sky, as well as project their thoughts upward hoping to see with the "same eye" looking down upon the earth. Much of the care and attention to cleaning the square ground is said to be for the benefit of the Sun, who is expected to note evidence of all this effort and, in consequence, benefit humans.[414] Indeed, in addition to the arbors and central fire, the pale ash mound is one of the most obvious features of a town when seen from the sky, especially when freshly mantled with lighter ashes from the old fire.

Like other human projects, mounds serve as the seen for the unseen. In the past, scholars assumed topography itself was the determining factor in the placement of mounds. Recent work on the spacings, alignments, and orientations among mounds indicate considerable involvement with the overarching sky. With proper dates for the occupation of a site, the sky from that time period can be simulated. While matching a pattern of mounds with an array of stars may well be impossible (or too easy, because

---

[413] Robert Hall, An Archaeology of the Soul ~ North American Indian Belief and Ritual 1997: 53.

[414] Similarly, hunters keep their camps clean and the bones of their game tidy in trees so the local spirit, flying over, can see and approve their conscientiousness, rewarding them with more success; See Adrian Tanner, Bringing Home Animals 1979: 75.

there are so many stars), links to the planets are readily made with the naked eye. The great precision afforded by modern scientific instruments further "gilds the lily".

Routine and fixed markers are sufficient for accuracy. The same fixed point for making observations, sight lines to landmarks, and simple devices like a gnomon provided consistency and accuracy.[415] Yet mounding was also an engineering feat and, as such, used standard measurements and techniques in construction. Such uniformity suggests a priesthood, or at least a guild of intertribal initiates ("masons"), who insisted on the special proprieties that made the religious aspects of this effort all the more worthy. For thousands of years, sites, such as the Newark Octagon and Cahokia, were positioned on the globe at precise spots with exact astronomical advantages. Each was positioned from a truly cosmic perspective, providing an orientation to stars or planets in terms of the best regional location on the geographic surface of the planet Earth.

Watching the sky relies on certain constants. Movements are east to west because of the earth's rotation. Spacing along the horizon, known as azimuth, assumes a circle (like the face of a clock) with 0/360° (@ 12 o'clock) at true north, 90° (@ 3) at east, 180° (@ 6) at south, and 270° (@ 9) at west. Each aspect has its own timing. The moon rises 50 minutes later each day, as well as waxing and waning with its phases. This synodic period (relative to the sun) is 29.53 days, while its nodical period (intersections of the lunar orbit with celestial equator) is 27.21 days. The conjunction of these two periods, every 47 new moons, produces a total eclipse of the sun and moon. Over 18.6 years the moon moves to "its southernmost setting on the western horizon". This is the most dramatic of the eight lunar standstills incorporated into the Newark Octagon (OH).

The solar day is 24 hours, but the stars have a sidereal revolution of 3 minutes and 56 seconds less, so stars seem to rise four minutes earlier each day. Constellations shift with the seasons. Winter skies show Orion, Taurus, and Canis Major, while summer has Cygnus, Lyra, and Sagittarius.

The sun, of course, is the most obvious object in the daytime sky, a potent instance of the seen for the unseen. Indeed, it is often called "the eye" of the Creator, and has gender as male, though often female in the Southeast. Since observations are made from a set location (a "seat"), landmarks along the horizon help to mark its passage. Oriented according to the sides of the body, its movement has four key positions (left, right, back, front), underscoring the sacred importance of the number 4. In the northern hemisphere, at the June 21 summer solstice ("sun stand"), the sun rises and sets at its furthest north on the longest day. At December 21 winter solstice, it is farthest south on the longest night. At the September 21 Fall and March 21 Spring equinox, the sun rises and sets due east and west on the horizon, midway between the solstice points.

Tamaroha of Poverty Point

Poverty Point, a famous Late Archaic site, is set on Macon Ridge near the Mississippi River in the northeast corner of Louisiana. Extensive research there for over a hundred years has provided background for understanding the human occupation of the

---

[415] Stephen Fabian, Patterns in the Sky, an Introduction to Ethnoastronomy 2001; Cf. Dianne Johnson, Night Skies of Aboriginal Australia 1998.

entire Southeast.[416] This upland provided abundant food resources from nearby swamps and forests. It lacked only one necessity – stone. Because it was on a major waterway, stone could be brought by the canoe load as trade goods or offerings at what must have long been a major attraction and sacred site.

From the start, Clovis founders stayed there and developed into Dalton 10,500 years ago, with a heavy reliance on nuts among other local foods. Lacking rock at a time before pottery when cooking used hot stones for boiling water in baskets or bags, locals molded clay soil into textured roundish lumps (PPO = Poverty Point objects) that served them well in the centuries before fired clay pots. People increasingly prospered during the early archaic (BP 9500-7500), and, in the middle archaic (BP 7500-4000), began to build earthen mounds as well as to cache bifaces (Turkeytail type) in pits. At the Watson Brake site nearby, eleven mounds, at varying heights on a connecting ridge, formed an oval ring (Chapter 3). During the Late Archaic (BP 4000-1000), Poverty Point itself developed (BP 3750-3300) into a complex array of six raised rings and six mounds, tapping into the vitalities of much more ancient ones anchoring their alignments.

With stone at a premium, it is significant that pieces were devoted to small carved effigies recognizable as *owl*, *fox*, and *locust*. All of these have ethnographic associations, particularly in terms of Choctaws, with souls, either born from the earth as locusts or transformed after death into owl or fox, which hunt at night and rest in dens (Miller 2015).

Jon Gibson has given much thought to the symbolism of mounds, based on his long career at Poverty Point, one of the "stilled places [where] wandering ... was arrested by resource richness and organization". He variously characterizes the results of all this earth moving as a

"vast security system, an invisible shield protecting the social and political heart of its folk ... as metaphors of creation and cosmos [with] the ability of encirclements, or 'broken circles,' to guard against dark forces and evil spirits lurking on the outside [and] the power of symmetry and alignment as barriers against those same supernatural forces [providing] architectural magic [such that] the scale on which they [were] laid out ... showed how much protection they felt they needed. That the massive system of security was installed at the same historical moment that long-distance exchange intensified suggests that exchange was a major source of up-welling fear and stress.[417]

"Mounds and plazas were special set-aside places, power places.... Poverty Point had both mounds and a plaza apart from the rings [that were] ... expressions of soul and home as well as safety nets for keeping evil spirits at bay. ... Rings were expressions of corporateness; they were manifestations of home" and pride.[418] Openings in the rings allowed for the passage of the sun,

---

[416] Jon Gibson, The Ancient Mounds of Poverty Point: Place of Rings 2001; Tamaroha, from Tunican words for 'mound' (*tama*) and 'cave' (*roha*), is treated in the Introduction, note 6.

[417] Gibson, The Ancient Mounds of Poverty Point 2001: 38-39, 105.

[418] Gibson, The Ancient Mounds of Poverty Point 2001: 100, 108-109.

as well as release of built-up negativities. During times of concern, they could be closed off ritually with ashes or water barriers. Beyond, six outer mounds formed a protective square around the entire occupied area."

Though a full octagon of rings was once imagined, wrongly assuming that the eastern side eroded into Macon Bayou, the site plan was probably more complex as a cosmology from mounded west to watery east. The enormous bird mound (A) to the west is the sky, the occupied ridge rings are the earth, and the area explicitly submerged below the bluff is the underworld. To further confirm its crescent shape, sites three hundred miles away, Claiborne and Cedarland, paired satellites at the mouth of the Pearl River (later to become Choctaw homeland), were also shaped as a half-circle (in U or C forms). While each was identical in form, they were very different in their specialized artifact assemblages, and both interacted with the hub at Poverty Point.

While Gibson saw the elaboration of rings and mounds at Poverty Point as a protective security device, it was equally the opposite (except for some well placed counterspells) as an attractor for human pilgrims and "tourists". To get people to bring much-needed stone, as well as other goods, locals, well fed and nicely situated, did what humans have always done. They built a lure, both local and regional.

In Europe, these have been novelties that ranged from standing stones, "follies", "whimsies", and cutouts into chalk hills to Gothic cathedrals, coliseums to sports arenas (for many), shrines to museums (for some), and now a host of tourist draws. Periodic gatherings were encouraged by conferences, trade shows, and world fairs, as well as Olympic sports venues. Churches staged festivals, morality plays, pilgrimages, and high holy days.

After Poverty Point, descendants moved away, later adopted the farming trinity and emerged as Mississippians after AD 1200. When Soto came through, they were likely Tunican and Natchezan speakers of the lower Mississippi River Valley.

Hopewell

More far-reaching than the prior localized Adena (Chapters 3, 4), the Hopewell more intensively reshaped their own Ohio River homelands. Consistently using the best soil (Fox series) for their massive efforts and placing them on a middle terrace above the flood plain, they built huge earthwork enclosures. In addition, ancient trails passed close to many of the sites, so access was not only by waterway. Major resources nearby fueled a far-flung trade. As noted, the Newark complex is nine miles from Flint Ridge, a high quality quarry; Tremper is near Ohio pipestone; Seip is close to red ocher; and small McKittrick adjoins the Old Scioto Salt Licks.[419]

The instigators of this trading, as well as the sanctifying, of these resources are now assumed to be persons who made the extra effort to link up with others like themselves far and wide. Today, they would be most like the "big men" of Melanesia,

---

[419] William Romain, Mysteries of the Hopewell ~ Astronomers, Geometers, and Magicians of the Eastern Woodlands 2000: 27-31, 67, 124, 129, 151, 168, 183.

though some of these "men" are women.[420] Indeed, recent study has shown that such big men are but the political aspect of a group of "great people" who try harder, do better, give more, and take charge. Their enthusiasm, ability, and goals carried others along, variously involving trade, travel, ritual, art, building, and learning useful knowledge, especially astronomical. Native conferences to recalibrate calendars and record celestial movements are in ethnography and probably took place prehistorically as well.[421]

Though seemingly (to some) mere combinations of circles, squares, and lines, the geometry of the Hopewell had a rich sophistication. While far apart in space, figures that were part of the same earthworks often shared the same dimensions and proportions. They literally could be nested within each other. This is proof, therefore, that the identical units of measurements were used to plan and build all these works. These units seem to be the equivalent of 1054 feet, subdivided into a half (½) of 526.5 and a quarter (¼) of 263.5 feet, with arm length the most basic unit. Like that of today's fraternal Masons, this geometry had symbolic and cosmological meanings.

Attempts to correlate features of these earthworks with sky events has shown that, in AD 250, a diagonal across the Hopewell Square was an almost perfect azimuth to the winter solstice sunrise, and Mound City aligned with summer solstice sunset. Of particular note, skeletons (four at the southeast, one at the northwest) marked the ends of the Mound City diagonal, when all the other Hopewell burials at this site were cremations. These burials marked on the ground what could be seen in the sky. They provided flesh and bone to feed the solar being known to thrive on humans, either by sacrifice or slain in battle.

Newark and High Bank Earthworks look like twins set at right angles. Moreover, they were once probably linked via the Great Hopewell Road. High Bank has been shown to have nine lunar and four solar alignments. Of these, the moon's maximum north rise is exact. Such extreme positions often are believed to be moments when the barriers between worlds and beings become thin, permeable, or passable (cf. Irish Celts, Chapter 4). Moreover, both include octagons, which can be linked to the eight phases of the moon as seen with the unaided human eye.

William Romain, relying on the expected patterning of native housing to copy the cultural understanding of the congruent shape of that universe, has proposed that the squares represent(ed) the sky and the circles represent(ed) the earth. Where three distinct forms were found at a site, they may represent the cosmic levels between water, earth, and sky. These associations are wholesale rather than particular or detailed. As he wrote, "it seems peculiar, and in some ways counterproductive, to have an earthwork the size of three football fields just to observe a lunar alignment that occurs once every nineteen

---

[420] Maria Lepowsky, Fruit of the Motherland ~ Gender in an Egalitarian Society 1993; Francoise Dussart, The Politics of Ritual in an Aboriginal Settlement ~ Kinship, Gender, and the Currency of Knowledge 2000.

[421] Jay Miller, North Pacific Ethnoastronomy ~ Tsimshian and Others, Earth & Sky ~ Visions of the Cosmos in Native American Folklore 1992 Chapter 11: 193-206.

years."[422] He strengthened the link between sky and square by noting today's use of the aptly named square grounds (Miller 2015) among southeastern tribes still celebrating the renewing Busk.[423] Yuchi refer to their own square as "in the rainbow house", elevated into the sky.

Where openings occurred in the outer walls of octagons and squares, a so-called gateway mound was placed just inside each gap. Excavations have shown these mounds are sterile, so it is their position rather than their contents that is significant. They prevent anyone from directly entering any of these openings, forcing a move to either side. Since some spirits and beings can only travel in straight lines, this would have prevented their entering the square, unless they could fly. It is encouraging to note, therefore, that flying was an ability of the good, but trudging the earth often went with the bad. At the Pawnee Four Pole, a similar mound, of soil excavated from the fireplace, stood outside in front of the opening into the earthen enclosure (Chapter 5).[424]

Earthwork circles, covering over the remains of an identical round palisade, often have a central burial mound, serving to anchor these ancestors to that place and to the earth in general. Martin Byers has referred to such a pivotal mound as an "iconic warrant" between living and dead kin.[425] Caches were also placed in these circles, offerings to further sanctify this space in earth and sky. The alignments of the famous Serpent Mound (Introduction), inspired by the same comet as seen at the Battle of

---

[422] Romain, Mysteries of the Hopewell 2000: 168; Ray Hively and Robert Horn, Geometry and Astronomy in Prehistoric Ohio 1982; Hopewellian Geometry and Astronomy at High Bank 1984. Missing from Romain's discussion is a full consideration of the modalities of light, from both fire and sun. Indeed, the model for *puwah* moving through the sky is a beam of light, while that moving on earth is water flow. Thus the gateway mounds occur at gaps in linear earthworks to manage this ray of vitality. See #11.

The answer to his question "why", of course, is that such massive construction is a prayer for a precise and orderly universe to forestall calamity and chaos by maintaining harmonious contact with vitality.

[423] While Romain "got it right", the impassioned, polemic work of Mann, taking scholars to task for misunderstanding Ohio mounds, insists that the circle is Sky and the square is Earth, though she is well aware of the Four Winds role in Ojibwa creation. These winds define the sky as four sided, and therefore a square, contra Barbara Alice Mann, Native Americans, Archaeologists, and the Mounds 2003.

[424] The location of these gateway mounds inside or outside the opening gap indicates the direction that *puwah* flows from or to, as well as the means of controlling, containing, or blocking it. That most gateway mounds block gaps in linear earthworks like squares and octagons enforces their associations with the sky and with light beams as the template for the flow of power there.

[425] Martin Byers, Social Structure and the Pragmatic Meaning of Material Culture: Ohio Hopewell as an Ecclesiastical-Communal Cult 1996.

Hastings, show a precise geography of triangles aligned by astronomy, positioning the three twists of the body, as well as the nose and the coiled tail, to lunar alignments and summer solstice sunset.

Though they were tending crops growing naturally in their region, before the addition of the trinity of maize-beans-squash, Hopewells were impacting their land, working the soil for food and goods, mining flint, and trading these resources. Even before farmers intensively prepared and cared for the land which became entailed in field cropping, sacred spaces and precincts were being constructed at scenic and strategic locales. In addition, elaborate burial rites involved charnel houses with lunar alignments, successive rehandling of the diminishing remains, and final deposition into an earth mound such as Cresap (Chapter 4) or within a reaccessible log tomb where others, such as family members, could later be successively and collectively interred.

The enclosures seem to have been for the living to interact as communities within earth circles or sky squares. Again, the associations are richly complex and multilayered, though aspects of gender are probably more important, but have been virtually ignored by scholars. Usually, curves are female, and angles are males, but local traditions delight in proclaiming their independence by deliberately reversing or modifying the obvious, as with a female Sun and male Moon.

Azimuths ~ Sky Alignments

At Toltec Mounds, near Little Rock, Arkansas, 18 mounds are placed around two plazas, with an embankment and ditch on three sides and a river oxbow on the fourth. Their geometry is complex. From the middle of mound C, all of the other mounds are intersected by lines radiating out at 60° intervals. Moreover, the overall layout suggests a standard unit of measurement, called the Toltec Module, of 47.5 (46~49) meters, though it more commonly appears doubled as 95 meters. The projected original height of Mound A is 1/3 of the module, and that of B is ¼, suggesting consistent, proportional applications.

It may be that this standard unit is based on a more human one, with an increment of 1.67 meters (5'6"), the height of a healthy male member of the elite ("a ruler"). Half of this measure is about the span of a stride, so 57 paces would equal 47.5 meters. A cubit, measured from elbow to tip of middle finger, would be ½ of a meter, repeated 95 times for the standard unit.

Excavation of some mounds indicated their different usages. Mound C holds burials, while B, D, E, S, and G had a succession of priestly homes. Of note, a line from the center of A to B has an angle of 61.5°, "precisely the azimuth of the rising summer solstice sun for the latitude of the site (34°18'15") at AD 700".[426] A sight line from A through G and H marks the 90° equinox sunrise. From H to B is the summer solstice sunset, from H to A is the equinox sunset, and from H to S is the winter solstice sunset. From A to R is the angle of the moon's 18.6 year southern-most setting.

---

[426] Clay Sherrod and Martha Ann Rolingson, Surveyors of the Ancient Mississippi Valley ~ Modules and Alignments in Prehistoric Mound Sites 1987: 5, 26, 30, 41, 65, 84, 98, 134.

Though stellar alignments are problematical, a line from E to A sees Polaris, the North Star, a steady and important celestial guide throughout the cultural world. It often served as the model for a steady, sure human leader (chief). The star Vega, prominent during the farming season, can be tracked via the mounds beside the oxbow along the northwestern side of the site.

Comparative studies on either side of the lower Mississippi, in the eastern Yazoo Basin and in western Red River Caddoan sites, confirmed solstice and equinox alignments. The Insley Site in Louisiana includes fascinating sight lines from its Mound A through an arc of seven mounds, each aligned with a different bright star that sets in winter. Strangely, lunar correlations were not attempted for the Caddoan sites, despite the obvious ethnographic fact that the Caddo priestly head was known by the title of Mr. Moon.[427]

Surveys done at the all-important Cahokia site near St. Louis, added further confirmation. Cahokia, occupied for 400 years, includes over 100 mounds within 15 square kilometers. The utter complexity of this site, clearly a Mississippian capital, indicates that much more was involved. Ridged-top mounds plot a diamond outline for the "downtown" core of the site. The focus of a huge trade network, it was also a religious complex, major attraction, and pilgrimage destination. Dominating the site is Monks Mound (# 38) with several terraces and an observation point (A) at the intersection of the geometry (geomancy) of the entire site. Later, a small mound was built on this spot, a bulge atop this much larger mass, a navel on the belly.

There is no doubt the entire arrangement was laid out with great precision. A map of the site indicated axis lines that have been confirmed by excavations. Key spots on the earth were marked by intense human activity, though the visible outcome might seem deceptively small. Precise engineering was serious business.

The most spectacular of these thus far was Mound 72 (see below), a low mound at the location of a projected main axis intersection. This nexus was proven by the remains of a huge marker post, placed about CE/AD 950. In addition, the mound was the grave of twin VIPs laid to rest above and below a falcon-shaped cloak of beads set between them. Hundreds of human sacrifices, who were buried at different times, surrounded them. Some grave goods originated from thousands of miles away. The sheer quantity and elaboration of these remains suggests that the actual burial rite did not take place at the time of death, when plans would have been necessarily hasty, but probably was held to coincide with some solar or solstice rite.

Given the complexity of all the earth, sky, and human relationships that seem to have been expressed at Cahokia, it is not surprising that specialized engineering transect devices have been proposed. Now called woodhenges, these were four or more circles (or perhaps arcs) of standing posts (tubes), another reflection of the human orientation to the sky also seen at Stonehenge in England. While they were probably used as calendars, solar markers, sacred enclosures, and a place to watch gnomon shadows shift in rotation, they could have also been used as surveyor instruments. Set up in a populous neighborhood of Cahokia, with posts that stayed in place for hundreds of years, sighting between a central and standing post provides obvious alignments for half of the mounds

---

[427] Jay Miller, Changing Moons 1996. Kolomoki in Georgia also conforms to the Toltec module.

at the site. More are possible but the tangible data are not at hand. Another factor for consideration was a consistent spacing of 1045 meters (22 times the Toltec module) among the mounds, suggesting widespread use of this basic unit.

In all, mound spacings and alignments convey a profound redundancy or overlapping of relationships. The same unit of measurement is simultaneous multiples and proportions of the length of a human stride, human height, dimensions of a plaza, aspects of the sky, and one or more of its phenomena in orbit. A mound, therefore, is not a single entity but instead the nexus and intersection of many, many concerns ~ concepts. What it does do in its own right, of course, is bulge, bulk, ballast, bank, focus, and bless – all of them at one place. Always, mounds obviously hold steady the earth, allowing continuous reuse of the same vital plot, rising steadily upward.

Mound 72, Cahokia

Cahokia, with over 120 mounds, provides the stellar example of a practical as well as symbolic community. At its heart rises Monks Mound, covering 14 acres, built in 14 stages at what seem to be 18 year intervals, from 900 to 1150 AD. Surrounding it were at least four administrative tiers decreasing from 1) the downtown of six square miles, 2) multimound clusters, 3) one mound villages, and 4) moundless farmsteads or hamlets. Melvin Fowler, the archaeologist who has devoted his career to systematic work, has proposed the use of a basic measuring unit of 1.055 meters or 3.46 feet (comparable to the Toltec module of 47.5 (46~49) meters). His careful mapping and confirming excavations have shown that this Mississippian capital was impressively planned, aligned, and engineered.[428]

The ramp on two-tiered Monk's Mound indicates that it faces south, with the tysic of the whole site at its southwest corner, aligned to an north-south axis that intersects the eastern side of Mound 72, as confirmed by evidence of huge post holes at these points. Its role in the master plan, mapping the Sky on the Earth, drew scholarly attention, though what was inside it soon dimmed other considerations as excavators prepared for a heroic feat. Four years were spent on this seven-foot high, ridged-top form, revealing six major episodes of burial and building that entombed about 300 people.[429]

The space was first claimed about 950 AD by a woodhenge of 48 posts set in a circle, serving as a celestial calculator, solar marker, and surveying station. Of notable significance, Cahokia is positioned at the latitude where solstice sight lines form a triangle of exactly 30 degrees per side (summer is 30° N of E, winter is 30° S of E). Given the Mississippian link between rulers and the Sun, it is significant that two mounds

---

[428] Biloine Whiting Young and Melvin Fowler, Cahokia ~ The Great American Metropolis 2000: 155, 183, 277.

[429] Young and Fowler, Cahokia 2000: 139-145, 155, 183, 238, 250, 277; Melvin Fowler, The Cahokia Atlas, Studies in Illinois Archaeology 6 1989; Melvin Fowler, Jerome Rose, Barbara Vander Leest, and Steven Ahler, The Mound 72 Area: Dedicated and Sacred Space in Early Cahokia 1999. Under pressure from AIM activists and waning funds, Features 107 and 356 were not excavated, clouding understanding of the body count.

were constructed opposite each other at the post marking the summer solstice sunrise (SSR at 72Sub1) and at the winter solstice sunset post (WSS at Mound 96). From the top of Monk's Mound, therefore, the far south horizon showed a ring of standing posts with paired low mounds, each pierced by a solar marker (tube).

Near the SSR post, mound 2Sub1 began as a black earthen platform arraying three groups of impressive burials. The twin central burials, resting against a cloak covered with shell disk beads that included the outline of a bird-head much like a falcon, was composed of men lying back-to-back, head-to-feet, offset by 10 degrees. Atop, the full skeleton was face-up, while the below man was exactly reversed, face down with feet under the skull above. Accompanying this pair were a range of human remains in various stages of curation, including a full skeleton, wearing a necklace of 700 shell disk beads, with a flexed right leg suggesting activity or burial alive. In two nearby pits, aligned to other posts in the woodhenge, were bone bundles and elaborate grave goods, including copper tubes, mica sheets (2 bushelfuls), hundreds of foreign arrows with stone points sorted by specimen type (to the delight of all classifiers) and two stacks of chunkey stones (10, 5 in each). All three of these burials were then covered by three feet of a north-south roundish mound (72sub1) with extensions to the east and west so that it had a lumpy cross (cruciform) shape. Its blue-black composition was then capped with dense off-white plaster that sealed and preserved it for a thousand years.

The flat rectangular top of the mound, approached by a ramp on the west side, was directly over the beaded burial. Later, the SSR post on its east side was replaced twice, and new burials, aligned to other posts, were positioned above earlier ones, indicating that adepts in charge of this mound had full knowledge of its contents. An altar basin was added to this mound, and then a final dark soil triangle.

Across the henge from the SSR post, another cruciform mound (#96) was built at the WSS post. Since it never had a plaster cap, it so deteriorated that it was identified as a mound only recently. Unexcavated, it is presumed to hold burials associated with the Earth, in balance with the Sky associations of Mound 72. Both include ramps leading toward the post that once protruded over its upper level.

Near 72Sub1, construction began on a companion mound (72Sub2) over the wall-trenches of a building that was probably a charnel house where bodies were curated for defleshing, resorting, bundling, and burial. It was dismantled and replaced by a low platform to display the remains of 13 humans sorted by bone size into three piles, along with four distinct bundle burials. Paired burials, two face-down men and paired face-up woman and face-down man, were set along the wall lines of the prior building. All of these remains were then covered by a two-terraced square mound (72sub2), to which were added a new post and two pit burials of females (numbering 22, 19), both in two layers. Later, a pit was dug to leave offerings of pottery, 36,000 shell beads, and 450 unhafted stone points. In the southeast corner, 24 females were buried in two layers, divided by mats and cloth, and covered with a ramp.

In three construction phases, the space between the two small mounds was filled in by unusual burials covered by small mounds. Eventually, a tiny ridge mound (72sub3) consolidated these and was topped by four men, with arms interlinked but missing their heads and hands, covered by a conical mound of alternating layers of light and dark sands. In a downslope pit, 50 young women (average age 21) were placed in two layers. Both burials were then buried under another mound of black soil (72Sub3A).

For a century, as 72Sub3 grew to include 72Sub2, 72Sub1 stood alone as the focus for offerings and sacrifices. Eventually, an overall ridgetop mound was planned, aligned to the solstices and the diagonal of the diamond-shaped border of the Cahokia "downtown". The axis ran parallel to Feature 229, where the humans on the bottom, which was lined with white sand, were a jumbled cross-section of 40 people, and the top level, separated by mats (shown by their remains), held 15 bodies that had been wrapped and placed on litters whose cedar poles provided a date of AD 1030. These sacrifices (of genetic kin) had lined up along the southern side of the pit, been struck at the back of the neck with a heavy weapon (perhaps a mace), and sprawled into the pit, where finger gouges convey their final agony. Other oval pits held extended burials.

Lastly, the henge posts were removed, and the ridged-top mound was capped with a hard surface of plaster, with triangular altars at each end enabling solar observation. Periodically, burials continued to be placed along the south side of the mound, indicating the continued vitality of these rulers.

In all, Mound 72 represented a thoroughly-engineered master plan that began with the 48 post woodhenge, followed by two roundish mounds (72Sub1, 96) at solstice points. Then 72 added a squarish one (72Sub2), built around another post. The intervening space was filled with a sacrificial ridge mound that expanded in tribute to free-standing 72Sub1. Together, these three mounds represent the full triple range of dome, platform, and ridge shapes occurring throughout Cahokia, repeatedly emphasizing two levels (and moieties) as both terraced mounds and layered burials. Periodic burials were made, including elite bodies, bundled bones, offerings, and sacrifices. Finally, all the 72 mounds were capped and sealed, though some offerings and burials continued to be made into pits dug along the south edge. Its tightened bulge hints at sealed songs still circulating inside it.

Mound 96 faced east at the winter solstice sunrise (WSR) in mirror image as 72Sub1 faced west at the summer solstice sunset (SSS). Cahokia has other mounds paired as round / long, as well as other buried pairs (dorsal/ventral males and females), reflecting an ancient twinning.[430] Within Mound 72 the twin birdmen burial, reversed (head to foot, face up and face-down) conjoined Earth and Sky (as moieties), while the marker posts [tubes] and solstice axis of the finished mound allowed the living to continue this alignment with their ancestors of the past and the world of the future.[431]

Its contents have been much discussed. The degree of human sacrifice has been argued to be evidence of an early state – in political terms, while the burials around the beaded cloak have been given a mythological interpretation based on the ballgame epic. Yet many of these remains had clearly been curated for some time, so a highly cosmological interpretation conjoining space and time seems the most likely explanation, reinforcing a sense of overall community rather than just elite rank, as was initially proposed.[432]

---

[430] Young and Fowler, Cahokia 2000, 250.

[431] Fowler, Rose, Leest, and Ahler, The Mound 72 Area 1999: 167-185.

[432] Patricia O'Brien, Cahokia: The Political Capital of the "Ramey" State 1989; James Brown, The Cahokia Mound 72-Sub 1 Burials as Collective Representation 2003. While O'Brien argued that the many sacrifices indicate a sanctioned or "legitimate" authority over life and death typical of early

Pawnee of Nebraska

While hills, mounds, and snakes have already been explored within the inner workings of this Caddoan farming society, their cultural elite focused on the sky. Historically, all but two of the dozen Skiri Pawnee villages belonged to a confederacy organized around a hierarchy of mystic bundles. There were several classes of bundles, variously associated with an individual, a village, and the whole confederacy. Every visionary assembled a personal bundle to represent his mystic partnership. When merited by prestige, warriors could request use of a special war bundle.

A village was defined in terms of its own mystic bundle such that the hereditary chief – expected to be wise, yet humble, strong yet placid, and generous yet reserved – was supposed to descend from its original owner, a Star who decided to live on the earth. Residence was matrilocal, with villages endogamous to safeguard its bundle.

In the sea of grass that was the American Plains, just as on the ocean (at sea), people relied on the stars to guide them at night. Pawnee towns were located on the basis of chiefly lines of inheritance and sacred bundles brought down from specific stars.[433] Their domed world was duplicated in the design of their winter earthlodges (Chapter 8) and in the holy hills where their animal guilds originated (Chapter 7). As such, these "homes" were a reminder that mounds too had insides and outsides, looming between earth and sky.

Within the lodge, the fireplace was the sun, the support posts represented fixed stars, the long entry faced east and sunrise, and the smokehole looked up into the sky. At night, this top opening showed crucial star clusters that played important roles in society, particularly for the Skiri. The North Star was chief, manifesting stability, reliability, and guidance. Nearby was the chief's council, the Corona Borealis.[434] On the other side of the sky were the Seven Stars (Pleiades), a close cluster that evoked unity. Above and

---

states, Brown saw the complexity of the "beaded burial" as portraying the founding epic of the ballgame in terms of antihero and hero. I concur with the excavators, however, that the falcon cloak more likely joins embodiments of the Earth and Sky moieties so typical of historic Siouans.

Goldstein correctly noted that the burials in 72 are a collective statement, covering a long time span of curated remains, not the status burial of an elite leader (or two); Cf. Lynne Goldstein, Mississippian Ritual as Viewed Through the Practice of Secondary Disposal of the Dead, <u>Mounds, Modoc, and Mesoamerica</u>: Papers in Honor of Melvin L. Fowler, Illinois State Museum Scientific Papers 18: 193-205 2000.

[433] Von Del Chamberlin, The Chief and His Council: Unity and Authority from the Stars, <u>Earth & Sky</u> – Visions of the Cosmos in Native American Folkore Chapter 14: 221-235 1992. Cf. Von Del Chamberlin, <u>When Stars Came Down to Earth</u>: Cosmology of the Skidi Pawnee Indians of North America 1982.

[434] The astronomy of science and of the Pawnee are not exactly the same, nor should they be. The chief's council actually includes all of the Corona Borealis as well as two stars in Bootes (Mu 1, Delta).

over all, unseen though always poised at the zenith was Tirawahat, the divine expanse of the heavens who was source and summary of radiating *puwah*. Polaris at night and the Sun by day were his seen avatars, showing he was always there.

Humans were created after a decision was made by this Sky chief's council. In the East lived the male beings and in the West the females. Father Morning Star (Venus) overcame many obstacles to sire a baby girl with mother Evening Star (Venus). Then Sun begat a boy with Moon. These became the parents of humanity, divided into communities, each led by a chief who had been a Star with a bundle that ("who") descended to earth. Among the four Pawnee bands, the Skiri towns confederated on the basis of set rotations among these chiefs and bundles, duplicating on earth what was happening in the sky.

Sky observations were made from fixed locations or seats. Some of these were outside to view landmarks along the horizon. Inside an earth lodge, a Pawnee priest sat west of the fire, at a place sacred to "mother" Evening Star, and looked up through the smoke hole at sunset and at dawn to plot the movements of stars, planets, and other sky beings such as Comets. Certain positions reached by stars signaled the timing of events. Early in February, the Corona appeared through the smokehole an hour before sunrise and the Pleiades showed up an hour after sunset. When a seated priest saw the Pleiades directly over the smokehole, the planting ceremonies began.

Throughout the year, the series of rites, based in stars and bundles, matched the pace of the earth, the sky, and the seasons with that of humans themselves. One of the Pawnee bundles included a star chart painted on an antelope hide that still fascinates and informs modern astronomers.[435]

The Skiri twin bundles of the Wonderful Skull and of the North Star represented all the confederated villages. Directly below these in degree of *puwah* were four bundles associated with the semi-cardinal directions, each with a leading chief who held authority over everyone for six month periods during an overall two-year sequence: Yellow Tent Bundle of the Northwest, Red Star of the Southwest, Big Black Star of the Northeast, and White Star of the Southeast. North bundles led during the winter, and South ones in summer. Complementing this sky-based system of priests and bundles were earth-based shamanic ~ doctor guilds, including the Medicine Lodge of the Pawnee (Chapter 8).

Overall, Pawnee society was organized around a series of overlapping triads, defining social classes and polity, pervaded by gender symbolism of Man and Woman, reflected in economics, ritual, and cosmology. These classes consisted of the elite "high" born, the ordinary ("good"), and the poor, sometimes with captives beyond the pale (outside society). Included in the elite were families noted for successive generations of chiefs, priests, and shamans. At a lesser rank were the families of warriors and other ambitious individuals without pedigree or ancestors of distinction. Chiefs benefited both from ancestry at particular stars and their own life-long training and public dedication.

In general, all these triplets reflected a basic one of leader/ manager/ commoner.[436] Significantly crossing these threefold segments was the duality of gender

---

[435] Von Del Chamberlin, <u>When Stars Came Down to Earth</u> 1982.

[436] These triplets range from leading chiefs/ priests/ doctors – to chiefs/ attendants/ members, leader shamans/ cult shamans/ ordinary doctors – to domestic roles organized as grandmaternal leader/ senior wives/ junior

reflected in bison and other hunting by men and in farming by women. Genders had different, complementing roles, functions, and responsibilities within the whole. For example, while the society was matrilineal, succession to office was generally patrilineal.

In all, this duality expressed a profound belief in the creative joining of opposites, expressed as Man and Woman, but this understanding was a guarded privilege known only to the elite, basic to their store of esoteric knowledge, together with titles and badges, bundle custody, and generosity. On the basis of this belief, some Pawnee recognized that death and destruction were more apparent than real. Time ran in cycles so life transmuted into successive forms. Thus, the death of plant crops at harvest allowed people to live until they too died and returned to the soil to nurture plants, each and all morphing to continue vitality. In all, Pawnee symbolic oppositions are:

MAN =	red	day	light	fire	dry	warfare	sky
Sun		winter		north	east		

WOMAN =	white	night	dark	rain	wet	farming	earth
Moon		summer		south	west		

The Skiri universe was composed of a plethora of metaphoric equations based on the fundamental genders, particularly represented in mythology and ritual by Morningstar Man and Eveningstar Woman. Each village bundle encouraged endogamy and internal solidarity, with its own cornfields and burial grounds. Maize was specifically identified as a Woman. Therefore, every cornfield was planted with an even number of hillocks to represent her breasts.

Alabama

For Native America, the sky and star lore of southern California Chumash, Plains Pawnee and Lakota, and Southwest Zuni are particularly well documented. The Southeast is not. A start has been made with a tale from the Alabama, suggesting the role of the Big Dipper in the coordination of the annual Busk.[437] Here is the summary, which abundantly indicates the power of song and trance to sustain and mobilize.

"People came from the sky in a canoe, singing and laughing. They got out on a prairie and played ball, presumable the two-stick ballgame. Then they went back into the sky. Some time later, they did all of this again. They became so predictable that a man positioned himself on a tree behind some bushes. When the ball went out of bounds near him, a woman ran to get it. He seized her, while the others hurriedly sang their way back into the sky, then married her and they had several children. When these were older, their

wives. The society as a whole consisted of hereditary families/ ambitious families/ ordinary families, including boys – aimless young and old men.

[437] Ray Williamson, The Celestial Skiff: An Alabama Myth of the Stars, Earth & Sky 1992: 52-66; Waselkov and Smith, Upper Creek Archaeology, Indians of the Greater Southeast, Alabamas: 248-9.

mother put them up to asking the father to go far away to hunt fresh venison. The man went off but became increasingly suspicious.

He returned home to find his wife and children singing in a canoe and rising toward the sky. He grabbed the canoe and pushed it down to the ground. Determined to return to the sky, the woman secretly made a small canoe while her husband went off hunting. When it was ready and he was gone, she got into the big canoe and put her children in the smaller one. They rose as they sang loudly. Alerted, the man rushed back and got the smaller canoe to the ground. His wife escaped.

The children pleaded to join their mother, and the father agreed. They took the canoe into the sky (by singing?). They came to an old woman and asked where their mother was. "Their mother is dancing over yonder all the time, having small round squashes for breasts." Then the woman gave them cooked squashes in pieces that kept replenishing themselves so that what looked like a tiny amount fed them amply. Then the old woman broke up a corncob and gave the pieces to her visitors. The family went on to another house, where they could see their mother dancing, inside rather than in an open plaza. As she went by, they threw a bit of corncob at her. They missed and she rushed on. The second time, they threw and she became startled, saying, "I smell something". The last time, they hit her and she realized her children had come. She joined them in the canoe and went back to the earth. After a time, the mother and children left in a canoe to return to the sky. For some time, the father tried living alone, but finally decided to go into the sky. He got into a canoe, singing, and rose up. Unwisely, he looked down, the canoe plummeted to earth, and he died.[438]

In his analysis of this tale, Ray Williamson suggests that the singing was what propelled the canoe, but he ignored the nautical necessity of paddling together to stay on course. The song probably set the tempo for paddle strokes. Moreover, these people are loud, which is not proper behavior anywhere in the Americas. The Tsimshian have an epic called the Revenge of Heaven, wherein their deity lured into the sky some noisy children who were playing games much too loudly and so restored quiet to the world.[439]

The timing of these canoe trips is assumed to coincide with the annual Busk of the Alabama. In addition to misunderstanding this as a Fall harvest feast – instead of a late Summer fast while the maize stands in the fields, one of the most compelling facts is overlooked. The mother's breasts are likened to squashes, and the children are fed tiny, inexhaustible squash slices. Ordinarily corn in the milk stage would have been the more likely analogy to the mother's breasts. During the Busk, however, there is a taboo on the touching, eating, and using of corn except at the ceremony, after the fasting, prayers, and purifications are over. It specifically relates to the new corn. Houses and town were cleaned out, and hearth fires were extinguished. These hearths were then rekindled from the new fire made in the center of the square. Old pottery, clothes, and, presumably, stored food were discarded.

---

[438] John Swanton, <u>Myths and Tales of the Southeastern Indians</u> 1929: 138-139.

[439] Jay Miller, <u>Tsimshian Culture</u> ~ <u>A Light Through the Ages</u> 1997.

The cob that was broken apart may have been from the past harvest, but a fresh cob would be more dangerous and require greater care. Because the husband and children lived in another world or dimension, they may not have been visible to the woman. From her constant dancing, she was in trance (Chapter 4). Her senses had to be alerted. By effort, her smell was awakened before her sight, either by the musty cob, by mortal human odors, or, more probably, a fresh cob then under taboo.

The Alabama Busk was held in June and until then "it was wrong to touch" corn. Each family brought roasted ears to the square, where they were placed on a cane-covered scaffold four feet high.[440] Everyone danced until midnight, the women forming an inner ring near the fire and the men an outer ring. Anyone who did not participate was ostracized. Some of the roasted ears were shelled, "and a few men took a handful (of kernels) apiece and threw them over the house. This was done four times." They ate what was left. A pot of medicine was brewed and heated. Then a man blew into it through a cane **tube** to make it bubble and receive special prayers. Men drank this medicine and then retired to purge.

The next dawn, a new fire was kindled in the woods and brought into the square. Women took embers from it to restart their kitchen fires. On each of the four nights of the Busk, roasted ears were brought to the scaffold, everyone danced until midnight, and handfuls of kernels were thrown over the house.[441]

In northern latitudes, only the three circumpolar constellations appear to swing down to earth and rise into the sky.[442] These are the Big Dipper (Ursa Major), Little Dipper (Ursa Minor), and Cassiopeia. Since the time on the ground was enough for a ballgame, which could last hours, only Ursa Major for Summer and Cassiopeia for early and late Spring would fit. Busk and ballgames, however, are Summer events so it has to be the Big Dipper. As confirmation, the Alabama name for the bowl of this constellation is indeed "canoe, watercraft" (Boat Stars).

In late July, the Big Dipper in the Alabama homeland appears to set at 1am and rises just after dawn. On the autumnal equinox, the sun rises at 6am and sets at 6pm, with an hour and twenty minutes of twilight, when the Big Dipper begins to set. The small canoe holding the children is probably one of the three stars in the handle, all of them bright. And they do indeed follow along with the body of the dipper's bowl.

Creek timing of their Busk occurs at the new full moon, but this over-simplifies. The dozen or so modern _talwa_ rotate the roles of host and guest throughout the Summer. After the full day when each town celebrates its Busk, other towns arrive in the evening to feast and to lead stomp dances in alternation all night long. Each town occupies a place in the series, which now also has to consider the demands of employment, as well

---

[440] This placement of the corn atop a scaffold recalls the first stages in some Southeast burial ritual, where the body is left on a platform to decompose before the bones are prepared for the temple.

[441] John Swanton, <u>Religious Beliefs and Medical Practices of the Creek Indians</u> 1928b: 602.

[442] Modern Creeks still have the sense that ancestors and others visit the earth, sometimes to attend Busks, using these stars as vehicles as they dip down at the horizon.

as ancient alliances. This means that weekends in July and August are devoted to the series of Busks now held by Creeks. Certain towns held their Busk on the weekend as close to the new moon as possible, with the other towns, knowing their own relative position before or after that of a key "mother" town, scheduling their own Busks accordingly in sequence.

In all, then, it is considerations of the sky, the earth, the crops, and the sequencing of towns hosting the Busks that must be taken into account in order to act appropriately as host or as guest at any of the vitalizing celebrations by modern Southeastern tribes, continuing mounds and other traditions enhancing vitalities from their Mississippian past.

Natchez

The Natchez[443] provide a last glimpse of a doomed Mississippian chiefdom before they were brutally dispersed by wars with the French in 1715, 1722, and 1730. Their language, remotely related to Tunican, was also spoken by the Avoyel and Taensa, whose temple was destroyed by lightning on 17 March 1700. Without that cataclysm and French attempts to halt the resulting infant sacrifices, this building would have gone unmentioned. Like ever-present churches in Europe, most foreign writers were oblivious to them,[444] or, in the case of missionary Catholic priests, actively hostile and seeking their destruction, as Pere Antoine Davion destroyed the Tunica temple without forfeiting his life because their great chief liked him.[445]

In British Louisiana (now the state of Mississippi), the Natchez had ten towns (half of them composed of refugees) near the Mississippi River, each ruled by a member of the same royal family. The head of that family, who was called and regarded as the Great Sun, ruled all the Natchez from a ceremonial center located across a creek from the main town. This center (now the Fatherland site) had three mounds, about six feet high, on a diagonal at the northeast end, the middle (dividing two plaza areas), and the southwest end. These mounds were on an axis that was 30.25° east of north, and therefore were crossed by a perpendicular that was close to the winter sunrise and summer sunset at the solstices.[446]

---

[443] Willard Walker, The Natchez: Ethnographic Notes 1979; Ian Brown, Natchez Indians and the Remains of a Proud Past, <u>Natchez Before 1839</u> 1989: 8-28; Karl Lorenz, The Natchez of Southwest Mississippi, <u>Indians of the Greater Southeast</u> 2000: 142-177.

[444] Though Pierre LeMoyne Ibbeville, <u>Gulf Journals</u> 1981: 62, 125, 129, 152, well describes temples for the Boyogoula, Natchez, and Taensa – writing explicitly that the Natchez chief's hut "is erected on a 10-foot mound of dirt carried there, 25 feet wide and 45 feet long.... Facing the chief's is the temple. These form a ring somewhat oval-shaped and enclose a public square about 250 yards wide and 300 long."

[445] John Swanton, <u>Indian Tribes of the Lower Mississippi Valley and Adjacent Coast of the Gulf of Mexico</u> 1911: 309.

[446] Clay Sherrod and Martha Ann Rolingson, Surveyors of the Ancient Mississippi Valley 1987, 3, 133; based on Anthony Aveni, Appendix VI: 176 in Robert

When the French arrived, the middle mound held the house of the living Sun, the southernmost had the temple, and the northern one was unused. Every dawn, the Sun greeted his ancestor and kin.[447] When he left the mound to travel, he was carried above the ground in a litter with a canopy.

In this warm climate, women wore a short skirt and men a front flap only. During winter, cloaks and robes were added. A sloped forehead was achieved by applying pressure with sand-filled weights to shape the heads of tiny infants. Tattoos marked rank and honor. Each nation also had an emblem ~ logo that was tattooed on the body and etched on weapons. That of the Natchez was a sun, while the Chakchiouma had a crayfish (Chapter 5) and the Bayogoulas an alligator.

Strategically located among the ten towns were three huge mound centers. Anna (1200-1350 AD) was located on a high bluff, and included eight platform mounds. Emerald (1500-1680 AD) itself consists of a huge pentagonal platform base (770 by 433 feet, second only to Monk's Mound) that today is 33 feet high and topped by rectangular mounds at each end and six square ones, arranged as threesomes along each side. Foster (CE 1350-1500) was transitional to Fatherland, the temple town attacked by the French. At each of these sites, the largest mound, often at the crucial intersection, probably housed the human Great Sun.[448] Though unoccupied during the Colonial era, some Natchez, especially Suns, would have worshiped at these sites of their ancient glory – venerably infused with *puwah* ~ vitality.

The Natchez temple visited by the French had a perpetual fire fed as a cross + by eight-foot logs, specially debarked and stockpiled around a special tree. The fire was maintained by eight men, two for each of the four quarters of the world. If the fire went out, they suffered death. On the temple roof were carvings of three large birds (eagles?), facing east and painted white with highlighted red feathers. The inside of the temple was divided by a wall. One section was twenty-feet wide and held the fire and an altar (6 by 2 feet on top and 4 feet high) that supported the remains of the last Sun kept in a cane basket. The bones of all prior Suns were kept in the other ten-foot wide room on the south side. Also inside were a carving of a rattlesnake, crystals, and stuffed owls, as well

---

Neitzel, Grand Village of the Natchez Revisited 1983. The alignment of the mounds to the solstices in a society whose major ceremonies occurred at the equinoxes further indicates how all-encompassing any theories of mounds and cultures should be.

[447] As Ray Fogelson is fond of noting, cultural bias is likely since Frenchmen were predisposed to solar rulers as this was the era of their own Sun Kings at Versailles – Louis XIV (1638-1715, crowned 1643) and Louis XV (1710-1774, with a regent until 1723), who was next in line as the surviving great grandson after many deaths in the intervening royal family. Death, even among the mighty, was ever present. Life is indeed uncertain.

[448] Karl Lorenz, The Natchez of Southwest Mississippi 2000, 146-7; William Morgan, Precolumbian Architecture in Eastern North America 1999: 166-170. Gordon precedes these three phases.

as stone figures, including the petrified first ancestor to come from the Sun in the sky.[449] The rattler was there to provide protection since the closely related Chitimacha believed that each family had a rattlesnake that would occupy and protect their home while they were away, then leave when they came back.[450]

Though it has been much debated among scholars, the Natchez probably observed the usual conventions of the Southeast for moieties divided into white and red. The French – looking for rank, class, and nobility – saw them in the Natchez and this has wrongly tainted the record. The French described four classes called Suns, Nobles, Honoreds, and Stinkards, who were said to speak another language. Suggesting an internally ranked moiety, the first three classes had to marry into the fourth, the other half. For both, membership was passed on only through the mother. Separate languages may not have been an issue since one Creek Red moiety was called "Those of Different Speech".

Most likely, therefore, Natchez had a system of matri-moieties, with one half including Earth women and the other Sky women, whose three internal rankings were based on closer or lesser degrees of mythic ancestry to the Sun. The key female figure was titled the White Woman, who was the senior woman, usually the mother of the present Sun and sister of the prior one. During the troubles with the French, her name was Tattooed Arm and she sabotaged a planned attack by her people that led to their own devastation.

Some could change their rank (and moiety), however, by valor in war or, during the funeral of a Sun, by offering a child as sacrifice or by acting as executioner of those who sacrificed themselves to join the Sun in death. One's membership was starkly revealed in the presence of the Great Sun, since those of lower rank had to respond with how! how! how! (three times) while higher ranks said it fewer times and fellow Suns whispered it once.[451]

Leadership was also divided between peace and war, White and Red. The Tattooed Serpent, who died on 1 June 1725, was the brother of the ruling Great Sun and the war chief of the nation. After he died, the French mounted a vigil to keep the grieving Great Sun from suicide. When Antoine Simon le Page du Pratz went to visit this

---

[449]   John Swanton, Indian Tribes of the Lower Mississippi Valley and Adjacent Coast of the Gulf of Mexico 1911: 159, 175, 269.

[450]   John Swanton, Indian Tribes of the Lower Mississippi Valley 1911: 318, 357. The Yurok of northern California hold the same belief that high ranking families had pet rattlers who protected their houses and treasures when they went away, see Lucy Thompson, To The American Indian 1916, 183-184; Cf. Thomas Buckley, Standing Ground, Yurok Spirituality 2002. The Tunica temple held idols of a woman and a frog, and while Swanton could associate the woman with the sun, who was female for Tunica, in sharp contrast to its maleness among their Natchez enemies, he was baffled by the frog. In Puget Sound, the epic of Starchild (Sun and Moon) includes a frog wife who eventually attaches herself to the face of Moon, see Jay Miller, Lushootseed Culture and the Shamanic Odyssey 1999: 55.

[451]   This is the Natchez equivalent of the Appalachee "$\underline{q^w\underline{a}}$".

Sun, he remarked that all of the home fires were drowned out and "the signal to extinguish the fires caused all the Natchez to tremble",[452] mimicking the unsteady state of the world. Later he entered the temple on the mound to find a room "full of Suns, nobles, and respected ones, all of whom were trembling" until he poured off the priming powder from the only gun there to keep the Great Sun from shooting himself.

Joining Tattooed Serpent in death, burial, and first funeral were his two wives, advisor, doctor, head of staff, pipe carrier, and some willing old women. Other people volunteered to be sacrificed as the funeral approached. Behind each one of these sacrificed retainers was a procession that was composed of those carrying, in turn, a 1) war club, 2) mat, 3) strangling cord, 4) skin (hood), 5) bowl holding six stupefying wads of powdered tobacco, 6) clay water bottle, and (7, 8) two men who would pull the cord tight. These eight items were used by or upon the retainer at the final moment. Tattooed Serpent and his wives were buried in the floor of the temple, then later dug up and defleshed ten months later. Their bones were put into burial baskets and given to kin to place in a temple. Remains of other sacrifices were taken away to be buried in their home villages.

The Great Sun himself presided at the two major rituals of the year, which marked the equinoxes (Spring on March 21, Fall on September 21). These were important because they signaled the transition in the ancient dual-year calendar from the summer farming part of the year to the winter hunting season. Villagers, both men and women, joined in work bees to plant, tend, and harvest each family's cornfield in turn. They also cared for the special fields of the Sun, and stored his harvest in a communal granary.

It is likely that the Natchez burned over their lands to encourage new growth. The Chitimacha tell of an angry man who set fire to a vast marsh, when Redwing Blackbird earned his bloody feathers trying to prevent him. Instead of causing hardship, however, the fire taught people the virtues of burning over the land and holding surrounds to hunt the escaping game.[453]

Each of the Natchez months, with the year beginning in March, was devoted to a particular food. In order, these were 1) deer at Spring equinox, 2) strawberries, 3) "little" corn, 4) melons, 5) grapes, 6) mulberries, 7) maize harvest with solemn feast at Fall equinox, 8) turkey, 9) buffalo, 10) bear, 11) geese, ducks, 12) chestnuts, and 13) nuts. What is notable is the division of the year into summer plants (2-7) and winter game (1, 8-11), with nuts (12-13), the important food since Archaic times, serving as the transition. The March rite (1) ended with a feast after a mock battle, divided into teams wearing white or red feathers that defended or menaced the Sun. The September rite (7) celebrated the maize harvested from the special field tended only by warriors and placed in a granary outside (or between towns), where temporary cabins were set up. It ended with a game of handball between red and white teams.

When the Sun himself died, his older family members were killed at his funeral. His remains were then placed on the altar in the temple, and those of his predecessor were moved into the smaller side room. His house was burned down, with another layer of earth added to cap the mound before a new home was built for the new Sun. Home fires were restarted from that rekindled in the temple, and the new Sun began each dawn

---

[452] Charles Van Tuyl, The Natchez 1979: 11, 14, 16, 25, 34.

[453] John Swanton, Indian Tribes of the Lower Mississippi Valley 1911: 359.

by greeting his relative in the sky, from atop the higher mound. By such repetitions, the world was protected and made safe, a community refuge ballasted, a temple sent on to parallel existences with Suns, and the sealed off layers holding the vitality of songs.

Conclusions

To the best of their abilities, natives transferred the precision of the skies onto the earth. As leaders traced their origins to Stars or the Sun, so mounds brought all people closer to the heavens. Built for pilgrimage and commerce, places like Poverty Point and the many Hopewell enclosures became powerful attractions over centuries. At Cahokia, itself a prime location, Mound 72 and its twin beaded burial fused together all aspects of their cosmos. The "higher" authority of earthly leaders was drawn from the sky. The top of a mound brought them upward and the insides of this same mound (duplicated within a dark section of the surmounting temple) took them downward.

While the celestial azimuths and alignments can still be traced by astronomers, they are meager testament to the greatness and wisdom of their makers. For a more comprehensive view, we looked to the fuller descriptions of the Pawnee, Alabama, and, especially, the ill-fated Natchez. Adding a new surface and house to an accretional mound whenever a new Sun was invested clearly associated the mound with renewal. For the workers, moreover, it was a labor of atonement and of hope. The past is covered over and sent onward, the future begins anew, and songs vitally sustain all.

Whether working with the earth or watching the sky, mounds involved cooperation among many forces, only some of them human. Earth moving was an expression of common effort, of working together toward an obvious goal. As a direct correlation, these efforts link past effort, numbers, and size in a way that still speaks to those of the present. Bigger is more, but smaller is not less since time may have taken a toll that actually heightened sanctity.[454]

A healthy and well-fed population built mounds. At first they were enhancing what nature provided as (garnered) food and materials, but later they were intensively farming the crop trinity. Living in towns entailed public works and projects for the benefit of all. Terracing hillsides and building canals around rapids required the approval of the earth, petitioned with offerings and prayers, but it made human life and transport easier. Undertaking such construction called for conscious effort and consensus. Assessed benefits included the obvious ease that resulted, but it also involved religious expressions to assure the wellbeing of the community. That people internalized this shaping of the earth and made it personal is suggested by the initial cranial shaping done to infant heads that began in the Adena period.

The intensity of the ballgame also reflects this communal impulse. In the Northwest, the non-farming Tsimshian lived ~ live on the bounty of salmon, other fish, game, berries, and plants. During the Summer, matrifamilies scattered to their clan-owned resource areas, and, during the Winter, they congregated in cedar-plank-house

---

[454] Saint's relics are an apt example that less is more, See Orin Starn, Ishi's Brain ~ In Search of America's Last Wild Indian 2004: 197, citing Peter Brown on their "inverse magnitude".

towns to stage impressive rituals, feasts, and public events. To transition, each town had a special Fall(-In) camp, where they gathered on their way back to the winter site to hold games and other competitions, learning again to work together in play after a summer apart.[455] This was a short-term solution.

By lasting over the long term, mounds also became an obvious embodiment of that fragile human community. Later people could add directly to the efforts of earlier ones, descendants could share common ground (literally) with ancestors. Providing an observation deck to the skies above, a haven in flood, and a gathering together of special earths once widely dispersed below; mounds, by public effort, made all these remote considerations manifestly visible. As blest ballast, bulk and banked bulge, they steadied the world, as canoes in epics transported people to the sky as well as along waterways, powered by the vitalizing rhythms of song.

Mounds anchor the earth after its creation. In Egypt, moreover, a mound stood at the center of creation itself: "the pyramid shape, which can be traced back to 1st Dynasty mounds left inside elite tombs ... built over the burial shaft ... represent[s] the earthen mound on which the primeval god stood to create the Egyptian cosmos."[456]

---

[455] Jay Miller, Tsimshian Culture ~ A Light Through the Ages 1997: 23.

[456] Zahi Hawass, Secrets from the Sand 2003: 44, 104.

8 ~ FINALE

Mounds touch freshly exposed earth, compressing it as a still place of safety in a tumultuous world, created by deliberate actions of Earth Diver, Father Sky and Mother Earth, Spider, Tricksters, Twins, Dismemberment, or Emergence. Its embodiments include snakes and other ground dwellers, often slithering reptiles and amphibians. While the outer form of mounds mirrors earth, hill, mountain, volcano, and sky; their insides evoke hollow heart, womb, spine, nest, den, and fortress. At other times, or even simultaneously, the inside is grave, cave, tube, and passage to the underworld, as well as conduit to new vitality.

Sustained by orderly human rituals and purifying efforts, mounding also acts as atonement for unintended human impacts on the earth. Once built up, they provide steadying ballast, bulk, bank, and bulge. More than just places for burials, community projects, or territory markers, mounds provide the means for humans to be bodily involved in a microcosm of the cosmic cycles, while also providing a vital haven from the precarious, unstable, and suddenly-violent world – given to pulsing, trembling, and occasional writhing turmoil that is not easily predictable or avoidable without some kind of supernatural aid and prophetic warnings.

Yet this anchoring also encouraged forecasting, in dream, vision, and trance. Northern hunters like the DunneZa believe they must first dream an encounter with the spirit of an animal in order to take its meat and release its spirit. Vision quests, where a youth sought a spirit to provide life-long help, are a hallmark of Native America.[457] Given its distribution, Paleo-Indiens probably arrived with this out-of-body tradition, localizing it in rituals that acclimated natives to be local residents. Powerful inspiration comes from above, approached from a high place. Placed in comparative perspectives, as pan-human aspects, the Irish, Shilluk, Dobu, and !Kung help illuminate Native America.

Stone as artifacts has ramifications beyond the archaeological record. Weight, color, and design aesthetics carry heavy symbolic meaning. Paleo-Indien caches added color to such offerings, while early Archaic burials at Windover actually pinned bodies to the watery ground. Mounds added their honored earth as ballast, though scholars were slow to sort out their makers by time, space, and tool kit. Later, in Wisconsin, mounds were given recognizable species shapes and appropriate habitat locations allied with kin groups and clans.

Moreover, a few constructions were intended to be unique attractions. For northeast Louisiana, such impressive centers lasted for over five thousands of years, as substantiated by Watson Brake, Poverty Point, Troyville, and others. Viewed in sequence, they drew distant visitors offering stones to such pilgrimage sites along the crucial lower Mississippi River, partaking of their banked blessings in a warm climate with few lithic resources.

Mounds mirror memory, too, as gateways. The Lower Illinois River study[458] indicates that that built environment of large and small Middle Woodland monuments served to re-create the cosmos, both vertically and horizontally, as well as providing a

---

[457] Ruth Benedict, <u>The Concept of the Guardian Spirit in North America</u> 1923.

[458] Jane Buikstra and Douglas Charles, Centering the Ancestors 1999: 208, 212, 216, 218.

forum for the intense negotiation of power relations among the living. It identified three loci of interments: a) at bluff crest knolls, b) at flood plain sand ridges, and c) at villages beside slackwater lakes. Atop bluffs, about seven thousand years ago (7000 BP), mounds begin "sequential additions of bodies [of young and middle-aged adults, tools, offerings] and enclosing sediments". Such bluff crests poise between the earth / sky and valley / uplands, so these Middle Archaic ancestors overlooked the living and "began the mound-building tradition." On the floodplain, featuring huge platform mounds later, at lakeside dwellings, young and infirm are buried in middens without offerings. Sand ridges held reburials with a high density and variety of offerings, clearly showing the expected reversal between living and dead because pottery decorated with raptors is always stacked below that with spoonbills, inverting the natural order of these birds.

In all, size and location distinguish an exclusive ancestral ~ political cult visible on knolls from an inclusive earth ~ fertility one on floodplain platforms. The former separated out kin units, while the latter integrated whole communities, sustained by these vital mounds. During mortuary rites, bodies carried over the locale, including time on raised scaffolding, provided both a reintegrative cosmological tour and a route for reaching the afterworld.

Along the Hocking, widening at the Plains of Athens and Ohio University,[459] a long-term study of landscape and mounds shows a steady increase in population, adoption of pottery to aid the processing of nut meats, a settlement shift to floodplain farming of corn (maize), and then, under drought aggravating maize-caused soil depletion, to better watered if more vulnerable banks of the Ohio River itself.

Beginning about 2500 years ago, mounds on ridgetops, like the Illinois bluffs, visible to each other, "mimic the natural landscape, thus cognitively associating the interred and the community with the land itself",[460] bundling together sentiments of identity, territory, sedentism, and gardening, against an intense sense of declining productivity and alienation from the land due to adverse climate changes. Overwhelmingly a religious expression – as plea, prayer, and atonement – mounds anchored the landscape.

The Plains became an "empty" ceremonial center for the dispersed Hocking population, hosting periodic gatherings to feast, pray, and build monuments, especially mounds and ten earthwork rings (circles), during the Hopewell "as an expression of grieving, honor, and memory of the dead".[461] Variations in the treatment of the deceased (interment, bundle, cremation, excarnation, log tomb, bark blankets, exotic artifact offerings, reburial) express the varied customs by an array of lineages or family lines.

In Ohio, mounds had long-range purposes as beacon, blessing, bank, and ballasting; monuments to place, people, pride, and profits from the land, vital for their own members as well as claims against others. Over eons, they securely placed people – unborn, living, and dead.

---

[459] Elliot Abrams and AnnCorinne Freter, <u>The Emergence of the Moundbuilders</u> 2005.

[460] Abrams and Freter 2005: 93, 178, 184.

[461] Abrams and Freter 2005: 99.

Mounds proliferated for the same reason as churches and banks do now; everyone wanted a safe haven directly, communally, and "personally" tapped to vital, life-giving divinity. Unlike right-angled buildings, mound fit organically into the land itself as a mark of genuine respect. Sizes and numbers of mounds are significant; upheld and enforced by the sanctions of neighboring opinion. Each mound's start or new earthen mantle mobilizes community effort, which was shown off and judged by intercommunity feasting and ceremony to legitimate that claim. Larger, more generous, strategic communities were entitled by popular opinion to bigger monuments.

This ranking of mounds created links between and among all the regional sites, such that single mound towns gained added stability because they were integrated with multimound centers, sometimes via actual constructed causeways above the ground. At least four levels can be assumed, given the universal importance of the number 4 in Native North America. Roughly these would be equivalent, in decreasing significance, to cathedral, church, chapel, and shrine. Surrounding walls or other barriers, like those now protecting both churches and banks, serve to concentrate *puwah* as defense against outside attack, theft, or siphoning off.

Today, at Creek ceremonies, people remark "they're looking good" both to themselves and to outsiders because the sacred precincts have been beautifully cleaned and cleared, and everyone is dressed in colorful finery. In the home camps, visitors are well fed and made welcome, adding to everyone's enjoyment. Work is done on the basis of ability. Older men as "arbor weights"[462] plan, direct, and advise, while younger men do the heavy, dirty, and arduous labor as work teams to hoe and rake the plaza, cut the fresh willows to roof the arbors, and harvest the special medicine plants to make the "herb water".

Men work together inside the enclosing ring, and women outside alone in their family camps. Men contribute directly while women reverse actions. Men are fasting and thirsting while they clean the ground and take ("touch") medicine; women, outwardly, are feeding visitors and exorcising the confines. Most obviously, men undertake the Feather Dance, devoted to birds and the heavens; while women, elaborately dressed, do the Ribbon Dance, wearing heavy leg rattles, often of turtle shells, holding them to the earth. Men raise river canes decorated with white feathers at the tip; each of the two lead women hold horizontally rigid a huge knife (*atassa*) carved of wood to butcher and remove any harm lurking on the grounds. Holding these knives absolutely still more effectively and thoroughly chops up harm in the reversed spiritual dimensions.

Mounds are not limited or unique to the Southeast. In the Northwest, Northeast, and Plains they are "holy homes", havens, burials, and offerings. Emblematic of the earth itself, Lushootseeds call their inhabitants Little Earths, and invoke them for the great *puwah* to enable shamans to travel to the afterworld safely and return with missing vitalities to cure a patient. Traveling in symbolic canoes, mounds painted at the base of empowered planks provided literal ballast for stability.

Other spirits, some under hills and mounds, are petitioned for help during quests and rituals. After the Abenaki Flood, humans and animals took on their subsequent identities, with emerging hills providing havens. While Osage no longer build mounds, except as tiny peyote altars, their rituals evoke Mississippian times, even to their bright

---

[462] Hill, Description of Hilabi Round House, 18, line 5; Haas and Hill 2015: 67.

use of shell and copper. Karuk make their mound from the sands of a boat landing, a protective haven at the end of a sometimes turbulent river crossing. By this mounding and embedding arrows, they fix for another year a world made unsteady by human faults. But human transgressions soon again start the imbalances that outweighs all this yearly good work. Until the 1600s, Huron placed violent deaths under a mound topped by a small hut, reminiscent of that inside the Calusa temple. Protecting against violent outbursts of the earth, Wichitas and other Caddoans propitiated special snake figures dug out in intaglios or sculptures.

Mound insides are more than mere empty hollows; they sing, as sound chamber, womb, nest, and den. Residents included snakes, insects, reptiles, and birds, with the ability both to sing and to provide humans with songs. Pawnee priests drew enclosures with a compass made of a string tightened between sharp sticks. Once piled up, bare mounds wore down by erosion typical of the earth itself. When grassed-over and stabilized, mounds serve as obvious permanent markers on the landscape. Their blessed insides sometimes included the dead and (c)remains, acting like seeds to revivify the land, becoming an oven, a charged repository, or incubator.

Cremation created a quick and sweet release of the souls from their mortal remains. Their very insubstantiality, however, was sometimes countered by the monumentality of mounds that came to hold their ashes. Offerings and other reminders added more substance. This rendering of the corpse served to ease and enhance the transmission of a immortal name and persona to its next holder, a successor who thereby became more secure in their distinctly new identity.

The Hochungara creation saga best characterizes this native world, in all of its instability. After several attempts, it became habitable for free-ranging animals after four island earth weights, brother water serpents, implanted themselves tail first at the four directional corners. They all now face east and the sunrise, to stretch, steady, and hold the earth. Rocks (as women) add bulk, weight, height, and ballast.

Throughout, snakes have vital roles, representing the earth itself for Pawnee doctors. Their "skin shedding" provides the poetic phrase for immortality. Closely allied with women, and the Moon Woman of the Skiri, these reptiles can either steady or shake the earth. Human care, attention, dance, and song play vital roles in influencing all outcomes to be orderly, though mounting human faults always take a heavy toll threatening to upset the earth.

Sky lore is also significant, especially correlations with Sun and Moon. As sky orbs, their motions and shapes visually set the time for events. Rising and setting along the horizon line, their half circle arcs duplicate the mound form. As stars and orbs move into the underworld, they are believed to be mirrored inside hollow mounds.

To the best of their abilities, natives transferred the precision of the skies onto the earth. Leaders traced their origins to Stars or the Sun, and mounds brought elite people closer to the heavens. Built for pilgrimage and commerce, places like Poverty Point and the many Hopewell enclosures became powerful attractions over centuries. At Cahokia, itself a prime location, Mound 72 and its beaded twin burial fuses together a complex cosmos. This "higher" authority of earthly leaders reflect the sky. As the top of a mound brought them upward, the insides of this same mound (duplicated within a dark section of the surmounting temple) led them downward.

While celestial azimuths and alignments agree with today's astronomers, their cultural imports varied among Pawnee, Alabama, and, especially, the ill-fated Natchez. Supplying a new surface and house to an accretional mound when a new Natchez Sun was invested clearly associated the mound with renewal. For the workers, moreover, it was a labor of atonement and of renewed promise. The past is covered over to be sent onward, and the future begins anew, as songs vitally sustain all.

Working with the earth and watching the sky, mounds involved many forces, only some of them human. Earth moving was an expression of common effort, of working together toward an obvious goal. Such efforts link time, numbers, and size with meaning in the present. Bigger is more, but smaller is not less since time may have diminished form but heightened sanctity.[463]

A healthy and well-fed population built mounds. At first they were enhancing what nature provided as (garnered) food and materials, but later they were intensively farming the crop trinity. Living in towns entailed public works and projects for the benefit of all. Terracing hillsides and building canals to travel around rapids required the approval of the earth, petitioned with offerings and prayers, to make human life and transport easier. Undertaking such construction called for conscious effort and sustained consensus. Assessed benefits included both new ease, as well as religious devotions assuring the wellbeing of the entire community. That people internalized and personalized this shaping of the earth is suggested by the coincidence of initial infant cranial shaping with rise of Adena mounds.

The intensity of the games also reflects this communal impulse. In the Northwest, the non-farming Tsimshian long lived on the bounty of salmon, other fish, game, berries, and plants. Seasonally, during Summer, matrifamilies scattered to their clan-owned resource areas, and, during Winter, they congregated in cedar-plank-house towns to stage impressive rituals, feasts, and public events. At the autumn transition, each town had a special Fall(-In) camp, where they camped returning to the winter town to hold games and other competitions, relearning to playfully work together after a summer apart.[464]

By lasting over the long term, mounds also became an obvious embodiment of any fragile human community. Later people could add directly to the efforts of earlier ones, descendants could share common ground (literally) with ancestors. Providing an observation deck to the skies above, a haven in flood, a gathering together of special earths once widely dispersed, and a public platform; public-effort mounds made all these secondary considerations manifestly visible. As blest ballast, bulk and banked bulge, they steadied the world, just as canoes in epics took people into the sky and along waterways, powered by the re
vitalizing song.

First and foremost, mounds impacted a place on the churned earth, setting it apart visually and substantially, as a weighted haven of compressed safety, security, and, obviously, solid~arity.

---

[463] Like Catholic saint's relics.

[464] Jay Miller, Tsimshian Culture 1997: 23.

~ BIBLIOGRAPHY ~

Abbott, Donald 1981 <u>The World Is As Sharp As A Knife</u>, An Anthology in Honour of Wilson Duff. Victoria: British Columbia Provincial Museum.

Abrams, Elliot, and AnnCorinne Freter, eds. 2005 <u>The Emergence of the Moundbuilders</u>. The Archaeology of Tribal Societies in Southeastern Ohio. Athens: Ohio University Press.

Adams, John 1973 <u>The Gitksan Potlatch</u>: Population Flux, Resource Ownership, and Reciprocity. Toronto: Holt, Rinehart and Wilson of Canada.

Adair, James
    1930 <u>History of the American Indian</u>. Samuel Cole Williams, ed. NY: Promontory Press. [1775, London]
    2005 <u>History of the American Indian</u>. Kathryn Holland Braund, ed. Tuscaloosa: University of Alabama Press.

Adamson, Thelma 1934 Folk-Tales of the Coast Salish. Memoirs of the American Folk-Lore Society 27.

Aftandilian, Dave, ed. 2007a <u>What Are the Animals to Us?</u> Approaches from Science, Religion, Folklore, Literature, and Art. Knoxville: University of Tennessee Press.
    2007b Frogs, Snakes, and Agricultural Fertility: Interpreting Illinois Mississippian Representations. <u>What Are the Animals to Us?</u> Chapter 4: 53-86.

Ahler, Steven, ed. 2000 <u>Mounds, Modoc, and Mesoamerica</u>: Papers in Honor of Melvin L. Fowler. Illinois State Museum Scientific Papers 18.

Ames, Kenneth, and Herbert Maschner 1999 <u>Peoples of the Northwest Coast</u>. Their Archaeology and Prehistory. London: Thames and Hudson.

Anderson, William, Jane Brown, and Anne Rogers, eds. 2010 <u>The Payne-Butrick Papers</u>. Six volumes in two books (1-3, 4-6). Lincoln: University of Nebraska Press.

Angulo, Jaime de 1990 <u>Indians in Overalls</u>. San Francisco: City Light Books. [1950]

Aveni, Anthony 1983 Astronomical Orientations at the Fatherland Site, Grand Village of the Natchez Revisited: Excavations at the Fatherland Site, Adams County, Mississippi, in 1972. Robert Neitzel, ed. Mississippi Department of Archives and History, Archaeological Report 12, Appendix VI, 176.

Baby, Raymond 1954 Hopewell Cremation Practices. The Ohio Historical Society, Papers in Archaeology 1, 1-7.

Bahn, Paul, ed. 2002 <u>Written in Bones</u>. <u>How Human Remains Unlock the Secrets of the Dead</u>. Devon, England: David and Charles.

Bailey, Garrick A, ed. 1995 <u>The Osage and the Invisible World</u>. From the Works of Francis La Flesche. Norman: University of Oklahoma Press.

Baird, W. David 1972 <u>Peter Pitchlynn</u>: <u>Chief of the Choctaws</u>. Norman: University of Oklahoma Press.

Baraga, Frederic 2004 <u>Short History Of The North American Indians</u>. Graham A MacDonald, ed and trans. From the 1837 French edition. Calgary: University of Calgary Press.

Bartram, John and William 1957 Bartram's America. Selections from the Writings of the Philadelphia Naturalists. Helen Gere Cruickshank, ed. New York: The Devin-Adair Company.

Bates, Dawn, Thom Hess, and Vi Hilbert 1994 Lushootseed Dictionary. Seattle: University of Washington Press.

Bell, Amelia Rector 1984 Creek Ritual. The Path to Peace. University of Chicago: PhD Anthropology.

　　1990 Separate People: Speaking of Creek Men and Women. American Anthropologist 92, 332-342.

Benedict, Ruth Fulton 1923 The Concept of the Guardian Spirit in North America. Memoirs of the Society for American Archaeology 29.

Bernal, Ignacio 1969 The Olmec World. Berkeley: University of California Press.

Berryhill, Alfred, ed. 2007 Este Mvskukvlke Svkvsmkv En Yahiketv ~ Muscogee People's Praise and Worship Hymns. Okmulgee, OK.

Betts, Colin M. 2003 Protohistoric Oneota Mound Construction: An Early Revitalization Movement. Midwest Archaeological Conference 29, Milwaukee.

　　2000 Symbolic, Cognitive, and Technological Dimensions of Orr Phase Oneota Ceramics. University of Illinois at Urbana-Champaign: PhD Dissertation.

Birmingham, Robert, and Leslie Eisenberg 2000 Indian Mounds of Wisconsin. Madison: University of Wisconsin Press.

Blaine, Martha Royce 1979 The Ioway Indians. Norman: University of Oklahoma Press.

Bloch, Maurice, and Jonathan Perry, eds. 1982 Death and the Regeneration of Life. Cambridge: University Press.

Bonney, Rachel, and J. Anthony Paredes, eds. 2001 Anthropologists and Indians in the New South. Tuscaloosa: University of Alabama Press.

Bossu, Jean-Bernard 1969 Travels in the Interior of North America, 1751-1762. Seymore Feiler, ed. and translator. Norman: University of Oklahoma Press.

Boyd, Robert 1999 The Coming of the Spirit of Pestilence. Introduced Infectious Diseases and Population Decline among Northwest Coast Indians, 1774-1874. Seattle: University of Washington Press.

Bowers, Alfred 1965 Hidatsa Social And Ceremonial Organization. Bureau of American Ethnology, Bulletin 194.

Bowne, Eric 2005 The Westo Indians. Slave Traders of the Early Colonial South. Tuscaloosa: University of Alabama Press.

Buffalohead, Eric 2004 Dhegihan History: A Personal Journey. Plains Anthropologist 49 (192), 327-343.

Bradley, R. B. 1993 Altering the Earth. Edinburgh: Society of Antiquities of Scotland, Monograph 8.

Brain, Jeffrey 1989 Winterville. Late Prehistoric Culture Contact in the Lower Mississippi Valley. Mississippi Department of Archives and History, Archaeological Report No 23.

Brookes, Sam 1997 Aspects of the Middle Archaic: The Atassa. Results of Recent Archaeological investigations in the Greater Mid-South. Proceedings of the 17th Mid-South Archaeological Conference, Memphis, Tennessee, 29-30 June 1996.

Charles McNutt, ed. The University of Memphis, Anthropological Research Center, Occasional Paper 18, 55-70.

Brose, David, James Brown, and David Penney 1985 <u>Ancient Art of the American Woodland Indians</u>. New York: Harry N. Abrams and Detroit Institute of Arts.

Brose, David, C. Wesley Cowan, and Robert C. Mainfort, Jr. 2001 <u>Societies in Eclipse</u>. Archaeology of the Eastern Woodlands Indians, AD 1400-1700. DC: Smithsonian Institution Press.

Brown, Calvin 1926 <u>The Archaeology of Mississippi</u>. University, MS: Mississippi Geological Survey.

Brown, Ian 1989 Natchez Indians and the Remains of a Proud Past. <u>Natchez Before 1839</u>, 8-28. Noel Polk, ed. Jackson: University Press of Mississippi.

Brown, James A. 1985 The Mississippian Period. <u>Ancient Art of the American Woodland Indians</u> , III, 93-145. David Brose, James Brown, and David Penny, eds. New York: Harry N. Abrams, Inc.

1996 The Spiro Ceremonial Center. An Archaeology of Arkansas Valley Caddoan Culture in Eastern Oklahoma. Ann Arbor: Memoirs of the Museum of Anthropology, University of Michigan, Number 29, 2 Volumes.

2003 The Cahokia Mound 72-Sub 1 Burials as Collective Representation. <u>A Deep-Time Perspective: Studies in Symbols, Meaning and the Archeological Record</u>. Papers in Honor of Robert L. Hall. <u>The Wisconsin Archeologist</u> 84 (1&2), 81-97.

2006a Where's the Power in Mound Building: An Eastern Woodlands Perspective. Brian M. Butler and Paul D. Welch, eds. <u>Leadership and Polity in Mississippian Society</u>. Carbondale, Il: Center for Archaeological Investigation, Occasional Paper 33.

2006b The Shamanic Element in Hopewellian Period Ritual. <u>Recreating Hopewell</u>. Douglas Charles and Jane Buikstra, eds. Gainesville: University Press of Florida, 475-488, Chapter 26.

2007 On the Identity of the Birdman Within Mississippian Period Art and Iconography Chapter 4, 56-106. <u>Ancient Objects and Sacred Realms</u>. Interpretations of Mississippian Iconography. Kent Reilly and James Garber, eds. Austin: University of Texas Press.

Bruce-Mitford, R. L .S. 1964 The Sutton Hoo Ship Burial. London: British Museum.

Buckley, Thomas 2002 <u>Standing Ground</u>, Yurok Indian Spirituality, 1850 -1990. Berkeley: University of California Press.

Buikstra, Jane, and Douglas Charles 1999 Centering the Ancestors: Cemeteries, Mounds, and Sacred Landscapes of the Ancient North American Midcontinent, 201-28. <u>Archaeologies of Landscape: Contemporary Perspectives</u>. Wendy Ashmore and A. Bernard Knapp, eds. Oxford, UK: Blackwell.

Bunny, George, Woodrow Haney, Rev. James Wesley, and Morina Wildcat 1998 <u>Nakcokv Esyvhiketv</u>. <u>Muckogee Hymns</u>. United Methodist Church, General Commission on Religion and Race, with the permission of Presbyterian Board of Christian Education, 1936.

Bushnell, David I. 1908 The Account of Lamhatty. <u>American Anthropologist</u> 10: 568-574.

1909 The Choctaw of Bayou Lacomb. Bureau of American Ethnology, Bulletin 48.

1910 Myths of the Louisiana Choctaw. American Anthropologist 12: 526-535.

1927 Burials of the Algonquian, Siouan, and Caddoan Tribes West of the Mississippi. Bureau of American Ethnology, Bulletin 83.

Byers, A. Martin 1996 Social Structure and the Pragmatic Meaning of Material Culture: Ohio Hopewell as an Ecclesiastical-Communal Cult, A View from the Core: A Synthesis of Ohio Hopewell Archaeology. Paul J. Pacheco, ed. Columbus: Ohio Archaeological Council.

Caldwell, Joseph 1953 The Rembert Mounds, Elbert County, Georgia. Bureau of American Ethnology, Bulletin 154.

Caldwell, Joseph, and Catherine McCann 1941 Irene Mound Site, Chatham County, Georgia. Athens: The University of Georgia Press.

Carlton, Kenneth 1996 Nanih Waiya. Mother Mound of the Choctaw. Common Ground 1 (1): 32-33.

1999 Nanih Waiya (22W1500): An Historical and Archaeological Overview. Mississippi Archaeology 34 (2): 125-155.

Cavalli-Sforza, Luigi Luca 2000 Genes, Peoples, and Languages. Mark Seielstad, trans. Berkeley: University of California Press.

Chafe, Wallace 1976 The Caddoan, Iroquoian, and Siouan Languages. The Hague: Mouton.

Claiborne, John FH 1880 Mississippi as a Province, Territory, and State, with Biographical Notices of Eminent Citizens. Jackson, Mississippi: Power and Barksdale.

Chamberlain, Von Del 1982 When Stars Came Down to Earth: Cosmology of the Skidi Pawnee Indians of North America. Ballena Press Anthropological Papers 26.

1992 The Chief and His Council: Unity and Authority from the Stars. Earth & Sky. Vision of the Cosmos in Native American Folklore: 221-235. Ray Williamson and Claire Farrer, eds. Albuquerque: University of New Mexico Press.

Chappell, Sally A. Kitt 2002 Cahokia – Mirror of the Cosmos. Chicago: University of Chicago Press.

Charles, Douglas, and Jane Buikstra 2006 Recreating Hopewell. Gainesville: University of Press of Florida.

Chaudhuri, Jean Hill, and Joyotpaul Chaudhuri 2001 A Sacred Path, The Way of the Muscogee Creeks. Los Angeles: UCLA American Indian Studies Center.

Clark, J., Jon Gibson, and J. Zeider 2010 First Towns In The Americas: Searching For Agriculture, Population Growth, And Other Enabling Conditions: 205-245. Becoming Villagers: Comparing Early Village Societies. Matthew Bandy and Jake Fox, eds. Tucson: University of Arizona Press.

Cleal, Rosamund, KE Walker, and R Montague 1995 Stonehenge in its Landscape. Twentieth-century Excavations. Wessex Archaeology. London: English Heritage, Archaeological Report 10.

Cloud, Henry Roe ~ Wa-na-xi-lay Hunkah 1929 Winnebago Cosmology. The Ohio Archaeological and Historical Society Publications 18. 4 May.

Coe, Joffre Lanning 1995 <u>Town Creek Indian Mound</u>. A Native American Legacy. Chapel Hill: University of North Carolina Press.

Conley, Robert 1993 <u>The Dark Way</u>. The Real People Series, 2. Norman: University of Oklahoma Press.

   2005 <u>Cherokee Medicine Man</u>. The Life and Work of a Modern-Day Healer. Norman: University of Oklahoma Press.

Crawford, Michael 1978 <u>The Mobilian Trade Language</u>. Knoxville: University of Tennessee Press.

Culin, Stewart 1907 Games. <u>Handbook of American Indians North of Mexico</u>. Frederick Webb Hodge, ed. Bureau of American Ethnology, Bulletin 30, Part I: 483-6, 484.

D'Anghera Martyr, Peter 1912 <u>De Orbe Novo</u>, The Eight Decades of Pietro d'Anghiera Martire. Francis Augustus MacNutt, translator. New York: GP Putnam's Sons. [1970]

Davis, R. P. Stephen, Patrick C. Livingood, H. Trawick Ward, Vincas P. Steponaitis 1998 Excavating Occaneechi Town. Archaeology of an Eighteenth Century Indians Village in North Carolina. CD-ROM Chapel Hill: University of North Carolina Press.

Deloria, Ella 1988 <u>Waterlily</u>. Lincoln: University Nebraska Press.

Dincauze, Dena and Robert Hasenstab 1989 Explaining the Iroquois: tribalization on a prehistoric periphery. <u>Centre and Periphery</u>: comparative studies in archaeology: 67-87. London: Unwin Hyman Ltd.

Dobyns, Henry F. 1983 <u>Their Number Become Thinned</u>. Native American Population Dynamics in Eastern North America. Knoxville: University of Tennessee Press.

Doran, Glen, ed. 2002 <u>Windover</u>. Multidisciplinary Investigations of an Early Archaic Florida Cemetery. Gainesville: University Press of Florida.

Dorsey, George, and James Murie 1940 Notes on Skidi Pawnee Society. Alexander Spoehr, ed. Field Museum of Natural History, Anthropological Series 27 (2): 65-119.

Dorsey, James Owen, and John Swanton 1912 A Dictionary of the Biloxi and Ofo Languages. Accompanied with thirty-one Biloxi Texts and Numerous Biloxi Phrases. Bureau of American Ethnology, Bulletin 47.

Dragoo, Don 1963 <u>Mounds for the Dead</u>: An Analysis of Adena Culture. Pittsburg: Carnegie Museum of Natural History.

Drechsel, Emanuel 1997 <u>Mobilian Jargon</u>. Linguistics and Sociohistorical Aspects of a Native American Pidgin. UK: Oxford Studies in Language Contact.

   2001 Mobilian Jargon in Southeastern Indian Anthropology. <u>Anthropologists and Indians in the New South</u>, Chapter 11: 175-183. Rachel Bonney and Anthony Paredes, eds. Tuscaloosa: University of Alabama Press.

Driver, Harold 1965 <u>Indians of North America</u>. Chicago: University of Chicago Press.

Drucker, Philip, Robert Heizer, and Robert Squier 1959 <u>Excavations at La Venta Tabasco, 1955</u>. Bureau of American Ethnology, Bulletin 170.

Du Bois, Cora 2007 <u>The 1870 Ghost Dance</u>. Lincoln: University Nebraska Press. [1939]

Duncan, Barbara R. 1998 <u>Living Stories of the Cherokee</u>. Chapel Hill: University of North Carolina Press.

Duncan, Barbara and Brett Riggs 2003 <u>Cherokee Heritage Trails Guidebook</u>. Chapel Hill: The University of North Carolina Press for the Museum of the Cherokee Indian.

Dussart, Francoise 2000 <u>The Politics of Ritual in an Aboriginal Settlement</u>. Kinship, Gender, and the Currency of Knowledge. DC: Smithsonian Institution Press.

Dyson, John 2003 Chickasaw Village Names from Contact to Removal: 1540-1835. <u>Mississippi Archaeology</u> 38 (2): 95-134, Winter.

Early, Ann 2000 The Caddos of the Trans-Mississippi South, 122-141. <u>Indians of the Greater Southeast</u>. <u>Historical Archaeology and Ethnohistory</u>. Bonnie McEwan, ed. Gainesville: University Press of Florida.

Eidlitz, Kerstin 1969 <u>Food and Emergency Food in the Circumpolar Area</u>. Studia Ethnographica Uppaliensis 32.

Emerson, Thomas 1982 Mississippian Stone Images in Illinois. Urbana-Champaign: Illinois Archaeological Survey, Circular 6.

Esarey, Duane 2004 Mississippian Spider Redux. St Louis: Joint Meeting of the 50th Midwestern Archaeological Conference and 61st Southeastern Archaeological Conference, 20-23 October.

Ethridge, Robbie 2001 Raiding the Remains: The Indian Slave Trade and the Collapse of the Mississippian Chiefdoms. Chattanooga, TN: Southeastern Archaeological Conference.
  2002 Shatter Zone: Early Colonial Slave Raiding and Its Consequences for the Natives of the Eastern Woodland. Riverside, CA: American Society for Ethnohistory, 7-12 November.
  2003 <u>Creek Country</u>. The Creek Indians and Their World. Chapel Hill: University of North Carolina Press.
  2010 <u>From Chicaza to Chicksaw</u>. <u>The European Invasion and the Transformation of the Mississippian World, 1540-1715</u>. Chapel Hill: University of North Carolina Press.

Ethridge, Robbie, and Sheri Shuck-Hall, eds. 2009 <u>Mapping the Mississippian Shatter Zone</u>. <u>The Colonial Indian Slave Trade and Regional Instability in the American South</u>. Lincoln: University Nebraska Press.

Ethridge, Robbie, and Charles Hudson 2002 <u>The Transformation of the Southeastern Indians, 1540-1760</u>. Jackson: University Press of Mississippi.

Evans-Pritchard, E. E. 1940 <u>The Nuer</u>. A Description of the Modes of Livelihood and Political Institutions of a Nilotic People. UK: Oxford University Press.

Fabian, Stephen 2001 <u>Patterns in the Sky</u>, an Introduction to Ethnoastronomy. Prospect Heights, Il: Waveland Press.

Faulkner, William 1939 <u>The Wild Palms</u>. New York: Vintage.
  1940 <u>Go Down, Moses</u>. New York: Vintage.
  1957 <u>The Town</u>. New York: Vintage.

Feeling, Durbin 1975 <u>Cherokee – English Dictionary</u>. Tahlequah: Cherokee Nation of Oklahoma.

Fienup-Riordan, Ann 1994 <u>Boundaries and Passages</u>, Rule and Ritual in Yup'ik Eskimo Oral Tradition. Norman: University of Oklahoma Press.

Fletcher, Alice. 1994 A Study of Omaha Indian Music. Lincoln: University of Nebraska. [1893, Harvard University, Archaeological and Ethnological Papers of the Peabody Museum 1 (5)]

Fletcher, Alice, and Francis LaFlesche 1992 The Omaha Tribe. Lincoln: University of Nebraska Press. [BAE AR 27, 1911]

Fogelson, Raymond 1961 Change, Persistence, and Accommodation in Cherokee Medico-Magical Beliefs. William N. Fenton, and John Gulick, eds. Symposium on Cherokee and Iroquois Culture. Bureau of American Ethnology, Bulletin 180: 213-225.

1984 Who Were The Ani-Kutani? An Excursion into Cherokee Historical Thought. Ethnohistory 31: 255-63.

Fogelson, Raymond, ed. 2004 Southeast. Handbook of North American Indians, 14. DC: Smithsonian Institution Press.

Forbes, Jack D. 1993 Africans and Native Americans. The Language of Race and the Evolution of Red-Black People. Urbana: University of Illinois Press.

Ford, James 1951 Greenhouse: A Troyville - Coles Creek Period Site in Avoyelles Parish, Louisiana. Anthropological Papers of the American Museum of Natural History, Volume 44, Part 1.

1969 A Comparison of Formative Cultures in the Americas. Diffusion or the Psychic Unity of Man. DC: Smithsonian Institution Press.

Fortune, Reo 1963 Sorcerers of Dobu. New York: EP Dutton & Co. [1932]

Foster II, H. Thomas 2007 Archaeology of the Lower Muskogee Creek Indians, 1715-1836. Tuscaloosa: University of Alabama Press.

Foster II, H. Thomas, ed. 2003 The Collected Works of Benjamin Hawkins, 1796-1810. Tuscaloosa: University of Alabama Press.

Fowler, Melvin 1989 The Cahokia Atlas. A Historical Atlas of Cahokia Archaeology. Springfield: Illinois Historic Preservation Agency, Studies in Illinois Archaeology 2. [1997 Revised]

Fowler, Melvin, Jerome Rose, Barbara Vander Leest, and Steven Ahler
1999 The Mound 72 Area: Dedicated and Sacred Space in Early Cahokia. Springfield: Illinois State Museum, Reports of Investigations, No 54.

Fox, William 2004 The North-South Copper Axis. Southeastern Archaeology 2 (1): 85-97.

Frison, George, and Bruce Bradley 1999 The Fenn Cache, Clovis Weapons & Tools. Santa Fe: One Horse Land & Cattle Company.

Fritz, Gayle 2000 Levels of Biodiversity in Eastern North America. Biodiversity and Native America. Chapter 8: 223-247. Paul Minnis and Wayne Elisens, eds. Norman: University of Oklahoma Press.

Gallay, Alan 2002 The Indian Slave Trade: The Rise of the English Empire in the American South, 1670-1717. New Haven: Yale University Press.

Galloway, Patricia 1982 Henri de Tonti du village des Chacta, 1702: The Beginning of the French Alliance. La Salle and His Legacy: 146-175. Patricia Galloway, ed.

1995 Choctaw Genesis, 1500-1700. Lincoln: University of Nebraska Press.

2006 Practicing Ethnohistory ~ Mining Archives, Hearing Testimony, Constructing Narrative. Lincoln: University of Nebraska.

Galloway, Patricia, ed. 1982 <u>La Salle and His Legacy: Frenchmen and Indians in the Lower Mississippi Valley</u>. Jackson: University Press of Mississippi.
 1997 <u>The Hernando de Soto Expedition</u>. History, Historiography, and "Discovery" in the Southeast. Lincoln: University of Nebraska Press.

Gatschet, Albert 1883 The Shetimasha Indians of St. Mary's Parish, Southern Louisiana. <u>Transactions of the Anthropological Society of Washington</u>, Volume II, 7 Feb to 15 May1882: 148-159.
 1884 A Migration Legend of the Creek Indians, With Linguistic, Historic and Ethnographic Introduction: I. DG Brinton, ed. Philadelphia: Library of Aboriginal American Literature.

Gatschet, Albert, and John Swanton 1932 A Dictionary of the Atakapa Language, Accompanied by Text Material. Bureau of American Ethnology, Bulletin 108.

Gehring, Charles, and William Starna, eds. 1988 <u>A Journey Into Mohawk and Oneida Country, 1634-1635</u>. The Journal of Herman Meyndertsz van den Bogaert. Syracuse University Press.

Gibbs, George 1855 Report ... to Captain Mc'Clellan on the Indian Tribes of the Territory of Washington. Pacific Railroad Report 1: 402-36. 33rd Congress, 2nd Session, Senate Executive Document 78 (Series # 758). [1972, Ye Galleon Press, 2015 George Gibbs Northwest Array].

Gibson, Arrell 1971 <u>The Chickasaws</u>. Norman: University of Oklahoma Press.

Gibson, Jon 1986 Earth Sitting: Architectural Masses at Poverty Point, Northeastern Louisiana. <u>Louisiana Archaeology</u> 13: 201-238.
 1996 Religion of the Rings: Poverty Point Iconography and Ceremonialism. <u>Mounds, Embankment, and Ceremonialism in the Midsouth</u>. Robert C. Mainfort and Richard Walling, eds. Arkansas Archaeological Survey Research Series 46: 1-6.
 2001 <u>The Ancient Mounds of Poverty Point</u>: Place of Rings. Gainesville: University of Florida Press.
 2006 Navels of the Earth: sedentism in early mound-building cultures in the Lower Mississippi Valley. <u>World Archaeology</u> 38 (2): 311-29.

Gibson, Jon, and Philip Carr 2004 <u>Signs of Power</u>. The Rise of Cultural Complexity in the Southeast. Tuscaloosa: University of Alabama Press.

Gifford, Edward 1931 The Kamia of Imperial Valley. Bureau of American Ethnology, Bulletin 97.

Gilbert, William Harlen 1947 New Fire Ceremonialism in America. Revista del Instituto de Anthropologia de la Universidad National de Tucuman. Publication #396, 3 (3) : 233-316.

Gilliland, Marion Spjut 1975 <u>The Material Culture of Key Marco, Florida</u>. Gainesville: University Presses of Florida.
 1989 <u>Key Marco's Buried Treasure</u>: Archaeology and Adventure in the Nineteenth Century. Gainesville: University of Florida Press.

Glob, P. V. 1969 <u>The Bog People</u>. Iron-Age Man Preserved. NY: Ballantine Books.

Goldman, Irving 1963 <u>The Cubeo Indians of the Northwest Amazon</u>. Illinois Studies in Anthropology, No. 2. [1979, University of Illinois Press]

Goldstein, Lynne 2000 Mississippian Ritual as Viewed Through the Practice of Secondary Disposal of the Dead, <u>Mounds, Modoc, and Mesoamerica</u>: Papers in

Honor of Melvin L. Fowler. Steven Ahler, ed. Illinois State Museum Scientific Papers 18: 193-205.

Gouge, Earnest 2004 Totkv Mocvse ~ New Fire. Creek Folktales. Jack Martin, Margaret McKane Mauldin, Juanita McGirt. eds. Norman: University of Oklahoma Press.

Granberry, Julian 1993 A Grammar and Dictionary of the Timucua Language. Tuscaloosa: University of Alabama Press.

Grange, Roger 1979 An Archaeological View of Pawnee Origins. Nebraska History 60 (2): 134-160.

Grantham, Bill 2002 Creation Myths and Legends of the Creek Indians. Gainesville: University of Florida Press.

Green, Michael 1979 The Creeks. A Critical Bibliography. Bloomington, Indiana University Press: Newberry Library Bibliography Series.

1982 The Politics of Indian Removal. Creek Government and Society in Crisis. Lincoln: University of Nebraska Press.

Haas, Mary 1941 Tunica. Handbook of North American Indian Languages 4: 1-143.

1946 A Grammatical Sketch of Tunica. Linguistic Structures of Native America. Harry Hoijer, ed. NY: Viking Fund Publications in Anthropology 6, 337-366.

1953 Tunica Dictionary. University of California Publications in Linguistics 6 (2): 175-332.

1969 The Prehistory of Languages. The Hague: Janua Linguarum, Series Minor 57.

Haas, Mary, and James Hill 2015 Creek (Muskogee) Texts. Jack Martin, Margarent McKane Mauldin, Juanita McGirt, eds. Berkeley: University of California Publications in Linguistics 150.

Hahn, Steven 2004 The Invention of the Creek Nation, 1670-1763. Lincoln: University of Nebraska Press.

Halbert, Henry S. 1899 Nanih Waiya, the Sacred Mound of the Choctaw. Mississippi Historical Society 2: 223-234.

Hall, Robert L. 1979 In Search of the Ideology of the Adena-Hopewell Climax. Hopewell Archaeology: The Chillecothe Conference. David Brose and N'omi Greber, eds. Kent, Ohio: Kent State University Press.

1997 An Archaeology of the Soul. North American Indian Belief and Ritual. Urbana: University of Illinois Press.

Hall, Jr., Joseph M. 2001 Making An Indian People: Creek Formation in the Colonial Southeast, 1590-1735. Madison: University Wisconsin, History PhD.

Hallowell, A. Irving 1969 Ojibwa Ontology, Behavior, and World View. Primitive Views of the World. Stanley Diamond, ed. NY: Columbia University Press. [1960, Culture in History: Essays in Honor of Paul Radin]

Hann, John 1988 Apalachee. The Land Between Two Rivers. Gainesville: University of Florida Press.

Hann, John, and Bonnie McEwan 1998 The Apalachee Indians and Mission San Luis. Gainesville: University of Florida Press.

Harrington, John P. 1932 Tobacco among the Karuk Indians of California. Bureau of American Ethnology, Bulletin 94.

Hawass, Zahi 2003 <u>Secrets from the Sand</u> ~ My Search for Egypt's Past. The American University in Cairo Press.

Hawkins, Benjamin 1848 A Sketch of the Creek Country in 1798 and 1799. <u>Collections of the Georgia Historical Society</u>, Volume III, Part I: 1-88. [1971, Kraus Reprint] 1916 Letters of Benjamin Hawkins, 1796-1806. Savannah: <u>Collections of the Georgia Historical Society</u> IX.

Hayden, Brian 1997 <u>The Pithouses of Keatley Creek</u>. Complex Hunter-Gatherers of the Northwest Plateau. Case Studies in Archaeology. New York: Harcourt Brace College Publishers.

Haywood, John 1823 <u>The Natural and Aboriginal History of Tennessee</u>, Up to the First Settlements there in by the White People in the Year 1768. [1959, Mary Rothrock, ed. Jackson, TN: McCowat-Mercer Press]

Heckewelder, John 1876. <u>History, Manners, and Customs of the Indian Nations Who Once Inhabited Pennsylvania, and Neighboring States</u>. Philadelphia: Publication Fund of the Historical Society of Pennsylvania. [1819; Arno Press, 1971].

Hedges, John 1984 <u>Tomb of the Eagles: Death and Life in a Stone Age Tribe</u>. NY: New Amsterdam.

Heizer, Robert, and Martin Baumhoff 1962 <u>Prehistoric Rock Art of Nevada and Eastern California</u>. Berkeley: University of California Press.

Heizer, Robert, ed. 1978 <u>California</u>. Smithsonian Handbook of North American Indians, Volume 8.

Helms, Mary 1988 <u>Ulysses' Sail</u> - An Ethnographic Odyssey of Power, Knowledge, and Geographical Distance. Princeton University Press.

Henning, Dale R., and Thomas D. Theissen, eds. 2004 Dhegihan and Chiwere Siouans in the Plains: Historical and Archaeological Perspectives. Part Two. <u>Plains Anthropologist</u> 49 (192), Memoir 36. [Blood Run]

Henri, Florette 1986 <u>The Southern Indians and Benjamin Hawkins, 1796-1816</u>. Norman: University of Oklahoma Press.

Hilton, Susanne, and John Rath 1983 Objections to Franz Boas's referring to eating people in the translation of the Kwakwala terms *baXwbakwalnuXwsiwe* and *hamats!a*. Portland State University: Working Papers of the 17th International Conference on Salish and Neighboring Languages, 9-11 August.

Hill, James H. Ms-a. Description of Hilabi Round House. Creek Texts by Mary R Haas and James H Hill. APS. www.wm.edu/linguistics/creek/hass-hill/texts.php. See Haas and Hill 2015.
    Ms-b. Origin of the Spokokaki. Creek Texts by Mary R. Haas and James H. Hill. APS. www.wm.edu/linguistics/creek/hass-hill/texts.php.

Hitchcock, Ethan Allen 1996 <u>A Traveler in Indian Territory</u>. Grant Foreman, ed. Norman: University of Oklahoma Press. [1930]

Hively, Ray, and Robert Horn 1982 Geometry and Astronomy in Prehistoric Ohio. <u>Archaeoastronomy</u> 4: S1-S20.
    1984 Hopewellian Geometry and Astronomy at High Bank. <u>Archaeoastronomy</u> 7: S85-S100.

Howard, James 1968 <u>The Southeastern Ceremonial Complex and its Interpretation</u>. Missouri Archaeological Society, Memoir 6.

Howard, James, with Willie Lena 1984 <u>Oklahoma Seminoles</u>. Medicines, Magic, and Religion. Norman: University of Oklahoma Press.

Howard, James, and Victoria Lindsay Levine 1990 <u>Choctaw Music and Dance</u>. Norman: University of Oklahoma Press.

Hudson, Charles 1976 <u>The Southeastern Indians</u>. Knoxville: University of Tennessee Press.

    1975 Vomiting for Purity: Ritual Emesis in the Aboriginal Southeastern United States. <u>Symbols and Society</u>. Essays on Belief Systems in Action. Carole Hill, ed. Southern Anthropological Society, Proceedings 9: 93-102.

    1990 Conversations with the High Priest of Coosa. <u>Lamar Archaeology</u>, Mississippian Chiefdoms in the Deep South: 214-230. Mark Williams and Gary Shapiro, eds.

    1997 <u>Knights of Spain, Warriors of the Sun</u>. Hernando de Soto and the South's Ancient Chiefdoms. Athens: University of Georgia Press.

    2003 <u>Conversations with the High Priest of Coosa</u>. Chapel Hill: University of North Carolina Press.

Hudson, Charles, ed. 1979 <u>Black Drink</u>. A Native American Tea. Athens: The University of Georgia Press. [2004 Reprint]

Hudson, Joyce Rockwood 2000 <u>Apalachee</u>. Athens: The University of Georgia Press.

Hugh-Jones, Stephen 1979 <u>The Palm and the Pleiades</u>: <u>Initiation and Cosmology in Northwestern Amazonia</u>. UK: Cambridge Studies in Social Anthropology.

Humes, Jesse, and Vinnie May James Humes 1973 <u>A Chickasaw Dictionary</u>. Ada: Chickasaw Nation.

Hurt, Douglas A. 2000 The Shaping of a Creek (Muscogee) Homeland in Indian Territory, 1828-1907. University of Oklahoma: PhD Geography.

Hurley, William 1975 <u>An Analysis of Effigy Mound Complexes in Wisconsin</u>. University of Michigan, Museum of Anthropology, Anthropological Papers 59.

Iberville, Pierre LeMoyne 1981 <u>Iberville's Gulf Journals</u>. Richebourge Gaillard McWilliams, ed. Tuscaloosa: University of Alabama Press.

Innes, Pamela, Linda Alexander, and Bertha Tilkens 2004 <u>Beginning Creek ~ Mvskoke Emponvkv</u>. Norman: University of Oklahoma Press.

Jackson, Jason 2003 <u>Yuchi Ceremonial Life</u>. Performance, Meaning, and Tradition in a Contemporary American Indian Community. Studies in the Anthropology of North American Indians. Lincoln: University of Nebraska Press.

James, Simon 1993 <u>The World of the Celts</u>. London: Thames and Hudson.

Jenkins, Ned 2009 Tracing the Origins of the Early Creeks, 1050-1700 CE. Ethridge and Shuck-Hall, <u>Mapping the Mississippian Shatter Zone</u>, Chapter 8: 188-249.

Jones, Calvin 1981 Excavations of an Archaic Cemetery in Cocoa Beach, Florida. Florida Anthropologist Interview with Calvin Jones, Part II. <u>Florida Anthropologist</u> 34 (2): 81-89.

Jones, Charles 1873 <u>Antiquities of the Southern Indians, Particularly the Georgia Tribes</u>. NY: D Appleton and Co. [1999, University of Alabama Press]

Johnson, Dianne 1998 <u>Night Skies of Aboriginal Australia</u>. University of Sidney: Oceania Monograph 47.

Johnson, Jay 1997 Stone Tools, Politics, and the Eighteenth-Century Chickasaw in Northeast Mississippi. <u>American Antiquity</u> 62 (2): 215-230.

2000 The Chickasaws, 85-121. <u>Indians of the Greater Southeast</u>. <u>Historical Archaeology and Ethnohistory</u>. Bonnie McEwan, ed. Gainesville: University Press of Florida.

Johnson, Jay, Gena Aleo, Rodney Stuart, and John Sullivan 2002 <u>The 1996 Excavations at the Batesville Mounds</u>. A Woodland Period Platform Mound Complex in Northwest Mississippi. Mississippi Department of Archives and History, Archaeological Report No 32.

Johnson, Jay, and Samuel Brookes 1989 Benton Points, Turkey Tails, and Cache Blades: Middle Archaic Exchange in the Midsouth. <u>Southeastern Archaeology</u> 8 (2): 134-145.

Johnson, Jay, Susan Scott, Jams Atkinson, Andrea Brewer Shea 1994 Late Prehistoric / Protohistoric Settlement and Subsistence on the Black Prairie: Buffalo Hunting in Mississippi. <u>North American Archaeologist</u> 15 (2): 167-179.

Kane, Allen 1989 Did the Sheep Look Up? Sociopolitical Complexity in Ninth Century Dolores Society. <u>The Sociopolitical Structure of Prehistoric Southwestern Societies</u>: 307-361. S. Upham, K. G. Lightfoot, and R. A. Jewett, eds. Boulder, CO: Westview Press.

Kan, Sergei 1989 <u>Symbolic Immortality</u>, The Tlingit Potlatch of the Nineteenth Century. Washington, DC: Smithsonian Institution Press.

Katz, Richard 1982 <u>Boiling Energy</u>. Community Healing among the Kalahari Kung. Cambridge: Harvard University Press.

Kehoe, Alice 2007 Osage Texts and Cahokia Data, Chapter 10: 246-261. <u>Ancient Objects and Sacred Realms:</u> Interpretations of Mississippian Iconography, Kent Reilly and James Garber, eds. Austin: University of Texas Press.

Kennedy, Roger 1994 <u>Hidden Cities</u>. The Discovery and Loss of Ancient North American Civilization. New York: The Free Press.

Kenyon, Walter A. 1986 <u>Mounds of Sacred Earth</u>. Burial Mounds of Ontario. Royal Ontario Museum, Archaeology Monograph 9.

Kimball, Geoffrey 1994 Making The Connection: Is It Possible to Link the Koasati to an Archaeological Culture. <u>Perspectives on the Southeast</u> ~ Linguistics, Archaeology, and Ethnohistory. Patricia Kwachka, ed. Southern Anthropological Society Proceedings 27: 71-79.

King, Duane Harold 1975 A Grammar and Dictionary of the Cherokee Language. University of Georgia: PhD Linguistics.

Klauber, Laurence 1982 <u>Rattlesnakes</u>, Their Habits, Life Histories, and Influence on Mankind. Abridged by Karen Harvey McClung. Berkeley: University of California Press.

Knight, Vernon James 1981 Mississippian Ritual. Gainesville: University of Florida, PhD Anthropology.

1986 The Institutional Organization of Mississippian Religion. <u>American Antiquity</u> 51 (4): 675-687.

1989 Symbolism of Mississippian Mounds. <u>Powhatan's Mantle</u> ~ Indians in the Colonial Southeast: 279-291. Peter Wood, Gregory Waselkov, and M. Thomas Hatley, eds. Lincoln: University of Nebraska Press.

1998 Moundville as a Diagrammatic Ceremonial Center. <u>Archaeology of the Moundville Chiefdom</u>: 44-62. Vernon James Knight, Jr. and Vincas P. Steponaitis, eds. DC: Smithsonian Institution Press.

2004 Ceremonialism Until 1500. <u>Southeast</u> 14: 734-741. Raymond Fogelson, ed. DC: Smithsonian Institution Press.

Knight, Jr., Vernon James, and Vincas P. Steponaitis, eds. 1998 <u>Archaeology of the Moundville Chiefdom</u>. DC: Smithsonian Institution Press.

Konrad, C. F. 1994 <u>Plutarch's <i>Sertorius.</i></u> A Historical Commentary. Chapel Hill: The University of North Carolina Press.

Korp, Maureen 1990 The Sacred Geography of the American Mound Builders. Lampetere, Wales: The Edwin Mellen Press, Ltd.

Krause, Richard 1996 Observations on the Excavation of a Mississippian Mound. <u>Mounds, Embankments, and Ceremonialism in the Midsouth</u>. Robert C. Mainfort, Jr. and Richard Walling, eds. Arkansas Archaeological Survey Research Series 46: 54-63.

Kroeber, Alfred 1925 <u>Handbook of the Indians of California</u>. Bureau of American Ethnology, Bulletin 78.

Kroeber, A. L., and E. W. Gifford 1949 <u>World Renewal</u>: A Cult System of Native Northwest California. University of California, Anthropological Records 13 (1): 1-156.

Kuper, Hilda 1963 <u>The Swazi</u>, A South African Kingdom. New York: Holt, Rinehart and Winston, Case Studies in Cultural Anthropology.

Kwachka, Patricia 1994 <u>Perspectives on the Southeast</u>. Linguistics, Archaeology, and Ethnohistory. Southern Anthropological Society Proceedings 27. Athens: University of George Press.

Lang, Julian, ed. 1994 <u>Ararapikva</u>. Creation Stories of the People. Traditional Karuk Indian Literature from Northwestern California. Berkeley: Heyday Books.

Lankford, George, ed. 1987 <u>Native American Legends</u>. Southeastern Legends: Tales from the Natchez, Caddo, Biloxi, Chickasaw, and Other Nations. Little Rock: August House.

Lankford, George 2007a The Great Serpent in Eastern North America, Chapter 5, 107-135. <u>Ancient Objects and Sacred Realms</u>: Interpretations of Mississippian Iconography. Kent Reilly and James Garber, eds. Austin: University of Texas Press.

2007b The "Path of Souls": Some Death Imagery in the Southeastern Ceremonial Complex, Chapter 8: 174-212. <u>Ancient Objects and Sacred Realms</u>: Interpretations of Mississippian Iconography. Kent Reilly and James Garber, eds. Austin: University of Texas Press.

Latta, Frank F. 1977 <u>Handbook of Yokuts Indians</u>. Santa Cruz: Bear State Books. [1949]

Lawson, John 1967 <u>A <i>New</i> Voyage to Carolina</u>. Hugh Talmage Lefler, ed. Chapel Hill: The University of North Carolina Press. [1709]

Lee, Richard 1984 <u>The Dobe !Kung</u>. New York: Holt, Rinehart and Winston, Case Studies in Cultural Anthropology.

Lepper, Bradley 2005 <u>Ohio Archaeology</u>, With Feature Articles Contributed By Over 20 Archaeologists and Scholars. Wilmington, OH: Voyager Media Group.

Leopold, Aldo 1978 A Sand County Almanac. New York: Ballantine Books.

Lepowsky, Maria 1993 Fruit of the Motherland, Gender in an Egalitarian Society, New York: Columbia University Press.

Levy, Jerrold 1998 In the Beginning ~ The Navajo Genesis. Berkeley: University of California Press.

Lewis, David, Jr., and Ann Jordan 2002 Creek Indian Medicine Ways. The Enduring Power of Mvskoke Religion. Albuquerque: University of New Mexico Press.

Lienhardt, Godfrey 1954 The Shilluk of the Upper Nile. African Worlds, Studies in the Cosmological Ideas and Social Values of African Peoples: 138-163. Daryll Forde, ed. London: Oxford University Press.

Lindauer, Owen, and John Blitz 1997 Higher Ground. Journal of Archaeological Research 5 (2), 169-207.

Linton, Ralph 1923 Annual Ceremony of the Pawnee Medicine Men. Chicago: Field Museum of Natural History, Anthropological Leaflet 8: 1-20.

Loeb, Edwin 1926 Pomo Folkways. University of California Publications in American Archaeology and Ethnology 19 (2).

Long, Fred, and George Scott 1998 *Nakcokv Esyvhiketv* ~ Muskogee Hymns. General Commission on Religion and Race, the United Methodist Church. [1936 by Presbyterians]

Lopatin, Ivan Alexis 1960 Origin Of The Native American Steam Bath. American Anthropologist 62: 977-992.

Lorenz, Karl 2000 The Natchez of Southwest Mississippi: 142-177. Indians of the Greater Southeast. Historical Archaeology and Ethnohistory. Bonnie McEwan, ed. Gainesville: University Press of Florida.

Loughridge, Rev. R. M., and David Hodge 1890 English and Muskokee Dictionary. [1964, Okmulgee Baptist Home Mission Board].

McEwan, Bonnie, ed. 2000 Indians of the Greater Southeast. Historical Archaeology and Ethnohistory. Gainesville: University Press of Florida.

McGhee, Robert, and James Tuck 1975 An Archaic Sequence from the Strait of Belle Isle, Labrador. National Museum of Man, Mercury Series, Archaeological Survey of Canada, Paper 34.

Mainfort, Jr, Robert C., and Lynne P. Sullivan 1998 Ancient Earthen Enclosures of the Eastern Woodlands. Gainesville: University Press of Florida.

Mainfort, Jr, Robert C., and Richard Walling, eds. 1996 Mounds, Embankment, and Ceremonialism in the Midsouth. Arkansas Archaeological Survey Research Series 46.

Mallam, Clark 1976 The Iowa Effigy Mound Manifestation: An Interpretative Model. Iowa City: Office of the State Archaeologist, Report 9.

  1982 Ideology from the Earth: Effigy Mounds in the Midwest. Archaeology 35 (4): 59-64.

  1984 The Serpent: A Prehistoric Life-Metaphor in South Central Kansas. Kansas Anthropological Association Journal 5 (2): 40-83.

Mann, Barbara Alice 2003 Native Americans, Archaeologists, and the Mounds. American Indian Studies Vol 14. NY: Peter Lang.

Marino, Mary Carolyn 1968 A Dictionary of Winnebago: An Analysis and Reference Grammar of the Radin Lexical File. Berkeley: University of California, PhD Dissertation.

Martin, Jack, and Margaret McKane Mauldin 2000 A Dictionary of Creek/Muskogee, with notes on the Florida and Oklahoma Seminole dialects of Creek. Lincoln: University of Nebraska Press.

Mason, Carol Ann Irwin 1963 The Archaeology of Ocmulgee Old Fields, Macon, Georgia. University of Michigan: Anthropology PhD.

Mathews, Darcy 2006 Burial Cairn Taxonomy and the Mortuary Landscape of Rocky Point, BC. University of Victoria: MA Anthropology.

Mathews, John Joseph 1961 The Osages. Children of the Middle Waters. Norman: University of Oklahoma Press.

Mavor, James, and Byron Dix 1989 Manitou. The Sacred Landscape of New England's Native Civilization. Rochester, VT: Inner Traditions International.

Maynor, Malinda 2000 Indians Got Rhythm: Lumbee and African American Church Song. American Indian Issue. North Dakota Quarterly 67 (3-4): 72-91. Summer/Fall.

Mayor, Adrienne 2005 Fossil Legends of the First Americans. Oxford: Princeton University Press.

Meltzer, David 1991 Altithermal Archaeology and Paleoecology at Mustang Springs, on the southern High Plains of Texas. American Antiquity 56 (2): 236-267.

Meltzer, David, ed. 1998 Introduction to Ephraim G. Squier and Edwin Davis, Ancient Monuments of the Mississippi Valley. Smithsonian Classics of Anthropology: 1-95. [1848, Smithsonian Contributions to Knowledge 1]

Milanich, Jerald 1998 Florida's Indians from Ancient Times to the Present. Gainesville: University of Florida Press.

   1999 Laboring in the Fields of the Lord. Spanish Missions and Southeastern Indians. DC: Smithsonian Institution Press.

   2000 The Timucua Indians of Northern Florida and Southern Georgia: 1-15. Indians of the Greater Southeast. Historical Archaeology and Ethnohistory. Bonnie McEwan, ed. Gainesville: University Press of Florida.

Milanich, Jerald, Ann Cordell, Vernon Knight, Jr., Timothy Kohler, and Brenda Sigler-Lavalle.

   1984 The McKeithen Weeden Island Culture. The Culture of Northern Florida A.D. 200-900. Orlando: Academic Press.

   1997 Archaeology of Northern Florida A.D. 200-900. The McKeithen Weeden Island Culture. Gainesville: University Press of Florida.

Milbrath, Susan 1999 Star Gods of the Maya. Astronomy in Art, Folklore, and Calendars. Austin: University of Texas Press.

Miller, Jay 1974a Why The World Is On The Back Of A Turtle. Man 9 (2): 306-308.

   1974b The Delaware As Women: A Symbolic Solution. American Ethnologist 1 (3): 507-514.

   1979 A 'Struckon' Model of Delaware Culture and the Positioning of Mediators. American Ethnologist 6 (4): 791-802.

   1980a High-Minded High Gods In North America. Anthropos 75: 916-919.

1980b The Matter of the (Thoughtful) Heart: Centrality, Focality, Or Overlap. Journal of Anthropological Research 36 (3) : 338-342.

1982 People, Berdaches, and Left-Handed Bears: Human Variation In Native North America. Journal of Anthropological Research 38 (3): 274-287.

1983a Numic Religion: An Overview Of Power In the Great Basin Of Native North America. Anthropos 78: 337-354.

1983b Basin Religion and Theology: A Comparative Study of Power (_Puha_). Journal Of California And Great Basin Anthropology 5 (1-2): 66-86.

1988 Shamanic Odyssey. The Lushootseed Salish Journey to the Land of the Dead. Menlo Park: Ballena Press.

1992a North Pacific Ethno-Astronomy: Tsimshian and Others. Earth And Sky: Visions of the Cosmos in Native American Folklore: 193-206. Claire Farrer and Ray Williamson, eds. Albuquerque: University of New Mexico Press.

1992b Earthmaker. New York: Putnam.

1996 Changing Moons: A History of Caddo Religion. Plains Anthropologist 41 (157): 243-259.

1997 Tsimshian Culture ~ A Light Through the Ages. Lincoln: University of Nebraska Press. [2001, Paperback]

1999 Lushootseed Culture and the Shamanic Odyssey. An Anchored Radiance. Lincoln: University of Nebraska Press.

2000 Indien Personhood II: Baby in the Oven Sparks Being in the World [Ovens of Incarnation]. American Indian Culture and Research Journal 24 (3): 155-160, Fall.

2001a Ashes Ethereal: Cremation in the Americas. American Indian Culture and Research Journal 25 (1): 121-137.

2001b Instilling the Earth: Explaining Mounds. Commentary. American Indian Culture and Research Journal 25 (3): 161-177.

2015 Ancestral Mounds ~ Vitality and Volatility Crossing Native America. Lincoln: University of Nebraska.

Miller, Jay, and Vi Hilbert 1993 Caring for Control: A Pivot of Salishan Language and Culture. American Indian Linguistics and Ethnography in Honor of Laurence C. Thompson: 237-239. Missoula: University of Montana, Occasional Papers in Linguistics 10.

Milner, George R. 1998 The Cahokia Chiefdom. The Archaeology of a Mississippi Society. DC: Smithsonian Institution Press.

2004 The Moundbuilders. Ancient Peoples of Eastern North America. London: Thames & Hudson.

Mochon, Marion Johnson 1972 Language, History, and Prehistory: Mississippian Lexico-Reconstruction. American Antiquity 37 (4): 478-503.

Mooney, James 1891 Sacred Formulas of the Cherokee. Bureau of American Ethnology, Annual Report 7. [1982, Cherokee, NC: Cherokee Heritage Books]

1982 Myths of the Cherokee. Cherokee, NC: Cherokee Heritage Books. [1900, Bureau of American Ethnology, Annual Report 19]

Mooney, James, and Frans M. Olbrechts 1932 The Swimmer Manuscript. Cherokee Sacred Formulas and Medicinal Prescriptions. Bureau of American Ethnology, Bulletin 99.

Moore, John 1994 Ethnoarchaeology of the Lamar People. Perspectives on the Southeast. Linguistics, Archaeology, and Ethnohistory: 126-141. Patricia Kwachka, ed. Southern Anthropological Society Proceedings 27. Athens: University of Georgia Press.

    2001 Ethnogenetic Patterns in Native North America. Archaeology, Language, and History: Essays on Culture and Ethnicity: 31-56. John Edward Terrell, ed. Westport, CT: Bergin & Garvey.

Mould, Tom 2003 Choctaw Prophesy. A Legacy of the Future. Tuscaloosa: University of Alabama Press.

    2004 Choctaw Tales. Jackson: University Press of Mississippi.

Mt Pleasant, Jane 2001 The Three Sisters: Care for the Land and the People. Science and Native American Communities ~ Legacies of Pain, Visions of Promise, Chapter 19: 126-134. Keith James, ed. Lincoln: University of Nebraska.

Morgan, David W. 1994 An Analysis of Historic Period Chickasaw Settlement Pattern. Tuscaloosa: University of Alabama: MA Anthropology.

Morgan, Lewis Henry 1959 The Indian Journals, 1859-62. Leslie White, ed. Ann Arbor: The University of Michigan Press.

    1962 League of the Iroquois. William Fenton, ed. Secaucus, NJ: Citadel Press. [1851]

    1963 Ancient Society, or, Researches in the Lines of Human Progress from Savagery through Barbarism to Civilization. Eleanor Burke Leacock, ed. Cleveland: The World Publishing Co. [1877]

    1965 Houses and House-Life of the American Aborigines. Paul Bohannan, ed. University of Chicago Press. [1881, Contributions to North American Ethnology IV]

Morgan, William 1999 Precolumbian Architecture in Eastern North America. Gainesville: University Press of Florida.

Munro, Pamela, and Catherine Willmond 1994 Chickasaw. An Analytical Dictionary. Norman: University of Oklahoma Press.

Murie, James 1914 Pawnee Indian Societies. Anthropological Papers of the American Museum of Natural History XI: 545-644.

    1981 Ceremonies of the Pawnee. Part I: The Skiri. Douglas Parks, ed. Smithsonian Contributions to Anthropology 27.

Nabokov, Peter, ed. 2015 The Origin Myth of Acoma Pueblo by Edward Proctor Hunt. New York: Penguin Books Classics.

Nairne, Thomas 1988 Muskhogean Journals. The 1708 Expedition to the Mississippi River. Alexander Moore, ed. Jackson: University Press of Mississippi.

Neitzel, Robert, ed. 1983 Grand Village of the Natchez Revisited: Excavations at the Fatherland Site, Adams County, Mississippi, in 1972. Mississippi Department of Archives and History, Archaeological Report 12.

Newcomb, W. W. 1956 The Culture and Acculturation of the Delaware Indians. University of Michigan, Anthropological Papers of the Museum of Anthropology 10.

    1961 The Caddo Confederacies. The Indians of Texas, Chapter 11: 279-313. Austin: University of Texas Press.

O'Brien, Patricia 1989 Cahokia: The Political Capital of the "Ramey" State. North American Archaeologist 10: 275-292.

O'Shea, John 1981 Social Configurations and the Archaeological Study of Mortuary Practices: A Case Study. The Archaeology of Death: 39-52. Robert Chapman, Ian Kinnes, Klavs Randsborg, eds. UK: Cambridge University Press.

Paige, Amanda, Fuller Bumpers, and Daniel Littlefield 2010 Chickasaw Removal. Ada: Chickasaw Press.

Parks, Douglas, ed. 1981 Ceremonies of the Pawnee by James Murie. Part I: The Skiri. DC: Smithsonian Contributions to Anthropology 27.

Parks, Douglas 2001 Pawnee. Plains. Handbook of North American Indians, Volume 13, Part I: 515-547. Raymond DeMallie, ed. DC: Smithsonian.

Parks, Douglas, and Waldo Wedel 1985 Pawnee Geography, Historical and Sacred. Great Plains Quarterly 5 (Summer): 143-76.

Parks, Douglas, and Lula Nora Pratt 2008 A Dictionary of Skiri Pawnee. Lincoln: University of Nebraska Press.

Parssinen, Martti, and Antti Korpisaari, ed. 2003 Western Amazonia – Amazonia Ocidental. Multidisciplinary Studies on Ancient Expansionistic Movements, Fortifications and Sedentary Life. University of Helsinki: Renvall Institute for Area and Cultural Studies.

Pauketat, Timothy R. 2007 Chiefdoms and Other Archaeological Delusions. NY: Altamira.

Phillips, Philip, James Ford, and James Griffin 1951 Archaeological Survey of the Lower Mississippi Alluvial Valley, 1940-1947. Papers of the Peabody Museum of Archaeology and Ethnology, Harvard University 60.

Phillips, Philip 1970 Archaeological Survey of the Lower Yazoo Basin, Mississippi, 1949-1955. Papers of the Peabody Museum of Archaeology and Ethnology, Harvard University 25.

Piker, Joshua 2004 Okfuskee ~ A Creek Indian Town in Colonial America. Cambridge: Harvard University Press.

Pluckhahn, Thomas 2003 Kolomoki – Settlement, Ceremony, and Status in the Deep South, AD 350-750. Tuscaloosa: University of Alabama Press.
    2010 The Sacred and the Secular Revisited: The Essential Tensions of Early Village Society in the Southeastern United States: 100-118. Becoming Villagers. Comparing Early Village Societies. Matthew Bandy and Jake Fox, ed. Tucson: University of Arizona Press.

Plutarch 1932 The Lives of the Noble Grecians and Romans. John Dryden, trans. Arthur High Clough, ed. New York: The Modern Library.

Powers, Stephen 1976 Tribes of California. Robert Heizer, ed. Berkeley: University of California Press. [1877]

Pratt, Richard Henry 1964 Battlefield and Classroom. Four Decades with the American Indian, 1867-1904. New Haven: Yale University Press.

Prentice, Guy 1986 An Analysis of the Symbolism Expressed by the Birger Figurine. American Antiquity 51 (2): 239-266.

Pursell, Corin 2004 Geographic Distribution and Symbolism of Colored Mound Architecture in the Mississippian Southeast. 20-23 October. St Louis: Joint

Meeting of the 50th Midwestern Archaeological Conference and 61st Southeastern Archaeological Conference.

Quattlebaum, Paul 1956 The Land Called Chicora. Gainesville: University of Florida Press.

Quintaro, Carolyn 2009 Osage Dictionary. Norman: University of Oklahoma Press.

Radin, Paul 1911 The Ritual and Significance of the Winnebago Medicine Dance. Journal of American Folk-lore 24 (92): 149-208.

1945 The Road of Life and Death. NY: Pantheon Books, Bollingen Series V.

1950 Winnebago Culture As Described by Themselves. The Origin Myth of the Medicine Rite: Three Versions. The Historical Origins of the Medicine Rite. Indiana University Publications in Anthropology and Linguistics, Memoir 3.

1990 The Winnebago Tribe. Lincoln: University of Nebraska Press. [1923]

Rankin, Robert ms. On Siouan Chronology. [1996]

2006 Siouan Tribal Contacts and Dispersions Evidenced by the Terminology for Maize and Other Cultigens. Histories of Maize: Multidisciplinary Approaches to the Prehistory, Linguistics, Biogeography, Domestication, and Evolution of Maize. John E. Staller, Robert H. Tykot, and Bruce F. Benz, eds. Amsterdam: Elsevier Academic Press.

2007 Siouian Tribes of the Ohio Valley: "Where did all these Indians Come From?" 16 May 2007 American Indien Studies Lecture Series, The Ohio State University. http://hdl.handle.net/1811/28545 {kb.osu.edu/dspace/browse ?value = Robert Rankin}.

Ray, Verne 1963 Primitive Pragmatists ~ The Modoc Indians of Northern California. Seattle: University of Washington Press, American Ethnological Society Monograph 38.

Rees, Alwyn, and Brinley Rees 1978 Celtic Heritage ~ Ancient Tradition in Ireland and Wales. London: Thames and Hudson.

Reilly III, F. Kent, and James Garber, eds. 2007 Ancient Objects and Sacred Realms ~ Interpretations of Mississippian Iconography. Austin: University of Texas Press.

Richards, John, and Melvin Fowler, eds. 2003 A Deep-Time Perspective: Studies in Symbols, Meaning and the Archeological Record. Papers in Honor of Robert L Hall. The Wisconsin Archeologist 84 (1 & 2).

Riddington, Robin 1968 The Medicine Fight: An Instrument of Political Process Among the Beaver Indians. American Anthropologist 70 (6): 1152-1160.

1969 Kin Categories Versus Kin Groups: A Two-Section System Without Sections. Ethnology 8 (4): 460-67.

1976 Wechuge and Windigo: A Comparison of Cannibal Belief Among Boreal Forest Athpaskans and Algonkians. Anthropologica 18 (2): 107-129.

1978 Swan People: A Study of the Dunne-Za Prophet Dance. Ottawa: National Museum of Man, Mercury Series 38.

1980 Trails of Meaning. The World Is Sharp as a Knife. An Anthropology in Honor of Wilson Duff: 265-68. Donald Abbott, ed. Victoria, BC: British Columbia Provincial Museum.

1988 Trail to Heaven. Knowledge and Narrative in a Northern Native Community. Ames: University of Iowa Press.

1990 Little Bit Know Something. Stories in a Language of Anthropology. Ames: University of Iowa Press.

Robbins, Lester 1976 The Persistence of Traditional Religious Practices among Creek Indians. Dallas: Southern Methodist University, PhD Dissertation.

Roe, Peter 1982 The Cosmic Zygote. Cosmology in the Amazon Basin. New Brunswick: Rutgers University Press.

Romain, William 2000 Mysteries of the Hopewell. Astronomers, Geometers, and Magicians of the Eastern Woodlands. Akron: The University of Akron Press.

Rooth, Anna Birgetta 1957 Creation Myths of North American Indians. Anthropos 52: 498-508.

Rouse, Irving 1992 The Tainos. Rise and Decline of the People Who Greeted Columbus. New Haven: Yale University Press.

Rowe, Chandler 1956 The Effigy Mound Culture of Wisconsin. Milwaukee Public Museum, Publications in Anthropology 3.

Sable, Trudy 1997 Multiple Layers of Meaning in the Mi'kmaw Serpent Dance. Papers of the 28th Algonquian Conference: 329-340.

Sabo III, George 1992 Paths of Our Children: Historic Indians of Arkansas. Arkansas Archaeological Survey, Popular Series 3.
     2003 Dancing into the Past: Colonial Legacies in Modern Caddo Indian Ceremony. The Arkansas Historical Quarterly 62 (4): 423-445.

Salzer, Robert, and Grace Rajnovich 2001 The Gottscall Rockshelter: An Archaeological Mystery. Maplewood, MN: Prairie Smoke Press.

Sassaman, Kenneth 1993 Early Pottery in the Southeast, Tradition and Innovation in Cooking Technology. Tuscaloosa: University of Alabama Press.

Saunders, Joe, Reca Jones, Thurman Allen, and Josetta LeBoeuf. ms. Ancient Mounds Heritage Area (Owner's Manual). Louisiana Regional Archaeology Program, (three-ring binder).

Saunders, Joe, Reca Jones, Thurman Allen, Josetta LeBoeuf, and Sunny Meriwether 2008 Indians Mounds of Northeast Louisiana. A Driving Trail Guide. Baton Rouge: Louisiana Division of Archaeology, Ancient Mounds Heritage Area and Trails Advisory Commission.

Saunt, Claudio 1999 A New Order of Things ~ Property, Power, and the Transformation of the Creek Indians, 1733-1816. UK: Cambridge Studies in North American Indian History.

Schele, Linda, and Peter Mathews 1998 The Code of Kings ~ The Language of Seven Sacred Maya Temples and Tombs. New York: Simon and Schuster.

Scherman, Katharine 1981 The Flowering of Ireland ~ Saints, Scholars, and Kings. Boston: Little, Brown, and Company.

Schoolcraft, Henry, ed. 1850s Information Respecting the History, Condition and Prospects of the Indian Tribes of the United States. 5 Volumes.

Schultz, Jack 1999 The Seminole Baptist Churches of Oklahoma ~ Maintaining a Traditional Community. Norman: University of Oklahoma Press.

Schweitzer, Marjorie 2001 Otoe and Missouria. Plains. Handbook of North American Indians, Volume 13, Part 1: 447-461. Raymond DeMallie, ed. DC: Smithsonian Press.

Science 1997 Volume 277, 19 Sept, 1761-1762, 1796-1799. [Watson Brake]

Seeman, Mark, and James Branch 2006 The Mounded Landscapes of Ohio: Hopewell Patterns and Placements. <u>Recreating Hopewell</u>, Chapter 6: 106-121, Douglas Charles and Jane Buikstra, eds. Gainesville: University Press of Florida.

Sears, William 1956 <u>Excavations at Kolomoki</u>. Final Report. Athens: University of Georgia Series in Anthropology 5.

Sellards, E. H. 1941 Stone Images from Henderson County, Texas. <u>American Antiquity</u> 7 (1): 29-38.

Seltzer, Frank M., and Jesse D. Jennings 1941 Peachtree Mound and Village Site, Cherokee County, North Carolina. Bureau of American Ethnology, Bulletin 313.

Shaffer, Lynda Norene 1992 <u>Native Americans Before 1492</u>. The Moundbuilding Centers of the Eastern Woodlands. Sources and Studies in World History. Armonk, NY: ME Sharpe.

Shambach, Frank 1996 Mounds, Embankments, and Ceremonialism in Trans-Mississippi South. <u>Mounds, Embankments, and Ceremonialism in the Midsouth</u>. Robert C. Mainfort and Richard Walling, eds. Arkansas Archaeological Survey Research Series 46: 36-43.

Shapiro, Warren 1970 The Ethnography of Two-Section Systems. <u>Ethnology</u> 9 (4): 380-388.

Sherfy, Michael J. 2005 Narrating Black Hawk: Indian Wars, Memory, and Midwestern Identity. Urbana: University of Illinois, History PhD Dissertation.

Sherrod, P. Clay, and Martha Ann Rolingson 1987 <u>Surveyors of the Ancient Mississippi Valley</u> ~ Modules and Alignments in Prehistoric Mound Sites. Arkansas Archaeological Survey Research Series 28.

Sherwood, Sarah, and Tristram Kidder 2011 The DaVincis of dirt: Geoarchaeological perspectives on Native American mound building in the Mississippi River Basin, <u>Journal of Anthropological Archaeology</u> 30: 69-87.

Shetrone, Henry Clyde 1930 <u>The Mound-Builders</u>. A Reconstruction of the Life of a Prehistoric American Race, Through Exploration and Interpretation of Their Earth Mounds, Their Burials, and Their Cultural Remains. NY: D. Appleton and Co.

Silverberg, Robert 1986 <u>The Mound Builders</u>. Athens: Ohio University Press. [1970]

Silberblatt, Irene 1989 Peru: The Colonial Andes. <u>Witchcraft and Sorcery of American Native Peoples</u>, Chapter 14: 311-22. Deward Walker, ed. Moscow: University of Idaho Press. [1970]

Skinner, Alanson 1924 <u>The Mascoutens or Prairie Potawatomi Indians</u>. Part I, Social Life and Ceremonies. Bulletin of the Public Museum of the City of Milwaukee, 6 (1): 1-262.

Smith, David Lee 1997 <u>Folklore of the Winnebago Tribe</u>. Norman: University of Oklahoma Press.

Smith, Marvin 1987 <u>Archaeology of Aboriginal Culture Change in the Interior Southeast</u> ~ Depopulation During the Early Historic Period. Florida Museum of Natural History, Ripley P. Bullen Series. Gainesville: University Press of Florida.

Snow, Dean, Charles Gehring, and William Starna, eds. 1996 <u>In Mohawk Country</u> ~ Early Narratives about a Native People. Syracuse University Press.

South, Stanley 1970 A Ceremonial Center at the Charles Towne Site. Columbia: South Carolina Institute of Archeology and Anthropology, Notebook II (6-7, June-July): 3-5.

    1972 Archeology on Albemarle Point – The Indian Ceremonial Center; Excavation of the Indian Ceremonial Center at the Charles Towne Site. Columbia: South Carolina Institute of Archeology and Anthropology, Research Manuscript Series 36: 202-248.

    1973 The Temple at Town Creek Indian Mound State Historic Site, North Carolina. Columbia: South Carolina Institute of Archeology and Anthropology, Notebook V (5, Sept-Oct): 145-172.

Speck, Frank G. 1907 The Creek Indians of Taskigi Town. American Anthropological Association, Memoir 2 (2): 100-164.

    1915a The Family Hunting Band as the Basis of Algonkian Social Organization. American Anthropologist 17: 289-305.

    1915b The Eastern Algonkian Wabanaki Confederacy. American Anthropologist 17: 492-508.

    1917a Game Totems Among the Northeastern Algonkians. American Anthropologist 19: 9-18.

    1917b 2. Malecite Version of the Water-Famine and Human Transformation Myth, Malecite Tales. Journal of American Folklore 30: 480-481.

    1928 Chapters on the Ethnology of the Powhatan Tribes. Indian Notes and Monographs 1 (5): 221-455.

    1934 Catawba Texts. Columbia University Contributions to Anthropology XXIV.

    1935 "Abenaki" Clans -- Never. American Anthropologist 37: 528-530.

    1942 The Tutelo Spirit Adoption Ceremony. Reclothing the Living in the Name of the Dead. Harrisburg: Pennsylvania Historical Commission.

    1945 The Iroquois: A Study in Cultural Evolution. Cranbrook Institute of Science. Bulletin 23: 1-94.

    1995 Midwinter Rites of the Cayuga Longhouse. Lincoln: University of Nebraska, Bison Books. [1949]

Speck, Frank, and John Witthoft 1947 Some Notable Life-Histories in Zoological Folklore. Journal of American Folklore 60 (238): 345-349.

Spier, Leslie 1933 Yuman Tribes of the Gila River. University of Chicago Press.

Springer, James Warren, and Stanley Witkowski 1982 Siouan Historical Linguistics and Oneota Archaeology. Oneota Studies. Guy Gibbon, ed. University of Minnesota Publications in Anthropology 1,.Chapter 5: 69-83.

Starn, Orin 2004 Ishi's Brain ~ In Search of America's Last Wild Indian. New York: W. W. Norton & Co.

Sunderhaus, Ted, and Jack Blosser 2006 Water and Mud and the Recreation of the World. Recreating Hopewell, Chapter 8: 134-145. Douglas Charles and Jane Buikstra, eds. Gainesville: University of Press of Florida,

Squier, Ephraim G. 1851 The Serpent Symbol and the Worship of Reciprocal Principles of Nature in America. New York: George F Putnam. [1975, Kraus Reprint]

Squier, Ephraim G., and Edwin Davis 1848 <u>Ancient Monuments of the Mississippi Valley</u>. Smithsonian Contributions to Knowledge 1. [1998, Smithsonian Classics of Anthropology]

Swan, Caleb 1855 Topical History: Position and State of Manners and Arts in the Creek, or Muscogee Nation in 1791. Information Respecting the History, Condition and Prospects of the Indian Tribes of the United States. Henry Schoolcraft, ed. Volume 5: 251-83 [Busk 267-68]. Philadelphia: J. B. Lippincott and Company.

Swanton, John 1911 Indian Tribes of the Lower Mississippi Valley and Adjacent Coast of the Gulf of Mexico. Bureau of American Ethnology, Bulletin 43.

1912 A Dictionary of the Biloxi and Ofo Languages. Bureau of American Ethnology, Bulletin 47.

1922 Tokuli of Tulsa. <u>American Indian Life</u>, by Several of Its Students. Elsie Clews Parsons, ed. New York: BW Huebsch, Inc.

1928a Social Organization and Social usages of the Indians of the Creek Confederacy. Bureau of American Ethnology, Annual Report 42 for 1924-25: 23-472.

1928b Religious Beliefs and Medical Practices of the Creek Indians. Bureau of American Ethnology, Annual Report 42 for 1924-25: 473-672.

1928c Aboriginal Culture of the Southeast. Bureau of American Ethnology, Annual Report 42: 673-726.

1928d <u>Chickasaw</u>. Bureau of American Ethnology, Annual Report 44: 169-273.

1928e The Interpretation of Aboriginal Mounds by Means of Creek Indian Customs. Smithsonian Institution Annual Report 1927: 495-506, 7 plates.

1929 Myths and Tales of the Southeastern Indians. Bureau of American Ethnology, Bulletin 88.

1931 Source Material for the Social and Ceremonial Life of the Choctaw Indians. Bureau of American Ethnology, Bulletin 103.

1932 Green Corn Dance. <u>Chronicles of Oklahoma</u> X (11): 170-195.

1998 <u>Early History of the Creek Indians and Their Neighbors</u>. Gainesville: University Press of Florida. [Bureau of American Ethnology, Bulletin 73, 1922]

Taborn, Karen 2004 *Momis Komet* ("We Will Endure"). The Indigenization of Christian Hymn Singing by Creek and Seminole Indians. City University of New York: Hunter College, MA.

Tacitus 1948 <u>Germania</u>. H Mattingly, translator. Penguin Classics.

Tanner, Adrian 1979 <u>Bringing Home Animals</u> ~ Religious Ideology and Mode of Production of the Mistassini Cree Hunters. London: C Hurst and Company.

Tedlock, Dennis 1985 <u>Popul Vuh</u>. New York: Simon and Schuster.

Teuton, Christopher, ed. 2012 <u>Cherokee Stories of the Turtle Island Liars' Club</u>. by Hastings Shade, Sammy Still, Sequoyah Guess, Woody Hansen. Chapel Hill: University of North Carolina Press.

Thomas, Cyrus 1985 Report on the Mound Explorations of the Bureau of Ethnology. Smithsonian Institution Press. [1894, Bureau of American Ethnology, Annual Report 12, 1890-91]

1980 The Cherokees in Pre-Columbian Times. AMS Press Reprint [1890, Fact and Theory Papers 4. NY: NDC Hodges]

Thompson, Lucy 1916 To The American Indian. Eureka, CA: Cummins Print Shop.

Thorne, Tanis 2003 The World's Richest Indian. The Scandal over Jackson Barnett's Oil Fortune. UK: Oxford University Press.

Timberlake, Lt. Henry 2007 Memoirs ~ The Story of a Soldier, Adventurer, and Emissary to the Cherokees, 1756-65. Duane King, ed. Cherokee: Museum of the Cherokee Indian.

Townsend, Richard 2004 Hero, Hawk, and Open Hand ~ American Indian Art of the Ancient Midwest and South. New Haven: Yale University Press.

Trigger, Bruce 1976 Children of Aataentsic: A History of the Huron People to 1660. Montreal: McGill-Queen's University Press.

Underhill, Ruth 1939 Social Organization of the Papago Indians. NY: Columbia University Press.

Van Nest, Julieann 2006 Rediscovering This Earth: Some Ethnogeological Aspects of the Illinois Valley Hopewell Mounds. Recreating Hopewell, Chapter 22: 402-426. Douglas Charles and Jane Buikstra, eds. Gainesville: U Press of Florida.

Van Tuyl, Charles 1979 The Natchez: Annotated Translations from Histoire de la Louisiane, A Short English-Natchez Dictionary. Oklahoma Historical Society, Series in Anthropology 4. [See also Walker 1979]

Vega, Garcilasco de la 1980 The Florida of the Inca. John and Jeannette Varner, trans. Austin: University of Texas Press.

Veniaminov, Rev. Ivan 1984 Notes on the Islands of the Unalaska District. Translated by Lydia T. Black and R. H. Geohegan, Edited with an Introduction by Richard A. Pierce. Kingston, Ontario: The Limestone Press. [1840]

Volpe, Edmond 1964 A Reader's Guide to William Faulkner. NY: Noonday Press.

Waddell, Gene 2004 Cusabo Southeast. Handbook of North American Indians, 14, 254-264. Raymond Fogelson, ed. DC: Smithsonian Institution Press.

Walker, Deward, ed. 1989 Witchcraft and Sorcery of American Native Peoples. Moscow: University of Idaho Press. [1970]

Walker, Willard 1979 The Natchez: Ethnographic Notes. Oklahoma Historical Society, Series in Anthropology 4. [See also Van Tuyl]

Walker, Winslow 1936 The Troyville Mounds, Catahoula Parish, La. Bureau of American Ethnology, Bulletin 113: 1-93.

Wallace, Ernest, and E Adamson Hoebel 1952 The Comanches ~ Lords of the South Plains. Norman: University of Oklahoma Press.

Warren, Stephen, and Randolph Noe 2009 "The Greatest Travelers in America". Shawnee Survival in the Shatter Zone. Mapping the Mississippian Shatter Zone, The Colonial Indian Slave Trade and Regional Instability in the American South, Chapter 7: 163-187. Robbie Ethridge and Sheri Shuck-Hall, eds. Lincoln: University Nebraska Press.

Waselkov, Gregory 1989 Indian Maps of the Colonial Southeast. Powhatan's Mantle. Indians in the Colonial Southeast, 292-343. Peter Wood, Gregory Waselkov, and Thomas Hatley, eds. Lincoln: University of Nebraska Press.

Waselkov, Gregory, John Cottier, and Craig Sheldon, Jr. 1990 Archaeological Excavations at the Early Historic Creek Indian Town of Fusihatchee (Phase I),

1988-1989). Report to the National Science Foundation. Auburn, AL: University of Auburn, Department of Sociology and Anthropology.

Waselkov, Gregory, and Kathryn E. Holland Braund, eds. 1995 <u>William Bartram on the Southeastern Indians</u>. Lincoln: University of Nebraska Press.

Waselkov, Gregory, and Marvin Smith 2000 Upper Creek Archaeology: 242-264. <u>Indians of the Greater Southeast</u> ~ <u>Historical Archaeology and Ethnohistory</u>. Bonnie McEwan, ed. Gainesville: University Press of Florida.

Watson, Robert 2000 Sacred Landscapes at Cahokia: Mound 72 and the Mound 72 Precinct. <u>Mounds, Modoc, and Mesoamerica</u> ~ Papers in Honor of Melvin L. Fowler. Steven Ahler, ed. Illinois State Museum Scientific Papers 18.

Weltfish, Gene 1965 <u>The Lost Universe</u> ~ The Way of Life of the Pawnees. NY: Ballantine Books. [1977, University of Nebraska Press].

Wermuth, Hans Fritz 1978 Crocodilia. <u>Encyclopedia Britannica</u>, Macropedia 5: 286-289 [HF We].

Wesson, Cameron Braxton 1997 Households and Hegemony: An Analysis of Historic Creek Culture Change. University of Illinois at Champagne-Urbana: Anthropology PhD.

   1999 Chiefly Power and Food Storage in Southeastern North America. <u>World Archaeology</u> 31: 145-165.

White, Leslie, ed. 1959 <u>Lewis Henry Morgan</u> ~ The Indian Journals, 1859-62. Ann Arbor: The University of Michigan Press.

White, Nancy Marie, Lynne Sullivan, and Rochelle Marrinan 1999 <u>Grit-Tempered</u> ~ Early Women Archaeologists in the Southeastern United States. Gainesville: University Press of Florida.

Whitman, William 1937 The Oto. Columbia University Contributions to Anthropology 28.

Wickman, Patricia Riles 1999 <u>The Tree That Bends</u> ~ Discourse, Power, and the Survival of the Maskoki People. Tuscaloosa: University of Alabama Press.

Widmer, Randolph 1988 <u>The Evolution of the Calusa</u>. Tuscaloosa: University of Alabama Press.

   2004 Explaining Sociopolitical Complexity in the Foraging Adaptations of the Southeastern United States: The Role of Demography, Kinship, and Ecology in Sociopolitical Evolution. <u>Signs of Power</u> ~ The Rise of Cultural Complexity in the Southeast: 234-253. Jon Gibson and Philip Carr, eds. Tuscaloosa: University of Alabama Press.

Wihr, William 1995 "You Toad Sucking Fool" ~ An Inquiry into the Possible Use of *Bufotenine* by Northern Northwest Coast Shamans. <u>Northwest Anthropological Research Notes</u> (<u>NARN</u>) 29 (1): 51-59.

Willey, Gordon 1998 <u>Archeology of the Florida Gulf Coast</u>. Gainesville: University Press of Florida. [1949, SMC 113]

Williams, Mark, and Gary Shapiro 1990 <u>Lamar Archaeology</u>. Mississippian Chiefdoms in the Deep South. Tuscaloosa: University of Alabama Press.

Williams, Stephen

   1990 The Vacant Quarter and Other Late Events in the Lower Valley. <u>Towns and Temples Along the Mississippi</u>: 170-180. David Dye and Cheryl Anne Coxe, eds. Tuscaloosa: University of Alabama Press.

1991 <u>Fantastic Archaeology</u>. The Wild Side of North American Prehistory. Philadelphia: University of Pennsylvania Press.

 2001 The Vacant Quarter Hypothesis and the Yazoo Delta, <u>Societies in Eclipse</u>. Archaeology of the Eastern Woodlands Indians, AD 1400-1700: 191-203. David Brose, C. Wesley Cowan, and Robert C. Mainfort, eds. DC: Smithsonian Institution Press.

Williamson, Ray 1992 The Celestial Skiff: An Alabama Myth of the Stars. <u>Earth & Sky</u> ~ Vision of the Cosmos in Native American Folklore: 52-66. Ray Williamson and Claire Farrer, eds. Albuquerque: University of New Mexico Press.

Wilson, Edmund 1960 <u>Apologies to the Iroquois</u>. NY: Farrar, Straus, and Cudahy.

Wood, Peter, Gregory Waselkov, and M. Thomas Hatley, eds. 1989 <u>Powhatan's Mantle</u>. <u>Indians in the Colonial Southeast</u>. Lincoln: University of Nebraska Press.

Wormington, H. M. 1964 <u>Ancient Man in North America</u>. Denver Museum of Natural History, Popular Series 4.

Worth, John 1998 <u>The Timucuan Chiefdoms of Spanish Florida</u>. Volume 1: <u>Assimilation</u>. Volume 2: <u>Resistance and Destruction</u>. Gainesville: University of Florida Press.

 2000 The Lower Creeks. Origins and Early History. <u>Indians of the Greater Southeast</u> ~ <u>Historical Archaeology and Ethnohistory</u>: 265-298. Bonnie McEwan, ed. Gainesville: University Press of Florida.

Wright, James Leitch 1981 <u>The Only Land They Knew</u> ~ The Tragic Story of the American Indians in the Old South. NY: The Free Press.

 1986 <u>Creeks and Seminoles</u>. The Destruction and Regeneration of the Muscogulge People. Lincoln: University of Nebraska Press.

York, Annie, Richard Daly, and Chris Arnett 1994 <u>They Write Their Dreams on the Rock Forever</u> ~ Rock Writings of the Stein River Valley of British Colombia. Vancouver, BC: Talon Books.

Young, Biloine Whiting, and Melvin Fowler 2000 <u>Cahokia</u> ~ The Great American Metropolis. Springfield: University of Illinois Press.

Zeisberger, David. 1910 <u>History of the Northern American Indian</u>. Archer Butler Hulbert and Reverend William Nathaniel Schwarze, eds. Columbus: Ohio Archaeological and Historical Quarterly 19 (1-2): 1-189. [1990, Arthur McGraw]

Zellar, Gary 2007 <u>African Creeks</u> ~ *Estelvste* and the Creek Nation. Norman: University of Oklahoma Press.

WHY NOW

Timing, people, place, and growing annoyance converged to urge me to self-publish my dozen long-languishing book drafts, making them widely and readily available to tribes and scholars who have been so very helpful over the years and deserve to have their contributions on record for posterity ~ my primary audience.

Approaching her 100th birthday, Amelia Susman Schultz (Columbia PhD 1939) wanted more brain stimulation to accompany her regular tai chi, yoga, helpfulness, and was told that "proof reading" was among the best mental challenges. She began by asking several friends and colleagues if they had manuscripts for her to work on, and, approaching me, I was only too happy to oblige with something I knew would interest her. After her requisite three reviews ~ for typos, grammar, perfection, she returned a superbly corrected copy. Others soon followed, though she is always urged to keep to her own pace. Thus began the process to correct my texts and prepare them for printing.

The Journal of Northwest Anthropology (JONA), where I am an editor, shifted in 2015 to Amazon self publishing for its journal issues and memoirs, including a collection (#9) of 25 of my own articles. This shift introduced me to the digital procedure as well as provided me with hands-on guidance as I began publishing my own works and improving my Create Space skills.

Another precipitating factor was the review and acceptance of an earlier manuscript by the academic press that has published several of my other volumes. This time, however, my Mounds draft was cut in half, and the reviewers (some my friends) were less than helpful, if not overly caustic and clueless. Self-publishing sidesteps these personal difficulties and preserves otherwise fraught friendships. In part, their startled reactions derive from my own limited participation in academic conferences, where my progress in data marshaling and interpretations would have been vetted during the writing-up process.

Along with these ongoing pressures and traumas, are factors of aging. Medical concerns arose that urged quick action, carrying me through awkward and frustrating misadventures with computers, programs, texts, and PDFs. Throughout, this endeavor has been creatively exciting, allowing me to choose my own cover illustrations, simplify punctuation, and make my own design choices.

Focusing on outcomes, held off distractions and conflicts as I concentrated more and more on final edits and revisions. While time and money are usually mutually exclusive for me, I suddenly had a bit of both, as more and more scholars espoused "digital humanities" despite incongruence with Indien country, where electricity can be beyond the means of families and native churches still rely on candlelight.

Finally, by making readily available these collaborations of decades, half a century in some cases, my life-long burdens are lifting and my future options include more freedoms, sharing, promise, and flexibility among wider choices.

Please help report Typo-Gnomes

Sold @ Amazon.com

Please help report & zap away Typo-Gnomes

Jay Miller's books & E-books @ Amazon.com

ACCULTURATING AMELIA ~ Round Valley 1937 California
ALASKA EDGE ISLAND ~ Siberian Yupiks of St Lawrence Island
ALLIED MOUNDS ~ Touching the Earth, Modeling the World, Reaching the Sky
ANIMAL PEOPLE ADVENTURES ~ Native North American Tribal Stories
AT BAY ~ Cultures Converging through Southwest Washington   > 5
BALLARD BULWARK ~
CHACO ECHOES ~ Pervasive Keresan Priesthoods
CHACOKIA ~ Chaco, Cahokia, Cities & Ceremonies ~ Bundles & Blood Lines Centuries Ago
CHINOOK CONCERNS ~ Emma Millett Luscier, Isabella Bertrand, Verne Ray
CIRCLING FOUR CORNERS ~ Re-Viewing Native American Indiens   > 10
CROSSING ~ LINES: An Educational Memoir of Native North America
DEL-AWARE ~ Lenape Legacies
DELAWARE INTEGRITY ~ Rituals, Removals, Reforms by Lenape Indiens
DISCLAIMING TREATIES I ~ Puget Tribes 1927 Testimonies
DISCLAIMING TREATIES II ~ Puget Tribes 1927 Testimonies   > 15
ELDERS' DIALOG ~ Ed Davis & Vi Hilbert Discuss Native Puget Sound Language, Culture, & Heritage
EVERGREEN ETHNOGRAPHIES ~ Hoh, Chehalis, Suquamish, and Snoqualmi of Western Washington
FEDERAL FISH FILES ~ Swindell 1942 Treaty Rights Report
GEORGE GIBBS NORTHWEST ARRAY ~ Full Reports, Place Names, Word List, Artifact Names, and Guide
GRASSROOTS JANET ~ Advancing Salish and Traditional Cultures   > 20
HERMAN HAEBERLIN REGAINED ~ Anthropology and Artifacts of Puget Sound 1916-17
HERSTORY NW ~ Women Upholding Native Traditions
INDIEN ~ ETHNOGRAPHY: Cultural Traditions of Native North America
INDIEN ~ ETHNOLOGY: Grounded, Gendered, Meaningful Cultural Traditions
LESCHI IN LOVE ~ A Novel of Native Puget Sound > x2   > 25
MARCO MUCK MASKS ~ Frank Cushing on Marshes and Mounds
MINTER BAY ~ Land, Lore, Loss, and Lucre in the South Salish Sea
NATIVE MET HOW ~ Improving Posterity
OLD LUKH ~ A Novel of Native Puget Sound Daily Life, Places, and Stories
OVER THE FALLS ~ Sdoqwalbixw Survivance Surrounding Seattle   > 30
PACIFIC PLATEAU PORTRAYALS ~ People Places Ponderings
RAY'S ARRAY ~ Raymond D Fogelson's Works
RIGHTING NATIVE PLACES ~ Adventures in Northwest Geography
SAHAPTINS STUDIES ~ Columbia River Plateau, Cora Du Bois, Homer Garner Barnett, Gerald Raymond Desmond
SDOQWALBIXW   > 35
SOUND SALISH STRAITS ~ Central Salish Sea Cultures
UNSETTLING SEATTLE ~ Arresting Local Talent and Academic Illiteracy
WRITING WORDS IN WARY WORLDS ~ World Wide Improved Spellings of Native America Languages

JONA Memoirs

RESCUES, RANTS, & RESEARCHES ~ A Re-View of Jay Miller's Writings on Northwest Indien Cultures ~ #9
TRIBAL TRIO of the Northwest Coast by Kenneth D Tollefson ~ #10
INTERWEAVING COAST SALISH CULTURAL SYSTEMS ~ Collected Works of Pamela Thorsen Amoss ~ #14

University of Nebraska Press

ANCESTRAL MOUNDS ~ Vitality and Volatility Crossing Native North America 2015
HONNE ~ The Spirit of the Chehalis 2015